Meeting the Standards in Secondary English

There is increasing pressure on students training to be secondary teachers to develop their subject expertise and classroom competence in a short space of time. All students on secondary Initial Teacher Training programmes must meet the requirements of DfEE Circular 4/98, *Teaching: High Status, High Standards* (DfEE, 1998). The authors guide students through what they need to know, using clear explanations and drawing on students' own knowledge of English.

Meeting the Standards in Secondary English provides:

- the pedagogical knowledge needed to teach English in secondary schools;
- support activities for work in schools and self-study;
- information on professional development for secondary teachers.

This practical, comprehensive and accessible book should prove invaluable for students on secondary Initial Teacher Training courses, PGCE students, lecturers on English education programmes and newly qualified secondary teachers. It is one of a series of books that provide subject knowledge and application in English, maths, science and ICT for primary and secondary students and teachers.

John Williamson is Lecturer in Education at the University of Newcastle-upon-Tyne. **Michael Fleming** is Senior Lecturer in Education and Director of Initial Teacher Training at the University of Durham. **Frank Hardman** is Senior Lecturer in Education and runs the secondary PGCE English course at the University of Newcastle-upon-Tyne. **David Stevens** is Lecturer in Education at the University of Durham and co-ordinator of the secondary PGCE English course at the Stockton Campus.

Meeting the Standards Series

Series Editor:
Lynn D. Newton, School of Education, University of Durham, Leazes Road, Durham, DH1 1TA

Meeting the Standards in Primary English
Angel Scott

Meeting the Standards in Primary Mathematics
Tony Brown

Meeting the Standards in Primary Science
Lynn D. Newton

Meeting the Standards in Primary ICT
Steve Higgins and Jen Miller

Meeting the Standards in Secondary English
John Williamson, Michael Fleming, Frank Hardman and David Stevens

Meeting the Standards in Secondary Science
Marion Jones and Ros Roberts

Meeting the Standards in Secondary ICT
John Halocha and John Ingram

Meeting the Standards in Secondary English

A Guide to the ITT NC

John Williamson, Michael Fleming, Frank Hardman and David Stevens

ROUTLEDGE / FALMER
Taylor & Francis Group

London and New York

First published 2001
by RoutledgeFalmer
11 New Fetter Lane, London EC4P 4EE

Simultaneously published in the USA and Canada
by RoutledgeFalmer
29 West 35th Street, New York, NY 10001

RoutledgeFalmer is an imprint of the Taylor & Francis Group

Typeset in Bembo by The Running Head Limited, Cambridge
Printed and bound in Great Britain by St Edmundsbury Press,
Bury St Edmunds, Suffolk

British Library Cataloguing in Publication Data
A catalogue record for this book is available from the British Library

Library of Congress Cataloging in Publication Data
Meeting the standards in secondary English/John Williamson . . . [et al.].
    p.   cm.
Includes bibliographical references and index.
1. English language – Study and teaching (Secondary) – Great Britain.
I. Williamson, John, 1946–
LB1631. M423   2001
428′.0071′2–dc21   00–051781

ISBN 0–415–23377–1

Contents

Illustrations

TABLES

FIGURES

Contributors

John Williamson is Lecturer in Education at the University of Newcastle-upon-Tyne. He taught English Language Studies in a college of higher education before moving to the university and has researched and published widely on aspects of language, grammar and Standard English. He lectures on aspects of Language Studies to both primary and secondary students on Initial Teacher Training programmes.

Michael Fleming is Senior Lecturer in Education and Director of Initial Teacher Training at the University of Durham where he is also co-ordinator of the secondary English programme. He has written extensively on the teaching of English and Drama including *Starting Drama Teaching* (1994) and *The Art of Drama Teaching* (1997), both published by David Fulton.

Frank Hardman is Senior Lecturer in Education, Sub-Dean of the Faculty of Education and tutor in charge of the secondary PGCE English course at the University of Newcastle-upon-Tyne. He taught English in comprehensive schools for 12 years and was head of an English department for five years before moving into higher education. He has researched and published widely in the area of language in education and communication skills.

David Stevens is Lecturer in Education (English) at the University of Durham's Stockton campus where he has been co-ordinating the secondary PGCE English course since 1996. He was previously Head of English in two secondary schools. He has published edited editions of Blake's poetry and *Frankenstein* for school use and, with Michael Fleming, *English Teaching in the Secondary School* (1998). He is currently Chair of the Cleveland National Association for the Teachers of English (NATE).

Series Editor's Preface

This book has been prepared for students training to be secondary teachers who face the challenge of meeting the many requirements for English specified in DfEE Circular 4/98, the DfEE's framework for Initial Teacher Training, *Teaching: High Status, High Standards* (DfEE, 1998). The book forms part of a new series of publications that sets out to guide students on Initial Teacher Training programmes, both primary and secondary, through the complex package of subject requirements they will be expected to meet before they can be awarded Qualified Teacher Status (QTS).

Why is there a need for such a series? Teaching has always been a demanding profession, requiring of its members enthusiasm, dedication and commitment. In addition, it is common sense that teachers need to know not only what they teach but also how to teach it most effectively. Current trends in education highlight the raising of standards (particularly in the areas of numeracy and literacy), the use of new technologies across the curriculum and the development of key skills for lifelong learning. These run alongside Early Learning Goals, Baseline Assessment, the requirements of the National Curriculum, Standard Assessment Tasks (SATs), interim tasks, GCSE examinations, new post–16 examination structures, BTEC qualifications . . . The list seems endless. Such demands increase the pressure on teachers generally and teachers in training in particular.

At the primary school level, since the introduction of the National Curriculum there is an even greater emphasis now than ever before on teachers' own subject knowledge and subject application. Trainees have to become Jacks and Jills of all trades – developing the competence and confidence to plan, organise, manage, monitor and assess all ten areas of the National Curriculum plus religious education. The increasing complexity of the primary curriculum and ever more demanding societal expectations make it very difficult for trainees and their mentors (be they tutors in the training institutions or teachers in schools) to cover everything that is necessary in what feels like a very short space of time. Four of the books in this series are aimed specifically at trainee primary teachers and those who are helping to train them:

- *Meeting the Standards in . . . Primary English*
- *Meeting the Standards in . . . Primary Mathematics*
- *Meeting the Standards in . . . Primary Science*
- *Meeting the Standards in . . . Primary Information and Communications Technology*

For those training to be secondary school teachers, the pressures are just as great. They will probably bring with them knowledge and expertise of their specialist subject, taken to degree level at least. However, content studied to degree level in universities is unlikely to match closely the needs of the National Curriculum. A degree in medieval English, applied mathematics or biochemistry will not be sufficient in itself to enable a trainee to walk into a classroom of 13- or 16-year-olds and teach English, mathematics or science. Each subject at school level is likely to be broader. For example, science must include physics, chemistry, biology, astronomy and aspects of geology. In addition, there is the 'how to teach it' dimension – subject application. Furthermore, secondary school teachers are often expected to be able to offer more than one subject. Thus three of the books in the series are aimed specifically at the secondary school level:

- *Meeting the Standards in . . . Secondary English*
- *Meeting the Standards in . . . Secondary Science*
- *Meeting the Standards in . . . Secondary Information and Communications Technology*

All the books deal with the specific issues that underpin the relevant Teacher Training Agency requirements identified in Circular 4/98. The very nature of the subject areas covered and the teaching phases focused upon means that each book will, of necessity, be presented in different ways. However, each will cover the relevant subject Annex from Circular 4/98. Thus, the books will deal with:

- subject knowledge – an overview of what to teach, the relevant subject knowledge that the trainees need to know and understand in order to interpret and teach the National Curriculum requirements for that subject;
- subject application – an overview of how to interpret the subject knowledge so as to design appropriate learning experiences for pupils, organise and manage those experiences and monitor pupils' progress within them.

The former is not presented in the form of a textbook. There are plenty of good quality GCSE and A level textbooks on the market for those who feel the need to acquire that level of knowledge. Rather, the subject knowledge is related to identifying what is needed for the trainee to take the National Curriculum for the subject and translate it into a meaningful package for teaching and learning. The latter is structured in such a way as to identify the generic skills of planning, organising, managing, monitoring and assessing the teaching and learning. The content is related to the specific requirements of Circular 4/98. The trainee's continuing professional development needs are also considered.

The purpose of the series is to give practical guidance and support to trainee teachers, in particular focusing on what to do and how to do it. Throughout each book there are directed tasks and activities that can be completed in the training institution, in school or independently at home. They serve to elicit and support the trainee's development of skills, knowledge and understanding that is needed to become an effective teacher.

Dr Lynn Newton
University of Durham
February 2000

1 Introduction Welcome to Your Teaching Career

JOHN WILLIAMSON

Teaching is without doubt the most important profession; without teaching there would be no other professions. It is also the most rewarding. What role in society can be more crucial than that which shapes children's lives and prepares them for adulthood?

Teaching: A Guide to Becoming a Teacher (TTA, 1998, p. 1)

So, you have decided to become a secondary English teacher. You will, no doubt, have heard lots of stories about teaching as a profession. Some will have been positive, encouraging, even stimulating. Others will have been negative and pejorative. But you are still here, on the doorstep of a rewarding and worthwhile career. Without doubt teaching *is* a demanding and challenging profession. No two days are the same. Children are never the same. The curriculum seldom stays the same for very long. But these things are all part of the challenge. Teaching as a career requires dedication, commitment, imagination and no small amount of energy. Yet, despite this, when things go well, when you feel your efforts to help children learn have been successful, you will feel wonderful. Welcome to teaching!

RECENT DEVELOPMENTS IN SECONDARY TEACHING

As with most things, the teaching profession is constantly buffeted by the winds of change. In particular, the last decade or so has been a time of great change for all involved in secondary education. At the heart of this change has been the Education Reform Act (ERA) of 1988. The act brought about a number of far-reaching developments, the most significant of which was the creation of the National Curriculum and its related requirements for monitoring and assessment.

Although there have always been guidelines from professional bodies (such as teachers' unions), local authorities and even official government publications, until

1988 teachers generally had freedom to decide for themselves *what* to teach and *how* to teach. Different approaches to curriculum planning and delivery have proved influential at different times. There has been a series of reports over the last quarter of a century which have impacted on the teaching of English in secondary schools that have largely arisen from ongoing concerns in government and other influential circles about the quality of provision in a subject which is seen as being of the highest importance. The Bullock Report (DES, 1975) went into great detail about all aspects of English teaching at both primary and secondary level but, in spite of saying a great deal which is still of value today, its recommendations went largely unheeded because, unlike National Curriculum documents, it did not have statutory force. Concerns about English teaching persisted and HMI produced a booklet *English from 5 to 16* (DES, 1984) which was the first of a series of important publications produced during the 1980s. Although this booklet was not universally welcomed by English teachers, it can be seen as the precursor of the first version of the National Curriculum. Another influence on the National Curriculum was the Kingman Report (DES, 1988) whose focus was 'explicit knowledge of the structure of the language' (p. iii). This has been a persisting theme running through the various forms of the National Curriculum for English. However, the most important work of this period was the Cox Report (DES, 1989) which laid out the framework for the first version of National Curriculum English (DES, 1990). This was generally, if cautiously, welcomed by English teachers but did not meet the demands of their political masters who set up a review chaired by Lord Dearing which led to the second version of National Curriculum English (DFE, 1995). In 1995, English teachers were assured that there would be no further curriculum changes for five years, an assurance which was adhered to quite punctiliously since 1999 saw the publication of the third version of National Curriculum English, which is the one which you will be implementing in (at least) the early years of your career. This brief narrative has been intended simply to help you place the National Curriculum in something of a historical context; the details will be explored in the following chapters of this book.

THE STANDARDS DEBATE

Parallel to the changing perspectives on curriculum has been an increasing emphasis on standards. There has, in essence, been a shift in perspectives from *equality in education* (as reflected in the post-war legislation of the late 1940s through to the 1970s) to the *quality of education*, the bandwagon of the 1980s and 1990s.

The term 'standard' is emotive and value-laden. According to the *Oxford English Dictionary*, among other descriptors of a standard, it is a weight or measure to which others conform or by which the accuracy of others is judged and also a degree of excellence required for a particular purpose. Both of these definitions sit well with the educational use of the term where it translates as acceptable levels of performance by schools and teachers in the eyes of the public and the politicians.

Over the last decade, the media has reported numerous incidents of falling standards and the failure of the educational system to live up to the degree of excellence required for the purpose of educating our young in preparation for future citizenship. We teachers have, purportedly, been measured and found lacking. It was this, in part, which was a major force behind the introduction of the National Curriculum.

In 1989, when the National Curriculum was introduced, the Department for Education and Science claimed:

> There is every reason for optimism that in providing a sound, sufficiently detailed framework over the next decade, the National Curriculum will give children and teachers much needed help in achieving higher standards.
>
> (DES, 1989, p. 2)

One of the major thrusts underpinning changes over the last decade or so has been the question of how we measure and judge the outcomes of the teaching and learning enterprise. To achieve the appropriately educated citizens of the future, schools of the present must not only achieve universal literacy and numeracy but also be measurably and accountably seen to be doing so, hence the introduction of league tables as performance indicators.

David Blunkett, the Secretary of State for Education and Employment at the time of writing, said in 1997:

> Poor standards of literacy and numeracy are unacceptable. If our growing economic success is to be maintained we must get the basics right for everyone. Countries will only keep investing here at record levels if they see that the workforce is up to the job.
>
> (DfEE, 1997a, p. 2)

While the economic arguments are strong, we need to balance the needs of the economy with the needs of the child. Few teachers are likely to disagree with the need to get the 'basics' right. After all, literacy and numeracy skills underpin much that we do with children in all areas of the curriculum. However, the increased focus on the 'basics' should not be at the expense of these other areas of experience. Children should have access to a broad and balanced curriculum if they are to develop as broad, balanced individuals.

All schools are now ranked each year on the basis of their pupils' performances in standardised tests and external examinations (GCSE and A level). The performances of individual children are conveyed only to their parents, although the school's collective results are discussed with school governors and also given to the local education authority (LEA). The latter then informs the DfEE which publishes the national figures on a school/LEA basis. This gives parents the opportunity to compare, judge and choose schools within the LEA in which they live. The figures indicate, for each school within the LEA, the percentage above and below the expected level – in other words, the schools that are or are not meeting the standard. This results in inevitable conclusions as to whether standards are rising or falling. Such crude measures as Standard Assessment Tasks (SATs) for comparing attainment have been widely criticised, notably by education researchers like Fitz-Gibbon (1996) who criticises the fact that such measures ignore the 'value added elements' – the factors which influence teaching and learning such as the catchment area of the school, the proportion of pupils for whom English is an additional language and the quality and quantity of educational enrichment a child receives in the home. Davies (1996) suggests that:

> Dissatisfaction [with standards] is expressed spasmodically throughout the year but reaches fever pitch when the annual national test results are published. Whatever the results they are rarely deemed satisfactory and targets are set which expect future cohorts of children to achieve even higher standards than their predecessors.
>
> (Davies, 1996, p. 162)

There are also targets for Initial Teacher Training (ITT) to redress the perceived inadequacies in existing course provision. These centre on a National Curriculum for Initial Teacher Training which prescribes the skills, knowledge and understandings which all trainees must achieve before they can be awarded Qualified Teacher Status (QTS). It follows, therefore, that as a trainee for the teaching profession you must be equipped to deal with these contradictory and sometimes conflicting situations as well as meeting all the required standards. So how will you be prepared for this?

ROUTES INTO A CAREER IN TEACHING

To begin, let us first consider the routes into teaching open to anyone wanting to pursue teaching as a career. Teaching is now an all-graduate profession, although this has not always been the case. Prior to the 1970s it was possible to become a teacher by gaining a teaching certificate from a college of higher education. However in the late 1960s and early 1970s, following a sequence of government reports, the routes were narrowed to ensure graduate status for all newly qualified teachers.

For many teachers in the United Kingdom this has been via an undergraduate pathway, reading for a degree at a university (or a college affiliated to a university) which resulted in the award of Bachelor of Education (BEd) with QTS. Such a route has usually taken at least three and sometimes four years. More recently, such degrees have become more linked to subject specialisms and some universities offer Bachelor of Arts in Education (BA (Ed.)) with QTS and Bachelor of Science in Education (BSc (Ed.)) with QTS.

Many other teachers choose to gain their degrees from a university first and then train to teach through the postgraduate route. This usually takes one year, at the end of which the trainee is awarded a Postgraduate Certificate in Education (PGCE) with QTS. In all cases, the degree or postgraduate certificate is awarded by the training institution but the QTS is awarded by the Department for Education and Employment (DfEE) as a consequence of successful completion of the course and on the recommendation of the training institution.

Whichever route is followed, there are rigorous government requirements which must be met by both the institutions providing the training and the trainees following the training programme before QTS can be awarded. In the 1970s and early 1980s, teacher training institutions had guidelines produced by a group called the Council for the Accreditation of Teacher Education (CATE). The guidelines identified key requirements that all Initial Teacher Training providers should meet to be judged effective in training teachers. Alongside the CATE criteria were systems of monitoring the quality of programmes.

During the late 1980s and early 1990s, there were a number of government documents which have moved Initial Teacher Training in the direction of partnership with schools. This has involved school staff taking greater responsibility for the support and assessment of students on placements and a transfer of funds (either as money or as in-service provision) to the schools in payment for this increased responsibility. Along with this responsibility in schools, staff have increasingly become involved in the selection and interviewing of prospective students, the planning and delivery of the courses and the overall quality assurance process.

More recent legislation has culminated in the establishment of the Teacher Training Agency (TTA), a government body which, as its name suggests, now has control over the nature and funding of Initial Teacher Training courses. This legislation is crucially important to you as a trainee teacher, since the associated documentation defines the framework for your preparation for and induction into the teaching profession. So how will the legislation affect you?

REQUIREMENTS ON COURSES OF INITIAL TEACHER TRAINING

In 1997, a government circular (DfEE Circular 10/97) introduced the idea of a national curriculum for Initial Teacher Training to parallel that already being used in schools (DfEE, 1997b). This was to be a major development in the training of teachers. In the circular there was an emphasis on the development of your professionalism as a teacher. This implies

> more than meeting a series of discrete standards. It is necessary to consider the standards as a whole to appreciate the creativity, commitment, energy and enthusiasm which teaching demands, and the intellectual and managerial skills required of the effective professional.
>
> (DfEE, 1997b, p. 2)

At the heart of this is the idea of raising standards. Circular 10/97 had specified:

1   the Standards which *all* trainees must meet for the award of QTS;
2   the Initial Teacher Training curricula for English and mathematics; and
3   the requirements on teacher training institutions providing courses of Initial Teacher Training.

Subsumed under the first set of criteria were groups of standards relating to the personal subject knowledge of the trainee, criteria related to his or her abilities to apply the skills, knowledge and understanding to the teaching and learning situation, and criteria related to the planning, management and assessment of learning and behaviour.

In April 1998, the DfEE issued Circular 4/98, *Teaching: High Status, High Standards*, in which the Secretary of State's criteria were revised and extended. As well as generic Standards for the award of QTS, the new document specified separate national curricula for Initial Teacher Training in English, mathematics and science at both primary and secondary levels, and a national curriculum for the use of Information and Communications Technology (ICT) in subject teaching to be taught to all trainees, regardless of phase focus. The fundamental aim of this new National Curriculum for ITT was to:

> equip all new teachers with the knowledge, understanding and skills needed to play their part in raising pupil performance *across the education system*.
>
> (DfEE, 1998, p. 3)

DfEE Circular 4/98 includes the following sections:

Annex A: Standards for the award of Qualified Teacher Status;
Annex B: Initial Teacher Training curriculum for the use of Information and Communications Technology in subject teaching;
Annex C: Initial Teacher Training curriculum for primary English;
Annex D: Initial Teacher Training curriculum for primary mathematics;
Annex E: Initial Teacher Training curriculum for primary science;
Annex F: Initial Teacher Training curriculum for secondary English;
Annex G: Initial Teacher Training curriculum for secondary mathematics;
Annex H: Initial Teacher Training curriculum for secondary science;
Annex I: Requirements for all courses of Initial Teacher Training.

So how does this affect you as a student teacher? In essence, it means that you must 'meet the Standards' before you can be awarded QTS. One of the major tasks facing you as an entrant to the teaching profession is that of wading through not dozens but hundreds of Standards and statements relating to your skills, knowledge and understanding. As a trainee, you must show that you have met these Standards by the end of your training programme so as to be eligible for the award of QTS. Courses in universities and other higher education institutions are designed to help you to do so, both in schools and in the institution, but the onus is likely to be on you to provide the evidence to show how you have met the requirements. This series of books, *Meeting the Standards*, is designed to help you with this task. This particular book focuses on those skills and competences you will need to acquire to show that you have met the requirements for secondary English.

There is more to teaching English than simply having a good knowledge and understanding of the subject as it is often taught in universities. One of the major tasks ahead of you is to develop your knowledge of the whole range that is covered by the

English component of the National Curriculum; this involves a knowledge of the literary texts which school pupils will encounter and of aspects of language study, drama and the media. Those coming to English via the BA plus PGCE route may be familiar with some of these elements but few will be prepared for all of them. Furthermore, you will need the ability to transform what you know and understand about English into worthwhile teaching and learning experiences for your pupils. You need to develop your *pedagogical skills, knowledge* and *understanding*. This is as important as your knowledge and understanding of the National Curriculum Order for English. The latter provides you with a framework of *what* to teach in English. It does not tell you *how* to teach it – how to plan, organise, manage and assess the learning of the 30 or so children in your class, each with varied and changing needs. This is left to your own professionalism. This book is designed to help you to make a start on this task.

AUDIT AND DEVELOPMENT OF SUBJECT KNOWLEDGE

Very few students on Initial Teacher Training programmes begin their courses with all the knowledge they will need to teach English effectively and often arrive with some apprehensions about teaching particular aspects of the subject. The ITT National Curriculum for secondary English states that all trainees need to be aware of the strengths and weaknesses in their own subject knowledge, to analyse it against the pupils' National Curriculum and examination syllabuses, and to be aware of gaps they will need to fill during training. It is likely therefore that at an early stage in the course you will be asked to audit your subject knowledge against the Standards to identify strengths and areas for development.

There are different approaches to subject audits. At worst they can take the form of a quiz which simply poses questions about decontextualised, isolated bits of knowledge and which embodies all the worst aspects of assessment in English (see Chapter 8). On the other hand an audit which simply asks you to state whether your own knowledge of specific aspects of English is adequate may be unhelpful because it does not give any guidance or means of determining what counts as 'adequate'. A balance between these two extremes is needed. It is important not to think of a subject audit as a 'one-off' exercise but as a focus for your own development throughout the course and during your teaching career. We give three broad approaches to subject audit that can be used alone or together to achieve the desired objective.

Placing your subject specialisms in rank order

The idea here is that you place the broad areas of English in rank order in terms of your own level of subject knowledge confidence. The task is not straightforward (for example you may have specialised in nineteenth century fiction but feel less confident about the modern novel). It is therefore helpful to use notes to record any specific observations about areas of strengths or areas for development. This approach represents a positive starting point because it asks you to think initially about the strengths in English that you bring to the course before concentrating on areas for development. The strengths you bring need not just be related to your first degree but may derive from other interests, walks of life or other professional experience. It also highlights the priority area that needs attention even though you may not at the start of a course have a real feel for the type of subject knowledge that is required. Members of a course can use the areas of English with which they feel most confident in order to provide support for others in a spirit of collaboration and mutual support. An example of a proforma for this type of initial broad audit is given in Appendix B. Having identified the areas with which you feel least confident the Initial Teacher Training National Curriculum for English can be used for a more detailed view of what is required.

Self-audit related to the Standards

This approach asks you to audit your own level of confidence against the Standards and has the advantage of bringing together knowledge and the effective teaching of secondary English which we term 'pedagogical subject knowledge'. The intention is that the self-audits are used at various points in the course to identify gaps in knowledge and as a basis for target setting. In completing the audit, cross reference is made to the National Curriculum for English for Key Stage 3 and Key Stage 4. Having completed the audit, targets should be set and discussions held with course tutors and subject mentors to determine how best to address the gaps identified (e.g. supported self-study, observation, planning and teaching specific topics/areas). A sample form is given in Appendix C.

Audit through focused questions

This approach to subject audit is more robust because it is less subjective, relying not on self-assessment but on responses to a set of test questions. The danger however is that it can give the absurd impression that subject knowledge is merely a matter of knowing facts. The audit and self-study guide, *English for Secondary Teachers* published by Letts, to some degree avoids this pitfall by providing feedback and explanations on each set of questions as an aid to further study. An extract from a sample question in the section on punctuation is given below:

> In the following sentences an underscore (_) is used to indicate the presence of a colon or semicolon. Decide which of these marks is most (*sic*) appropriate in each case.
>
> (f)   Debbie dropped her bag and out spilled the contents _ a large bunch of keys _ her husband's wallet that she had been asked to keep _ a calculator for the shopping and a rather crumpled handkerchief.

> (g)   They talked all day without mentioning the one topic on their minds _ the robbery.
>
> (h)   I once had a Jaguar car _ it was the best I had ever driven.
>
> (i)   The sun shone _ the birds sang _ I was happy.

Read in isolation such questions present a rather reductive view of English but the feedback, explanations and advice on improving subject knowledge are helpful.

> Semi-colons are often misused. They are sometimes similar to commas and sometimes like full stops. They are used like a comma in lists where the items are phrases, rather than single words. They are used like full stops to separate linked main clauses to indicate a relationship between them where a full stop would otherwise be used.
>
> Colons are used to indicate a list of following items or where a simple item follows before a quotation or speech in a play.

Whatever method of audit is used on your own course it is up to you to make the best use of the outcome by using it as a focus for your own development both during your training and in your teaching.

OVERVIEW OF THIS BOOK

As suggested above, very few students on Initial Teacher Training programmes begin their courses with all the subject knowledge they will need to teach English effectively. Nor are you likely to have expertise in the teaching and learning process although you will all have experienced it in some shape or form. While such experience and expertise does vary from person to person, you all have one thing in common – *potential*. You have successfully cleared the hurdles of the application form and the interview and have been offered a place on an Initial Teacher Training course. Your tutors have decided that you have the necessary personal qualities which indicate that you are capable of acquiring the skills, knowledge and understanding needed to become effective teachers. In other words, you have shown evidence that you have the *potential* to meet the Standards.

This book is designed to help you to do this, but it is only a part of the picture. It will be most useful to you if you read it in conjunction with the other experiences offered to you on your training programme. These will range from theoretical to practical in the following way.

- *directed reading*: reading might be handouts related to lectures, books and articles for assignments or professional newspapers and magazines simply to broaden your own professional base;
- *taught sessions*: these could take the form of formal lectures, informal practical workshops or combinations of either, whether in schools or in the institution;

- *talks/discussions*: again, these could be held in school or in the institution and can range from formal structured seminars with a group to more informal one-to-one discussion, usually with the aim of integrating theory and practice;
- *tutorial advice*: one-to-one sessions with a tutor, mentor or teacher to plan for and reflect upon your practical experiences;
- *observations*: opportunities to watch your mentor and other experienced teachers at work in their classrooms;
- *restricted experience*: opportunities to try out, under the guidance of your mentor or other teachers, limited teaching activities with a small group of children, perhaps building up to a whole-class session;
- *teaching practice*: a block placement where you take responsibility for the planning, teaching and assessment of classes of children, under the guidance of your school mentor and tutor and usually within defined parameters.

What is important about all of these is the amount of effort you put in to them. No one else can do the work for you. Your tutors, your mentors in school and other teachers can all offer you advice, guidance and even criticism, but how you respond is up to you. This, once again, is a reflection of your professionalism.

The book is written with the aim of giving you a general introduction to teaching English in secondary schools. It is set out in such a way that the sections and chapters also link directly to the clusters of Standards in Annex F of the DfEE Circular 4/98. For your information, Annex F is reproduced in full as Appendix A in this book, with permission from the DfEE. The book will also link indirectly into the more generic Standards specified in Annex A to be met by all trainees regardless of phase or subject specialism. Each chapter can stand alone. Two chapters are devoted to language study and one each to drama and media because in our experience trainee teachers of English are particularly keen to develop their knowledge and understanding of these areas. ICT is not discussed in detail because it is treated separately in one of the books in this series. Each chapter has clear sub-headings, so you can relate them directly to your institution's training programme for English and to the experiences you have in school. Throughout, whenever appropriate, there is reference to recent research into topics and issues in English teaching and suggestions for further reading.

REFERENCES/SUGGESTIONS FOR FURTHER READING

In addition to the references we recommend texts at the end of some chapters which are of specific relevance to the chapter's contents; the following are recommendations for some particularly valuable books which deal with English teaching as a whole.

Cox, B. (1991) *Cox on Cox: An English Curriculum for the 1990s*, London: Hodder and Stoughton
Cox, B. (1995) *Cox on the Battle for the English Curriculum*, London: Hodder and Stoughton
Davies, C. (1996) *What is English Teaching?*, Buckingham: Open University Press
DES (1975) *A Language for Life* (The Bullock Report), London: HMSO
DES (1984) *English from 5 to 16*, London: HMSO

DES (1988) *Report of the Inquiry into the Teaching of English Language* (The Kingman Report), London: HMSO

DES (1989) *English for Ages 5 to 16* (The Cox Report), London: HMSO

DES (1990) *English in the National Curriculum*, London: HMSO

DFE (1995) *The National Curriculum*, London: HMSO

DfEE (1997a) *Excellence in Schools*, London: HMSO

DfEE (1997b) *Teaching: High Status, High Standards* (Circular 10/97) *Requirements for Courses of Initial Teacher Training*, London: HMSO

DfEE (1998) *Teaching: High Status, High Standards* (Circular 4/98) *Requirements for Courses of Initial Teacher Training*, London: HMSO

Fitz-Gibbon, C.T. (1996) *Monitoring Education: Indicators, Quality and Effectiveness*, London: Cassell

Fleming, M. and Stevens, D. (1998) *English Teaching in the Secondary School*, London: David Fulton Publishers

TTA (1998) *Teaching: A Guide to Becoming a Teacher*, London: Teacher Training Agency

2 What Do We Mean by Secondary English Teaching?

FRANK HARDMAN

This chapter will consider the question of what it means to be a teacher of secondary English by considering a range of viewpoints and will ask you to think about your own rationale for teaching English in the light of this discussion. It is designed to address the aims and purposes of English teaching related to current debates and issues and your own professional development as a teacher. It will look briefly at the various historical processes that have come to shape the current English curriculum and try to get you to think about how it can be developed into something better.

In discussing the aims of English teaching, the Cox Report (DES, 1989) attempted to define the role of English in the curriculum in order for it to take its place as a core element in the National Curriculum in England and Wales. Drawing on the literature of the history of English teaching in England, it outlined five different views of the subject that it claimed are 'not sharply distinguishable and certainly not exclusive' (paragraph 2.20). Cox (1991) also claimed that they give a broad approach to the curriculum that can unite the profession as they acknowledge the utilitarian functions of English teaching and yet place them in a wider cultural and imaginative framework. The Cox Report (paragraphs 2.21–2.27) listed them as follows:

> A 'personal growth' view focuses on the child: it emphasises the relationship between language and learning in the individual child, and the role of literature in developing children's imaginative and aesthetic lives.

> A 'cross-curricular' view focuses on the school: it emphasises that all teachers have a responsibility to help children with the language demands of different subjects on the school curriculum . . .

> An 'adult needs' view focuses on communication outside the school: it emphasises the responsibility of English teachers to prepare children for the

language demands of adult life, including the workplace, in a fast changing world . . .

A 'cultural heritage' view emphasises the responsibility of schools to lead children to an appreciation of those works of literature that have been widely regarded as amongst the finest in the language.

A 'cultural analysis' view emphasises the role of English in helping children towards a critical understanding of the world and cultural environment in which they live. Children should know about the processes by which meanings are conveyed, and about the ways in which print and other media carry values.

Activity 1   Place Cox's five models into your order of priority for the teaching of English and rank them in terms of the importance of their influence on classroom practice. You may wish to review your priorities and answers, having read the following sections, at different stages in your training course.

Before considering research into the views of English towards the five models, the next section traces the historical roots of the current curriculum and the controversy that has surrounded its formulation since 1989.

A HISTORICAL PERSPECTIVE

Throughout its history as a school and university subject there have always been tensions and contradictions within English. Indeed the term itself is ambiguous, as English can include the study of the language, literature or culture. Therefore, none of the contemporary debate about the aims of English teaching is new: the justification for the place of English in the curriculum having always been contested and rested upon different priorities at different stages in its history. The 1921 Newbolt Report, set up in response to government concern about the high level of illiteracy revealed by conscripts during the First World War, emphasised literary values in order to make available to all the civilising and humanising literary values of the public school. In this way a 'liberal education' would be a feature of all schools, at the heart of which was to be the nation's greatest literature. Prior to Newbolt, the English curriculum in state schools had been made up of Standard English and grammatical correctness, emphasising an instrumental or utilitarian approach. Throughout the history of English teaching in England, the literary/creative and the linguistic/vocational have remained the two main themes of the debate.

The teaching of English has always been an ideological weapon and in tracing the development of the National Curriculum for English, as Cox (1991, 1995) in his discussion of the curriculum makes clear, it is difficult to ignore the political context in which it was produced. As suggested above, the debate has centred around two views of English: one which tried to provide the general skills of language use that pupils would need throughout life (what Cox calls the 'adult needs' view); another which saw its purpose as introducing young people to their national literature, its appreciation and attendant values (what Cox calls the 'cultural heritage' view). In the 1960s, commentators like John Dixon tried to reconcile the two separate notions of literature and literacy by proposing that the main purpose of English teaching was to help pupils use language in order to do things like build their 'own representational world' because 'In ordering and composing situations that in some way symbolise life as we know it, we bring order and composure to our inner selves' (Dixon, 1967, p. 20).

Dixon suggested the imaginative and symbolic explorations of human experience and relationships could be brought together with subject-specific notions of literacy in which pupils' language resources are developed through the exploration of their individual human experiences and relationships. This literary-creative or 'personal growth' model therefore grew out of the 'cultural heritage' one as it got beyond restricting literature to the 'great tradition' by including literature which got closer to children's interests and experience. Such a view of English teaching reflects Cox's description of the 'personal growth' model that emphasises the relationship between language and learning in the individual child, and the role of literature in developing children's imaginative and aesthetic lives.

The 'personal growth' view of English teaching was also very influential on the Bullock Report (DES, 1975) that was set up in response to government concerns about falling literacy standards and the effects upon economic performance which endorsed the role that English teaching can play in developing the literacy skills needed to access the pleasures and insights of aesthetic/imaginative writing and to produce such forms of writing for oneself. However, this extensive report was concerned with all aspects of teaching the use of English, including reading, writing and speech. In other words, it was concerned with the teaching of general literacy skills that went beyond the scope of what could be covered in the curriculum slot designated as English. It explored the literacy skills needed to cope with the demands of studying different subjects at school and those that people encounter as citizens or as workers. The report therefore put forward a language curriculum that went beyond the scope of what could reasonably be covered in the English subject area. It introduced what Cox calls a 'cross-curricular' view, focusing on the role that all teachers have for helping pupils with the languages demands of the different subjects on the school curriculum and an 'adult needs' view, focusing on communication outside the school and emphasising the responsibility of teachers to prepare pupils for the language demands of adult life, including the workplace.

CHALLENGES TO THE LITERARY DOMINATION
OF ENGLISH STUDIES

However, during the 1970s and 1980s, the literary view of English teaching was being criticised from two directions – political and intellectual. There was concern over standards of literacy and the new academic disciplines in universities were questioning the intellectual and philosophical values of Leavisite literary criticism: its traditional notions of textual unity, organic wholeness and belief in literature as morally educative. Up to the 1960s there was always a close relationship between the study of English literature in universities and the teaching of English in schools because of its civilising mission and sense of a 'common culture' which spread through the educational system downwards. In practical terms this meant that the teaching of English in universities was very important in the training of teachers, as many English graduates went into teaching, and until recently there was relatively little difference between university and sixth-form English teachers in terms of both pedagogical practice and status. Similarly there was relatively little difference between what was studied at school and university as the same texts were selected from a shared canon with similar terms and methods of textual analysis applied to them.

This sense of a shared purpose and status started, however, to break down because of the challenge to the nature of literary criticism. English studies saw the development of a variety of literary specialisms and a turning away from criticism in Leavisite terms, where the study of literature was an exercise in value judgement. This culminated in the 1980s in the emergence of self-conscious 'literary theorists' and the introduction of a whole plethora of critical and theoretical approaches to literature (e.g. structuralism, linguistics, semiotics, sociology, Marxism, feminism and post-structuralism). And in the same period, largely as a result of the Chomskyan revolution, linguistics moved from being an esoteric and highly specialist area of study to one which seemed to offer insights into a whole range of fields of intellectual endeavour. The study of language began to offer new insights not only into language itself but also into the understanding of the human mind and human society. It also began to impinge on the study of literature itself, directly through the concept of stylistics and indirectly through the role of linguistics as one major source of the structuralist movement.

Such developments led to the questioning of English as a subject and what can or cannot be counted as 'English'. The growth of cultural studies, communication and media departments in universities led to a significant reconsideration of what constitutes a text, moving beyond the traditional study of literary texts, so that 'English' has been reconstituted as a cultural or social semiotic study. This is reflected in recent innovations in the study of language, where language is viewed as a meaning making system and where all texts are worthy of analysis; they were also being joined by the study of popular culture and the media and by new theoretical approaches to the study of literature. The development of such theoretical approaches to the study of language, literature and the media throughout the 1980s has been very influential in bringing about the growth of the 'cultural analysis' model in the teaching of English. It was given official recognition in the Cox Report when media education became a central and compulsory part of the English curriculum. It was also complemented by the new emphasis on sociolinguistics concerned with developing children's knowledge about language through the close study and critical analysis of language as it is used. It brought with it new approaches to texts and embraced an understanding and critical awareness of all forms of language and media texts, thereby aiming to contribute to the literacy demands of citizenship by providing young people with tools for understanding the modern world.

The 1980s saw the publication of *English from 5 to 16* (DES, 1984) produced by Her Majesty's Inspectorate (HMI) which marks the first tentative step in the direction of a National Curriculum for English and provided a template for all subsequent attempts at arriving at such a curriculum. It set out the aims for teaching English as a subject area and adopted the 'four modes of language' (i.e. speaking, listening, reading and writing) of the Bullock Report but without the cross-curricular perspective. It therefore blurred the distinction between specialist English and general literacy and, according to some critics (see Davies, 1996), set up unrealistic expectations about what could and could not be achieved within the curriculum slot called English. It also added another concept to the English curriculum that eventually became known as 'knowledge about language'. It was introduced as 'a fourth aim which applies over all the modes of language. This is to teach children about language . . . so that they achieve a working knowledge of its structure and of the variety of ways in which meaning is made, so that they have a vocabulary for discussing it, so that they can use it with greater awareness, and because it is interesting (paragraph 1.7)'.

The *English from 5 to 16* report led to the report of the Kingman Committee's Inquiry into the Teaching of English Language set up in early 1987 by Kenneth Baker whose terms of reference were 'to recommend a model of the English language as a basis for teacher training and professional discussion, and to consider how far and in what ways that model should be made explicit at various stages of education'. The report's main task was to give substance to the stated aims for teaching about language as set out in *English from 5 to 16*. There were fears in the English teaching profession that it would be an attempt to reintroduce a prescriptive grammar into the teaching of English as set out in a 44-page pamphlet, *English our English* by John Marenbon, published by the Right-wing Centre for Policy Studies in 1987 (Marenbon, 1987). In the event the Kingman Report (DES, 1988) emphasised the development of pupils' linguistic competence and offered some fairly academic kinds of linguistic knowledge to move English teachers in a linguistic direction but away from the fixed notions of Standard English and grammatical correctness that the educational right was seeking to reinstate into state schools.

On the day the Kingman Report was published, and with teaching knowledge about language firmly on the English curriculum agenda, the Cox Committee was set up charged with writing the real English curriculum which was to take its place along with nine other subjects in the National Curriculum – see Brian Cox's *Cox on Cox* (1991) for a detailed account of the design of the English curriculum. To the educational right, the committee appeared to be in safe hands as Brian Cox had been one of the authors of the Black Papers in the early 1970s which had been critical of what they saw as progressive trends in education. The key structural characteristics of the

Cox Report reflected those of *English from 5 to 16* by maintaining that report's division into the four 'modes' of speaking, listening, reading and writing. It also picked up where the Kingman Committee (of which Cox had been a member) had left off by taking forward the report's focus on teaching and learning about language by trying to develop its fundamentally academic ideas into programmes of study.

When the Cox Report was published it summarised the five views of English teaching (i.e. personal growth, cross-curricular, adult needs, cultural heritage and cultural analysis) in an attempt to acknowledge and create some consensus between the different subject ideologies in the hope that such differences might be reconciled through informed debate. Because of its liberal consensus, the report came as a considerable relief to English teachers as it had none of the repressive spirit that English teachers had feared. After further revisions owing to political pressure (see *Cox on Cox*, Cox, 1991) in which the assessment criteria were placed before the programmes of study, the statutory version was published in March 1990.

Despite the many strengths of the statutory version of the Cox curriculum, many teachers found its overall organisation difficult to work with as it amounted to a set of checklists. There was little integration of the four language modes and a lack of clear signposting for the reader through which one might chart a clear and logical course. However, as teachers set about implementing the wide range of demands of the first version of the English curriculum, media education and drama were being taught in most secondary schools along with the study of non-literary texts and active approaches to Shakespeare. English teachers also began to take on the teaching of knowledge about language with pupils learning about such things as the history of the language and the differences between dialect and Standard English so that they could articulate and explore their own understanding about language and the skills of using it. It also complemented the developments in post-16 English teaching where, since the mid-1980s, English language was offered as a separate A level which drew on the academic study of linguistics and included the study of media and non-literary texts and students' own writing. In order to support this initiative the Language in the National Curriculum (LINC) project was created to produce materials for training teachers about language and ways of teaching it in the classroom.

The teaching of media education, along with the new emphasis on developing children's knowledge about language, gave further impetus to the cultural analysis model in the teaching of English which had been growing throughout the 1980s. It brought with it new approaches to texts and embraced an understanding and critical awareness of all forms of language and media texts, thereby aiming to provide young people with tools for understanding the modern world. However, such initiatives were short lived because of changes in the curriculum soon after it had first been implemented.

REVISING THE ENGLISH ORDER

In July 1992, only two years after English teachers had started to teach English in the National Curriculum, the Conservative government published a document called

National Curriculum English: The Case for Revising the Order (NCC, 1992). The aim of this document, despite claims to the contrary, was to impose a right-wing agenda by reintroducing fixed notions of Standard English, grammatical correctness and the teaching of a traditional English literary canon as set out in John Marenbon's *English our English* (1987). The following statement reflects how the professional officers in the National Curriculum Council (NCC) tried to accommodate the views of the educational right by trying to phase their insistence on simple rules for correctness rather than appropriateness with some academic respectability. The linguistic concept of 'Standard English' was now replaced by the term 'Standard English' and was given a more prominent place in the subject's conceptual hierarchy:

> The one explicit reference to standard English in the statements of attainment focuses on the need to develop 'an awareness of grammatical differences between spoken standard English and a non-standard variety' (level 6). This is not the same thing as being able to use standard English in conversation and will not necessarily encourage pupils to speak clearly, accurately and confidently . . . These requirements need to be based on a clear definition of standard English.

These views were backed up in the press by David Pascall, then chairman of NCC on secondment from British Petroleum, who famously demanded that all children should be taught to speak in Standard English, even in the playground! It was in this political climate that the decision to revise the whole English curriculum was made along with the sudden abandonment of the LINC project which was too sociolinguistic in focus and had failed to come up with a few rules for correct English.

The agenda for the teaching of English was obviously shifting from the liberal consensus envisaged in the Cox Report with its five models of English teaching. The radical right's cultural offensive, through the highly partisan appointments to the National Curriculum Council and the Schools Examination and Assessment Council (SEAC), was evident in the proposed revisions to the English Order and new assessment arrangements. Their view of English teaching, articulated in Marenbon's *English our English*, that English teaching is simply a matter of grammar and great books, was now central to the government's agenda for English. Cox summed up the situation in a lecture broadcast on Channel 4 and published in *The Times* (1 March 1993):

> The extraordinary situation today is that this small group of sentimental dogmatists is in a position to impose its will on all teachers of English in state education – and is doing so . . . The rightwingers are attacking the present curriculum because they want to restore a unity and stability based on the hegemony imposed by the upper and middle classes in the 1930s and before. The texts they prescribe often seem more suited to the days of British imperialism.

To Cox it seemed that the 'cultural heritage' model, with its emphasis on the teaching of a literary canon, together with a narrow language/linguistic competence view of English, was being given dominance over the other models of English teaching, particularly the 'cultural analysis' view which did most to challenge the privileged status of English literature. This was illustrated in the proposal from the NCC to drop media education from the English curriculum in order to reduce overload and force a return to 'basics' in the subject. The move towards an understanding of contemporary culture was seen as destroying the teaching of great literature and undermining the values of English education which such literature is supposed to promulgate. The offensive on the Cox curriculum was also accompanied by the introduction of Key Stage 3 English testing whose design bore little resemblance to the teaching and attainments specified in the National Curriculum. The tests introduced out-moded forms of study through comprehension questions on anthologies of literary extracts and they made the study of Shakespeare into a major element within the English curriculum. The insensitive manner in which the testing of Key Stage English was introduced led to widespread protest and boycotting of the tests and the resignation of John Marenbon who had been appointed chair of the Schools Examination and Assessment Council and was responsible for administering the tests. Sir Ron Dearing was also brought in to simplify the whole of the National Curriculum and establish a period of stability in the world of education.

ENGLISH IN THE NATIONAL CURRICULUM IN 1995

The English curriculum was to go through three drafts before arriving at the 1995 version and not surprisingly there was general relief at the pragmatic compromise that was finally reached. As a result of the political compromises, for example, greater emphasis was given to the explicit teaching of language structures at word, sentence and text level and to the teaching of Standard English (although it avoids any definition of this concept) in each of the language modes. Under reading, two pages of highly detailed specifications about the kinds of literature to be studied were provided but there was a superficial treatment of the multi-cultural dimension. Study of the media was also mentioned briefly under reading, although the revised curriculum insisted that any magazine, newspaper, radio, television or film texts that are studied 'should be of high quality', thereby confusing the whole issue (see Chapter 7).

More generally, the 1995 English curriculum was given the major responsibility for teaching about general literacy; other subjects were expected to contribute to standards of linguistic correctness, especially in writing. However, the School Curriculum and Assessment Authority did try to redress the balance of responsibility by publishing *Use of Language: A Common Approach* (SCAA, 1997) in which the responsibility for language development is shared with other subjects enabling pupils to develop skills of reading, writing and oracy in order to get access to, organise, analyse and report their learning across the whole school curriculum.

ENGLISH TEACHERS' VIEWS OF COX'S MODELS

Although discussion of Cox's original five views of English teaching has been miss-ing in subsequent versions of the English curriculum, they still remain useful as a way of exploring teachers' thinking and their priorities for teaching English (as you read through this section, look back at your own priorities for the teaching of English under Activity 1). Davies (1996) suggests that while four out of five views of English offered in the report do not seem to present the prospect of any major philosophical conflict because they implicitly or explicitly take for granted the privi-leged status of English literature, the cultural heritage and cultural analysis models must be seen as two alternative views of the subject despite Cox's claim that they are not mutually exclusive. As has been suggested in the previous section, Cox's formu-lation of the two models reflects the growing polarisation of views over the English curriculum with the educational right giving priority to the cultural heritage view with its emphasis on the teaching of a literary canon together with a narrow language/ linguistic competence view of English. This was in sharp contrast to the cultural analysis view of English teaching which embraces an understanding and critical aware-ness of all forms of language and media texts to equip young people with tools for coping with the demands of the twenty-first century.

Research (Goodwyn, 1992) was carried out to validate the models in terms of the beliefs and opinions of working teachers and to investigate the extent to which teachers' ideology influences their interpretation and application of the National Curriculum requirements in their schools. Goodwyn's surveys suggests that English teachers recognise and use all five models posited by the Cox Report, but that they do not give equal weighting to each model. He found that the personal growth model was the one that most teachers subscribed to and that the cultural analysis model was growing in importance so that these models were developing into a composite of both. The cultural heritage model, although present in a number of ways, was given a low status in terms of personal priorities and influence on classroom practice by the teachers in the survey.

Given the fact that many trainees would have already been debating the conflicting subject philosophies at university prior to starting their PGCE course, Hardman and Williamson (1993) carried out a similar survey to Goodwyn's to investigate whether the models posed a problem for trainee teachers making the transition from being students of English as an academic discipline in higher education to training to be teachers of English in secondary schools. We were also interested to discover their views on the subject philosophies posited by Cox, at an early stage in the course, to see if any changes were discernible throughout the course of the year.

Goodwyn's questionnaire (1992) was applied to the 24 trainees on the Newcastle PGCE course to compare their views with those of the teachers studied by Goodwyn concerning the Cox models and their influences on classroom practice. It was in two parts: the first section asked respondents to rank the models in order (see Table 2.1); the second part asked them to respond to 20 individual statements (see Table 2.2). An open-ended questionnaire was also provided to allow trainees to expand upon their views to the survey.

Table 2.1 Personal priorities for teaching secondary English

Teachers		Trainees	
1.43	Personal growth	1.28	Personal growth
2.50	Cultural analysis	2.50	Cultural analysis
3.50	Cross-curricular	3.31	Adult needs
3.70	Adult needs	4.00	Cross-curricular
3.70	Cultural heritage	4.50	Cultural heritage

Current influence

Teachers		Trainees	
2.10	Personal growth	2.95	Personal growth
2.50	Cross-curricular	3.00	Cultural analysis
3.30	Cultural analysis	3.00	Adult needs
3.50	Cultural heritage	3.04	Cross curricular
3.60	Adult needs	3.70	Cultural heritage

Activity 2 Compare the findings of the first part of the survey (Table 2.1) with your own rankings for Activity 1 and consider how you would respond to the 20 individual statements (Table 2.2).

When asked to rank the five models in order in terms of personal priorities and current influence in the classroom, the order that emerged is shown in Table 2.1. In each case the figures given are the total for each model divided by the number of respondents.

The percentages of teachers and trainees supporting and disagreeing with the 20 statements are given in Table 2.2; neutral responses were not recorded except when they are particularly significant. Where Goodwyn had not given a complete breakdown of his figures, an asterix was used.

The ranking of personal priorities and perceived influence of the models on classroom practice by both teachers and trainee teachers showed that personal growth was perceived as being the most important model and thought to be the most influential on classroom practice. Similarly, cultural analysis was seen as the second most important personal priority by both teachers and trainees. For the teachers, however, cultural analysis was not considered very influential on practice in a general way whereas the trainees thought it was very important in the classroom, alongside adult needs. Differences emerged over the adult needs model, with the teachers placing it last on their list of personal priorities and last as a current influence on English teaching. Their rejection of the adult needs model was also reflected in their response to statement 15 concerning the importance of preparing 16-year-olds for the world of

Table 2.2   Statements on secondary English teaching

	% agreeing/disagreeing	
	Teachers	Trainees
1 English teachers should use all five models in their teaching.	nearly 100	91/4
2 Media education belongs principally in English.	15/25	34/34
3 English teachers should teach their pupils to resist the influence of the media.	15/40	3/60
4 English teachers should teach their pupils to be more discriminating about the media.	nearly 100	96/4
5 English teachers should teach pupils to resist the influence of popular culture.	5/40	4/82
6 In English, the study of the media is as important as the study of literature.	20/40	35/22
7 It is more important for pupils to have knowledge of a range of texts than of the conventional literary canon.	80/*	73/4
8 Knowledge about language is a welcome addition to English.	80/*	82/4
9 Knowledge about language builds on existing good practice in English.	60/*	69/17
10 Linguistics is an increasing influence in English.	20/50	47/13
11 The influence of linguistics is improving English teaching.	15/*	17/21
12 Ultimately, knowledge about language is more important than knowledge about literature.	25/45	13/65
13 Language across the curriculum is chiefly the responsibility of English teachers.	13/70	17/52
14 All teachers of language (i.e. English, ESL, other languages) should co-operate closely.	70/*	78/4
15 It is more important for pupils aged 16 to be prepared for the world of work than for studying for A level.	*/70	21/43
16 All pupils should study literature at Key Stage 4.	90/*	87/4
17 The study of literature and of language should play equal parts at Key Stage 4.	85/*	69/8
18 The study of literature has a civilising influence. (30 neutral)	70	26/52
19 The study of literature helps moral development. (30 neutral)	70	30/39
20 Pupils' personal response to literature is very important.	98/2	96

work, over and above the study of A level English: over 70 per cent of the teachers rejected this idea; in the case of the trainees only 43 per cent felt that it was important to place more emphasis on preparing pupils for A level than for work. Clearly the adult needs model had much more importance in the trainees' thinking and was not seen in opposition to the personal growth model. In the case of the teachers, Goodwyn suggests that it reflects the long-standing tension in the teaching of English between helping pupils prepare for the functional demands of the adult world and trying to develop their literary sensibilities.

Differences also appeared between the trainees and the teachers in their attitudes to the cultural heritage model. Both in terms of their personal priorities and current influence on the teaching of English, trainees ranked cultural heritage last. Similarly, in response to the statements reflecting the influence of the cultural heritage model on the teaching of English (18 and 19), only 26 per cent agreed with the statement that literature has a civilising influence and 30 per cent agreed with the view that it helped moral development. This contrasted with the 70 per cent agreement by the teachers to both statements, showing that the cultural heritage model was still influential.

The trainees' responses to the statements about media education (statements 2–6) also showed some interesting differences and suggested a stronger support for the cultural analysis model where media education has been very influential. While only 34 per cent of the trainees agreed that media education belongs in English for statement 2, with 32 per cent remaining neutral (compared with 15 per cent of the teachers agreeing and 60 per cent remaining neutral), 60 per cent disagreed with the statement that English teachers should teach their pupils to resist the influence of the media (statement 3); this compared with only 40 per cent of the teachers disagreeing with this statement. In response to the statement that English teachers should teach pupils to resist the influence of popular culture (statement 5), over 82 per cent of the trainees disagreed with the statement compared with only 40 per cent of the teachers. When asked if the study of the media is as important as the study of literature (statement 6), most of the trainees, 43 per cent, remained neutral, 35 per cent agreed and 22 per cent were against. This compared with 40 per cent of the teachers remaining neutral, 20 per cent agreeing and 40 per cent disagreeing. Both teachers and trainees were almost unanimous in their support of pupils becoming more discriminating about the media, but in the case of the trainees it seemed there was stronger support for the role that media education could play in this process.

Differences also appeared in response to the cluster of statements relating to the role of linguistics in the teaching of English (8 to 12): over 50 per cent of English teachers said that linguistics was not an increasing influence on English (statement 10), with only 20 per cent agreeing that it was. In the case of the trainees, 47 per cent thought it was an increasing influence, 13 per cent disagreed and 39 per cent were undecided. There was less certainty among the trainees, however, that linguistics was improving English teaching (statement 11): only 17 per cent of the trainees agreed, compared with 11 per cent of teachers, and most remained neutral. Goodwyn suggested that the perceived lack of the influence of linguistics may have been due to the fact that they failed to see knowledge about language as linguistics. Both trainees and teachers were enthusiastic about knowledge about language, however, with over 80 per cent from each survey agreeing that it is a welcome addition to English (statement 8). Goodwyn suggested that this was evidence of the increasing importance of the cultural analysis model, as the analytical approaches being developed through knowledge about language were also necessary for dealing with media texts.

In both surveys, literature continued to dominate. In fact the majority of trainee teachers thought knowledge about literature was more important than knowledge about language: 65 per cent disagreed with statement 12 that knowledge about language is more important than knowledge about literature compared with 45 per cent of the English teachers; only 13 per cent of the students thought that it was more important compared with 25 per cent of teachers. Like the teachers in Goodwyn's survey, literary texts featured strongly in the trainees' views on English teaching but they were not confined to the narrow range of texts of the cultural heritage model. Both trainees and teachers strongly supported statement 7 stating that it was more important to have knowledge of a range of texts than of the conventional literary canon. Similarly, there was a high degree of support, by both trainees and teachers, for literature at Key Stage 4 (statement 16), although this was balanced by support being given to statement 17 on the study of language and literature playing equal parts at Key Stage 4. Goodwyn suggested that this reflected support for the personal growth model which fostered a balance between language and literature at all stages of the curriculum. Support for the personal growth model was also reflected in the almost unanimous agreement to the final statement concerning the importance of pupils' responses to literature by both teachers and trainees.

In response to the statements concerning the cross-curricular model (13 and 14) there seemed to be broad agreement that cross-curricular English is not solely the responsibility of the English teacher; nor did the cross-curricular model rank highly in either the trainees' or teachers' personal priorities, although it was seen as quite a strong influence in the classroom by the English teachers.

The results from the questionnaires suggested that the trainee teachers, like the teachers in Goodwyn's survey, recognised all five models of English teaching and that there was broad support for the models. While different priorities were given to each of the models, with personal growth and cultural analysis being viewed by the trainees as the most important both in terms of personal priority and influence in the classroom, the findings supported Cox's contention that they gave a broad approach to the curriculum. Nor did the models seem to present the trainees with any of the major philosophical or ideological difficulties which critics claim are posed by the cultural analysis model; as with the teachers in Goodwyn's survey, the trainees seemed to take a pragmatic view, borrowing from all five models.

From both surveys it seemed that the high degree of support for the personal growth and cultural analysis models suggested that the cultural analysis model, developed during the 1980s, was having an increasing influence in the classroom and that it was being accommodated into the personal growth model, in the same way that the personal growth model developed from the cultural heritage model. Media education, along with knowledge about language, was seen as providing common ground between personal growth and cultural analysis so that the models were developing into a composite of both.

While both trainees and teachers broadly supported the personal growth and cultural analysis models, significant differences did emerge over the adult needs model which appeared to be an unresolved conflict for the teachers who placed it last as a personal priority and current influence on classroom practice. The trainee teachers showed more support for meeting pupils' linguistic needs in order to function effectively in society, although it was not seen solely as the responsibility of the English teacher, as the trainee responses in an open-ended response to the cross-curricular model suggested, and they ranked adult needs second alongside cultural analysis in terms of its influence on the classroom. The teachers, however, showed more support for developing pupils' literary sensibilities and for the values of Leavisite literary criticism in which many English teachers had been trained.

THE TEACHING OF LITERATURE AND THE PLACE OF MEDIA EDUCATION IN THE ENGLISH CURRICULUM

Evidence of the growing importance of the cultural analysis view of English teaching following the introduction of the Cox curriculum was also supported by a further survey of 60 teachers (Williamson and Hardman, 1994). We decided to explore teachers' thinking and classroom practice in two areas that had become central to the debate over revisions to the Cox curriculum: the teaching of literature and the place of media education in the curriculum. The attitude questionnaire was made up of 30 statements drawn from a review of the literature on the teaching of literature and media education. Table 2.3 shows the degree of agreement/disagreement to each statement as expressed by the teachers.

The response to the questionnaire revealed that far from abandoning the teaching of literature, as the radical right were arguing, 93 per cent of the teachers in the survey (statement 30) agreed that literature had an important part to play in developing pupils' sensitivity and 62 per cent agreed with statement 18 that it had a civilising influence and is important in the moral development of a pupil. Here we see the strong influence of the personal growth model of English teaching with its emphasis on the role of literature in the development of a child; we also see it in statement 2 where 85 per cent of teachers agreed that the study of culture should include everyone's creative and communicative experience. The sample was, however, divided over the question of adult needs: 40 per cent agreed with statement 17 that English should be more concerned with developing pupils' literary sensibilities than preparing them for the world of work, 32 per cent disagreed and 28 per cent remained neutral. The teachers seemed suspicious of a narrow, utilitarian approach to English which this statement suggests and this, together with a belief in the moral educative value of literature, reflects the strong influence that the values of Leavisite literary criticism continue to exert over many English departments.

There was little support however for a cultural heritage view which restricted teachers' and pupils' choice of literature to a narrow range of texts made up of a traditional literary canon: 92 per cent of teachers disagreed that the reading curriculum should be made up of a compulsory canon of literary works (statement 23) and

Table 2.3 Survey of teachers' beliefs on the teaching of literature and media in the secondary English curriculum (percentages have been rounded to the nearest 5)

		Agree/disagree
1	English teachers should aim to bring their pupils into as much contact as possible with first rate literature so as to provide them with standards and powers of discrimination against which the offerings of the mass media will be cut down to size.	58/22
2	The study of culture should go beyond established art forms to include everyone's creative and communicative experience.	85/3
3	Popular forms of culture deserve curriculum space and should be analysed in the classroom alongside more traditional forms.	83/2
4	Great literature has an important part to play in training children in traditional values.	33/35
5	The subject 'English' should be replaced by a term like cultural studies that would make it possible to think about books and television programmes, films and newspapers as part of a totality.	13/58
6	The teaching of English should aim to promote a cultivated understanding of the history of English literature which is inseparable from its appreciation.	35/37
7	The mass media is a major contributor to the social and moral decline of society.	22/50
8	We should not be concerned with putting books, plays, television and comics into a universal scale of cultural values, but with valuing how people relate to their cultural experience.	50/2
9	By seeing all texts, whether print, audio or visual, as worthy of study, media education will fail to teach children to discriminate and appreciate great works of art.	7/85
10	Popular culture impairs children's capacity to appreciate more valuable aspects of culture like literature and theatre.	15/77
11	Visual literacy is as important as print literacy.	60/22
12	In the language of literature we find the values of the past, and thence we shape the values of the present.	27/35
13	Knowing that texts are open to different interpretations and that audiences bring meanings to a text is an essential part of learning how texts work.	98/0
14	Media education should be at the heart of the English National Curriculum.	38/42
15	Understanding and using audio-visual technologies ought to be taken as seriously as reading and writing verbal language.	37/38
16	It is important that children develop knowledge of a range of texts that goes beyond the traditional literary canon.	93/3
17	English should be concerned with developing children's literary sensibilities rather than preparing them for the world of work.	40/32

Table 2.3   (continued)

		Agree/disagree
18	Studying literature has a civilising influence and is important in the moral development of a child.	62/12
19	Media education should aim to develop pupils' critical awareness of the way in which the media is actively involved in the process of constructing or representing 'reality' rather than transmitting or reflecting it.	82/5
20	The traditional English canon should be central to the English curriculum.	23/47
21	The literary canon should be seen as an artificial concept, constructed by particular people for particular reasons at a certain time.	47/23
22	Our task in English should be to analyse discourses for their ideological content.	22/37
23	The reading curriculum in schools should be made up of a compulsory canon of literary works.	0/92
24	We should broaden the traditional literary canon to ensure women's writing, black writing and working class writing stand strongly alongside the texts of privileged white men.	82/8
25	Books and plays are of more value than TV programmes or comics.	38/30
26	As literature is pushed out of the English curriculum, the general level of literacy will continue to fall.	37/32
27	English should be concerned with the study of language as it is used, taking in all kinds of texts whether they be from literature, advertising, journalism, comics, pop music or soap operas.	88/5
28	Works of literature studied in the classroom should be unquestioned masterpieces, for children can learn to read and enjoy literature only through knowing the best of it.	8/82
29	Specifying a compulsory canon of great works will squeeze out of the curriculum many of the books which help young people to develop as confident, responsive and discerning readers.	93/0
30	As teachers of English we aim to awaken the sensitivity of our pupils to human emotions.	93/5

Activity 3   How would you respond to each of the statements in Table 2.3? Do your views differ greatly from those expressed by the teachers in the survey?

82 per cent disagreed that it should be made up of unquestioned masterpieces (statement 28). The idea of a broad reading curriculum was strongly supported: 93 per cent agreed that pupils should develop knowledge of a range of texts beyond the traditional literary canon (statement 16), 93 per cent thought that a compulsory canon would deprive young people of many of the books that help them to develop as confident,

responsive and discerning readers (statement 29) and 82 per cent thought that the traditional literary canon should be broadened to include women, black and working class writers (statement 24).

Similarly, there was little support for statements traditionally associated with a cultural heritage model. Only 23 per cent of teachers agreed with statement 20 that the traditional English canon should be central to the English curriculum, with most disagreeing (47 per cent) or remaining neutral (30 per cent) and, on the question of whether great literature has a part to play in training children in traditional values (statement 4), only 33 per cent agreed with 36 per cent disagreeing and 31 per cent remaining neutral. Statement 6, on whether English should promote a cultivated understanding of the history of English literature which is necessary for its appreciation, got a mixed response with 35 per cent agreeing, 37 per cent disagreeing and 28 per cent remaining neutral, as did statement 12 on whether the literature of the past can shape the values of the present with 27 per cent agreeing, 35 per cent disagreeing and 38 per cent remaining neutral. On the question of whether standards of literacy would fall if literature was pushed out of the curriculum (statement 26), opinions were again mixed with 37 per cent agreeing, 32 per cent disagreeing and 31 per cent remaining neutral. The ambiguity of what is meant by literature may have contributed to the uncertainty reflected in the responses to statement 26; the declining influence and rejection of the cultural heritage model, however, was reflected in the above statements, particularly of the simplistic and narrow definition of the canon which the educational right wanted to reimpose.

Support for a text-based approach was clear but it was one which went beyond traditional literary forms to embrace a full range of media, literary and non-literary texts. Eighty-three per cent of teachers thought popular culture should be studied in the classroom alongside more traditional forms (statement 3) and 77 per cent disagreed with statement 10 that it impairs pupils' capacity to appreciate more 'valuable' aspects of culture like literature and theatre. Similarly only 22 per cent thought the mass media was a major contributor to the social and moral decline of society (statement 7) with 50 per cent disagreeing and 28 per cent staying neutral. The growing influence of media education on teachers' thinking, a key element of the cultural analysis model, was also reflected in statement 19, where 82 per cent of the sample supported its role in developing a critical awareness of the way in which media texts are constructed, in statement 11, where 60 per cent of teachers thought visual literacy was as important as print literacy, and in statement 9, where 85 per cent disagreed with the statement that using media texts in the classroom would be a corrupting influence.

Critical approaches to language and text, the other main strand of the cultural analysis approach to English, were also strongly supported in statement 13, which statistically produced the most significant result, where 98 per cent of teachers agreed with the view that knowing that texts are open to different interpretations was an essential part of how texts work. Similarly in response to statement 27, 88 per cent of teachers agreed that English should be concerned with language as it is used, taking in all kinds of texts, thus reflecting the sociolinguistic influence on knowledge about language. It also reflected the fact that teachers frequently made use of a variety of media texts – in terms of subjects such as the language of newspapers or advertising – to teach about the varieties of language structure. While just under a half (47 per cent) agreed that the literary canon was an ideological construct (statement 21), there was less commitment to analysing discourses for their ideological content (statement 22) with only 22 per cent agreeing, 37 per cent disagreeing and most, 41 per cent, remaining neutral. Perhaps fears of political indoctrination which such work can evoke were evident in the responses to this statement.

Although in principle the cultural analysis model is value free, moving away from an established hierarchy of values that a literary canon will impose, teachers in the survey still wanted to develop some form of evaluation and judgement in pupils' responses to literary and media texts; in other words some form of discrimination but not resistance to the media. Not surprisingly there were some conflicting responses to this issue, perhaps reflecting the paradoxical nature of a model that aims to be value free and yet enhance and extend an individual's ability to make personal judgements through analysis and reflection. Just over a half (52 per cent) thought it was wrong to have a universal scale of cultural values against which to judge literary and media products (statement 8), with 46 per cent remaining neutral; 58 per cent of the teachers saw literature as offering a yardstick against which the mass media could be judged (statement 1) and, on the statement that books and plays had more value than TV programmes or comics (statement 25), 38 per cent agreed, 30 per cent disagreed and 32 per cent were neutral.

When it came to the more general question of the place of media education in the English curriculum (statement 14) opinions were equally divided: 38 per cent agreed that media education should be at the heart of the English national curriculum, 42 per cent disagreed and 20 per cent remained neutral. On the question of whether the subject of English should be replaced by a term which would embrace the study of all kinds of texts beyond the study of literature (statement 5), only 13 per cent agreed, 58 per cent disagreed and 29 per cent remained neutral. The responses to these statements suggested that teachers were uncertain about how far to accept media education as a normal part of their work. Statement 15, concerning the role of audio-visual technologies in media education, also revealed uncertainty about approaches to the media in the classroom beyond text-based work, with 37 per cent agreeing that understanding and using audio-visual technologies ought to be taken as seriously as reading and writing verbal language, 38 per cent disagreeing and 25 per cent remaining neutral.

The research supported Cox's view (1991), Goodwyn's view (1992) and our earlier findings (Hardman and Williamson, 1993) that English teachers favoured a broad approach to the curriculum in which personal response to and critical analysis of a wide range of literary, media and non-media texts were seen as essential to ensure the personal growth of the pupil. The broad approach to language and text was also reflected in the fact that teachers in the survey drew little distinction between literature and media work as both are considered forms of reading – as in the National Curriculum where media education mainly comes under the reading attainment targets for English – and they used a whole range of texts to teach about language structure.

THE COX MODELS REVISITED

In a follow-up to his original survey, Goodwyn and Findlay (1999) found that English teachers are increasingly opposed to what many saw as the prescriptive nature of the 1995 English curriculum underpinned by the cultural heritage model. They found that the curriculum was perceived as irrelevant and impersonal and that teachers were holding on to the personal growth and the value of literature in developing personal responses as revealed in earlier surveys. They also found that English teachers are increasingly adopting a more cultural analysis stance to their teaching mainly through their belief in the importance of media education despite its official downgrading in the 1995 curriculum.

In the 1997 survey, in response to the statement 'Media study has a place in English because it represents a significant element in students' lives', 58 per cent of English teachers were in strong agreement, 29 per cent were in agreement and only 4 per cent were in disagreement. Similarly, 82 per cent of English teachers were in disagreement with the statement 'Media study has no place in English'. However, there was a more equivocal response to the statement 'In English the study of media is as important as the study of literature': 19 per cent strong agreement, 25 per cent agreement, 30 per cent neutral, 17 per cent disagreement and 9 per cent strong disagreement; effectively 44 per cent for equality for media and 26 per cent against. As in the earlier surveys, these responses reflect the tensions and uncertainties that remain over the teaching of English. However, compared to Goodwyn's original survey, the 1997 study reveals a movement over time: in 1991 only 20 per cent of teachers were in support of equality for media within the English curriculum. In other words, despite the reduction of media work in the 1995 English curriculum, it is growing and becoming established.

Overall, the survey supports the earlier research findings which suggest teachers of English are pragmatic and favour a broad church approach to the teaching of the subject in which personal growth and cultural analysis are given prominence in the face of the constraints of the National Curriculum. All three surveys reveal there was little support for a cultural heritage view of English teaching which restricted teachers' and pupils' choice of literature to a narrow range of texts made up of a traditional canon of English literature. Such cultural stability was felt to be inappropriate in a rapidly changing world and the idea of a broad reading curriculum which included women, black and working class writers was strongly supported. Support for a text-based approach which went beyond traditional literary forms to embrace a full range of media, literary and non-literary texts was clear. The studies also revealed the growing influence on teachers' thinking of media education, a major element of the cultural analysis view of English teaching, with its emphasis on the role of English in helping children towards a critical understanding of the world and cultural environment in which they live.

There was a great deal of support for a critical approach to the way media texts are constructed to develop pupils' critical awareness, but one which would develop some form of evaluation and judgement in pupils' responses to literary and non-literary texts to promote discrimination but not resistance to the media. Here we also see the continuing influence of the personal development model with its emphasis on the relationship between language and learning in the individual child, and the role of literature in developing children's imaginative and aesthetic lives. Indeed, much of the media work surveyed in our research centred on the study of literary texts as the study of literature and media education were seen as complementary rather than mutually exclusive.

Critical approaches to language and text, designed to develop in pupils an understanding that texts are open to different interpretations, were also strongly supported. Similarly teachers agreed that English should be concerned with language as it is used, taking in all kinds of text, thus reflecting a strong sociolinguistic influence which was present in the Cox curriculum and the suppressed LINC training materials. The findings also imply that English teachers, as experienced professionals, know how and when to employ the different models of English teaching, whereas to its critics the National Curriculum attempts principally to enforce one inappropriate model on all teachers. The results of Goodwyn's survey suggest that secondary English teachers want a much more relevant pupil-centred and flexible curriculum that allows space for the exercise of their expertise and professional judgement. The question is: will the third version of the National Curriculum address these concerns?

A CURRICULUM FOR THE TWENTY-FIRST CENTURY

The third version of the National Curriculum for English (DfEE, 1999) forms the basis of the curriculum for the start of this millennium. In the introduction to the curriculum, it is stated that the revised version is designed to be less prescriptive and to address the needs of young people at the start of the twenty-first century. This is in terms of the rapid expansion of communication technologies, changing modes of employment, and new work and leisure patterns resulting from economic migration and the continued globalisation of the economy and society.

In structure, it appears very similar to the 1995 curriculum although with slightly different emphases. For example, more attention has been given to recent literature written for young people and adults and from different cultures and traditions, to the use of drama and ICT, and to the explicit teaching about language at word, sentence and text level. A revised statement on use of language across the curriculum also makes clear the ways in which all subjects can contribute to the literacy development beyond concerns with linguistic correctness. Small changes have also been made to the study of the media so that it is not limited to material of 'high quality' and includes more critical engagement with media texts. Compared to the original Cox curriculum, however, the coverage of media education and drama in the English curriculum is still fairly superficial.

Commentators on the National Curriculum (e.g. Davies, 1996; Williamson and Goodall, 1996; Carter, 1997) have highlighted key issues for the study and teaching of English for the year 2000 and beyond so as to encourage critical literacy practices. They assert the importance of a cultural analysis stance to the teaching of English in preparing young people for the twenty-first century in which the study of text in all its forms is central. They suggest that knowledge of the characteristics of different forms of spoken and written discourse and of their social place can and should be taught so that pupils can identify, analyse and use different genres in order to acquire the intellectual and linguistic resources to progress academically and to negotiate systems of power. This would entail a detailed knowledge of how language works; in the words of Kress and Knapp (1992) 'a knowledge of grammar as a means of gaining a full understanding of the range of things which it is possible to mean, to say, to write in a particular culture, and to do with its language'. The emphasis, therefore, is on meaning and function and on what language is doing and being made to do by people in specific situations in order to make particular meanings. In this social theory of language, the most important unit is the text that is a socially and contextually complete unit of language, rather than parts of speech and the rules governing their form and combination or the structure of the sentence.

Similarly Stubbs (1990) argues that 'an understanding of spoken and written discourse helps people to understand how meanings are expressed by being able to interpret language in use and the points of view from which language is produced. In what he calls critical linguistics, grammar is used as a tool of analysis so that patterns of discourse which contribute to the meanings of texts are made explicit so that points of view or ideologies can be explored. In other words, he is advocating access to power through textual analysis, as meanings are expressed in grammar and people need to understand how points of view are constructed through the selection and omission of particular grammatical options or rhetorical devices; and they require abstract descriptive categories to state them so study of grammar is essential in order to identify and talk about such meanings.

In discussing what a discourse approach to English will look like, Carter (1997) proposes that the study of modern English language should be rooted in texts and contexts in which different varieties of language, spoken and written, are compared and contrasted, and in which language and literature can be integrated so they are mutually informing and enriching, and which draw on recent developments in critical and cultural theory. In addition to highly valued canonical texts it would also include examples of popular fiction, advertisements and political speeches as well as media texts, such as television soap opera and radio comedy programmes, so that literary texts would be seen as continuous with all other kinds of texts. By ensuring that the study of modern English language is principled and systematic the curriculum would enable pupils increasingly to understand how language is used across a range of genres.

Whatever the shape of the next curriculum, it seems clear that the teaching of language is likely to become an increasingly important part of the English curriculum not only in terms of its history or particular textual qualities, but also as an object of linguistic, rhetorical and grammatical theory across a range of literary, media and non-literary texts. Those of you who have followed an entirely literature-orientated training in higher education will probably need to address gaps in your knowledge as outlined in Chapters 3 and 4. We do not, however, foresee the demise of the study of literature: literary study will continue to play a central part in English studies approached from a variety of critical perspectives and the systematic study of the English language will make a significant contribution to its study.

> **Activity 4** Compare and contrast the latest version of the English curriculum with the 1995 version. Is the 2000 curriculum less prescriptive and more broad-based in its view of the teaching of English? Will it address the needs of young people at the start of this millennium?

REFERENCES/SUGGESTIONS FOR FURTHER READING

Carter, R. (1997) *Investigating English Discourse*, London: Routledge

Cox, B. (1991) *Cox on Cox*, London: Hodder and Stoughton

Cox, B. (1995) *The Great Betrayal*, London: Hodder and Stoughton

Davies, C. (1996) *What is English Teaching?*, Buckingham: Open University Press

DES (1975) *A Language for Life* (The Bullock Report), London: HMSO

DES (1984) *English from 5 to 16: Curriculum Matters 1*, London: HMSO

DES (1988) *Report of the Committee of Inquiry into the Teaching of English Language* (The Kingman Report), London: HMSO

DES (1989) *Report of the English from 5 to 16 Working Party* (The Cox Report), London: HMSO

DfEE (1999) *English: The National Curriculum for England*, London: HMSO

Dixon, J. (1967) *Growth Through English*, Oxford: Oxford University Press

Firth, S. (1990) 'The Cox Report and the University', *Critical Quarterly*, 32, 2, pp. 68–75

Goodwyn, A. (1992) 'English Teachers and the Cox Models', *English in Education*, 28, 3, pp. 4–10

Goodwyn, A. and Findlay, K. (1999) 'The Cox Models Revisited: English Teachers' Views of Their Subject and the National Curriculum', *English in Education*, 33, 2, pp. 19–31

Hardman, F. and Williamson, J. (1993) 'Student Teachers and Models of English', *Journal of Education for Teaching*, 19, 3, pp. 279–92

Kress, G. and Knapp, P. (1992) 'Genre in a Social Theory of Language', *English in Education*, 26, 2, pp. 4–15

LINC (undated) *Language in the National Curriculum: Materials for Professional Development*, Department of English Studies, University of Nottingham

Marenbon, J. (1987) *English our English*, London: Centre for Policy Studies

NCC (National Curriculum Council) (1992) *National Curriculum English: The Case for Revising the Order*, York: National Curriculum Council

NCC (National Curriculum Council) (1993) *English in the National Curriculum: A Report to the Secretary of State for Education on the Statutory Consultation for Attainment Targets and Programmes of Study in English*, York: National Curriculum Council

SCAA (School Curriculum and Assessment Authority) (1994a) *English in the National Curriculum: Draft Proposals*, London: HMSO

SCAA (School Curriculum and Assessment Authority) (1994b) *The National Curriculum Orders*, London: HMSO

SCAA (School Curriculum and Assessment Authority) (1994c) *Evaluation of the Implementation of English in the National Curriculum at Key Stages 1, 2 and 3 (1991–93)*, London: HMSO

SCAA (School Curriculum and Assessment Authority) (1997) *Use of Language: A Common Approach*, London: HMSO

Stables, A. (1992) *An Approach to English*, London: Cassell

Stubbs, M. (1990) *Knowledge about Language: Grammar, Ignorance and Society*, Institute of Education, University of London

The Times (1993) 'Why the Right is Wrong', 1 March

Williamson, J. and Goodall, C. (1996) 'A Vision for English: Rethinking the Revised National Curriculum for English in the Light of Contemporary Critical Theory', *English in Education*, 30, 3, pp. 4–13

Williamson, J. and Hardman, F. (1994) 'Abridged too far: Evidence from Teachers against the Case for Revising the Cox Curriculum', *Educational Review*, 46, 3, pp. 233–46

3 What Do We Mean by Standard English and Language Study

JOHN WILLIAMSON

Many students come into teacher training with little or no formal training in language study. This partly reflects the relatively low priority which was placed on this area during their own school years; priorities have now changed, especially since the advent of the present pupils' National Curriculum, and Standard English and Language Study is now an element in each profile component (speaking and listening, reading and writing) at each key stage. Even among English graduates knowledge about language is often limited because their prime interest lies in the study of literature and they do not choose language or linguistics options. The ITT National Curriculum for secondary English notes that

> For some [students] the narrowness of their background subject knowledge may mean that they do not feel confident about, or competent in, all the English which they are required to teach. All trainees need to be aware of the strengths and weaknesses in their own subject knowledge, to analyse it against the pupils' National Curriculum and examination syllabuses, and to be aware of the gaps they will need to fill during their training.
>
> (DfEE, 1998, p. 99)

This chapter provides an introduction to that subject knowledge.

STANDARD ENGLISH

Standard English and other dialects

Quotation 1   And the Gileadites took the passages of Jordan before the Ephraimites: and it was so that when those Ephraimites which were escaped said 'let me go over' that the men of Gilead said to him, 'Art thou an Ephraimite?' If he said 'Nay' then they said

> unto him, 'Say now "Shibboleth"'; and he said 'Sibboleth' for he could not frame to pronounce it right. Then they took him and slew him at the passages of Jordan; and there fell at that time of the Ephraimites forty and two thousand.
>
> Judges XII: 5–6

As the above quotation suggests, forms of language have been important for a very long time and they continue to arouse strong feelings today. In countries such as Canada and Belgium there are major divisions between groups of people who are separated from each other through the use of different languages. One of the main languages of former Yugoslavia is generally known as Serbo-Croatian but even before the troubles it was important to Croats and their sense of identity to maintain that there was no such language; they argued that there was Serbian and there was Croatian but no Serbo-Croatian (Wardhaugh, 1992).

Historically, England has known no such divisions (although the same cannot be said of Ireland, Scotland or Wales). In the years since the Second World War, England has become a multilingual country but only English has official status and English is essentially the language of education so we will not be dealing in this section with the rich variety of languages from around the world which many of us encounter in our everyday lives.

This does not mean, however, that there is no variation in the English used in this country. In fact, English varies in many ways but our focus in this section is on differences in dialect and accent. The distinction between these terms is important and these two aspects of linguistic variation are treated quite differently from each other in the pupils' National Curriculum. The term dialect 'refers to a variety of the language that is identified geographically or socially by certain vocabulary or grammatical features' (Carter, 1995, p. 37). 'Accent' refers only to varieties of pronunciation. It should be noted that by definition every speaker of English speaks with an accent and in a dialect (or, quite commonly, with more than one). Your accent is simply your way of pronouncing English and your dialect is the collection of vocabulary and grammatical features which you use. Accents and dialects are not the prerogative of foreigners or people from rural or inner-city areas.

We mentioned geographical and social factors in the definitions; in fact the relationship between these factors is quite complex. Essentially, the higher up the social scale you go, the less regional distinctiveness there tends to be. So, for example, working-class speakers from Newcastle have an accent which is easily distinguished from the accent of similar people from Sunderland and Ashington, neither of which is more than 15 miles away. On the other hand, middle-class speakers – doctors, lawyers, most teachers and so on – might be identified as having a northern rather than a southern accent but they probably couldn't be precisely located. At the top of the social scale is a regionless accent which reflects merely the speaker's social status and not his or her geographical origins; this accent is known as Received Pronunciation (almost always referred to as 'RP'); 'received' is used in the Victorian sense of 'accepted' which perhaps indicates the social confidence of speakers of RP.

The situation with regard to dialect is rather different in some important respects. The majority of people in England have an accent with some regional component:

'It has been estimated that only about three per cent of the English population speak RP' (Hughes and Trudgill, 1987, p. 3). However far fewer people speak with a non-standard dialect; one study of children's speech in four widely separated parts of England found that about one-third of the sample used no non-standard dialect features at all (Hudson and Holmes, 1995). At some time in our lives all of us at least attempt to use Standard English (if only in writing) and many of us use it all the time. This is not true of RP.

A second important feature of English dialects is that they share so much in common.

> **Quotation 2**   Yes, classes influence language, introduce into the language their own specific words and expressions and sometimes understand one and the same word or expression differently. . . . [But] such specific words and expressions, as well as cases of difference in semantics, are so few in language that they hardly make up even one per cent of the entire linguistic material. Consequently, all the remaining overwhelming mass of words and expressions, as well as their semantics, are *common* to all classes of society.
>
> Joseph Stalin

Now, Stalin probably had his own agenda in this debate and we needn't perhaps take Soviet statistics of the period very seriously but the point made is a very important one. We tend to think of dialects as being entirely separate entities, each separated from the others. This is not at all the case, in two senses. On the one hand, words and grammatical constructions have their own patterns of geographical distribution that sometimes cut across dialect boundaries. For example, the word *bairn*, meaning a child, is used all over Scotland and the north east of England whereas *wean*, meaning the same, is restricted to a relatively small part of Scotland only. On the other hand, one major national study of non-standard dialects found that 97.5 per cent of schools surveyed reported the use of *them* as a demonstrative adjective in constructions like 'Look at them big spiders' (Cheshire, Edwards and Whittle, 1993, p. 65).

Now we come to a very important point: the tendency for all dialects to share words and constructions applies also to Standard English because Standard English is a dialect by our definition. If we look at the example above, 'Look at them big spiders', we can note that the words *look*, *at*, *big* and *spiders* are all used with exactly the same meaning as they would have in Standard English. Grammatically there are shared features, too, including the use of the imperative *look* and the adjective *big* premodifying the noun *spiders*.

Standard English has been mentioned several times now and it is perhaps time to try to define it.

> **Quotation 3**   Any standard language is no more than a dialect with an army and a navy.
> Cited in Carter, 1995, p. 149

Carter's somewhat jocular reference highlights the point that Standard English is in many ways a dialect which carries with it a particular power and prestige. Standard English is, in fact, a notoriously difficult term to define but one helpful way is to think about the uses to which it is put. Trudgill (1983, p. 17) suggests:

> Standard English is that variety of English which is usually used in print, and which is normally taught in schools and to non-native speakers learning the language. It is also the variety which is normally spoken by educated people and used in news broadcasts and other similar situations.

This should be illuminating for anyone with a good knowledge of the use of English in this country although it does leave the specifics of the grammar and vocabulary unmentioned. Wardhaugh (1992, p. 30) offers another way of thinking about the issue:

> *Standardization* refers to the process by which a language has been codified in some way. That process usually involves the development of such things as grammars, spelling books, and dictionaries, and possibly a literature . . . Standardization also requires that a measure of agreement be achieved about what is in the language and what is not.

It may be helpful, then, to think of Standard English as being that dialect of the language whose grammatical features, spelling and vocabulary can be verified in authoritative sources such as those mentioned. However, it should be noted that there is a danger of circularity here. What is Standard English? It's what you find in grammars and dictionaries. What gets put into grammars and dictionaries? Standard English. Good grammarians and lexicographers (dictionary-makers) try to avoid this difficulty by basing their work on studies of what people actually say and write. Of course, the 'measure of agreement' that Wardhaugh mentions probably covers the majority of features of Standard English (which as we have seen are shared by all British English dialects) but we should be aware that the boundaries of Standard English are not clear-cut for several reasons. One of these is illustrated by Activity 1.

Activity 1   Which, if any, of the following sentences are not examples of Standard English?

1 Between you and I there's nothing wrong with these sentences.
2 I don't know why people have to constantly look for mistakes.
3 None of the mistakes here are serious.
4 It's different to speaking in a foreign language.
5 Hopefully, we will be more tolerant in the future.

Well, the answer is, it depends on who you are talking to. Many people would regard all of these as perfectly normal examples of Standard English but many would object to them; in fact the sentences are based on a list of common complaints to the BBC about non-standard language. (You can find the grounds for some people's objections at the end of this chapter.) There are, to sum up, cases of divided usage where people disagree about what precisely constitutes Standard English.

Secondly, Standard English has no clearly definable boundaries because it is always changing. All language changes through time and we must adapt our views of what constitutes Standard English to accommodate this phenomenon. For example, there is no entry for *microchip* in the 1964 edition of the *Concise Oxford Dictionary* but there is in the 1995 edition.

Finally, different parts of the world have different varieties of Standard English. Even Scottish Standard English differs from the English version, with words like *ashet* (a serving dish) and constructions like 'My hair needs washed' as opposed to 'My hair needs washing'.

Attitudes towards accent and dialect

We saw at the start of this chapter that many people have powerful feelings about the languages spoken in their country. This is also true of the accents and dialects which people use.

Quotation 4	The accent of one's birthplace lingers in the mind and in the heart as it does in one's speech.
	Rochefoucauld

Quotation 4 highlights the way in which one's native speech can be an important part of one's sense of identity and of belonging to particular groups within society. The way a child speaks when he or she comes into school is something shared with parents, brothers and sisters, aunts and uncles and probably just about everyone he or she knows personally. The language forms of a community are an important aspect of that community's sense of itself.

Unfortunately, a less positive feature of dialect variation in Britain is that many British people have strong antipathies to the language of groups that they do not themselves belong to.

Quotation 5	It is impossible for an Englishman to open his mouth without making some other Englishman despise him.
	George Bernard Shaw

Shaw, not uncharacteristically, overstates his case somewhat but there is no doubt that there are strong prejudices within society which are largely based on social class divisions and which operate both upwards and downwards on the social scale. Many working-class communities with non-standard dialects have terms for middle-class speech forms that they regard as affected. There are many opprobrious epithets applied to middle-class speakers and, often, to members of one's own community whose speech forms are changing as they advance through the educational system: you may be familiar with terms like *talking posh*, *talking with a marble in your mouth*, *talking pan loaf* (a Scottish reference to the more genteel of the two kinds of sliced bread to be found in that country) and *talking lah di dah* (some of you may remember 'Mr lah di dah gunner Graham' from the television series *It Ain't Half Hot, Mum*).

However, middle-class prejudices towards working-class forms of language are far more important because of the power relationships within our society. A child who does not use Standard English in school may be seriously disadvantaged and application letters for many kinds of jobs may be frowned upon if not written in Standard English.

Quotation 6	Dialect words – those terrible marks of the beast to the truly genteel.
	Thomas Hardy

Many erroneous attitudes to non-standard dialects have persisted since Hardy wrote. Sometimes non-standard dialect users will be said to 'have no grammar'. This is wrong on two counts: firstly, as we have seen, non-standard dialects share most of the grammatical features of Standard English; secondly, where they vary from Standard English it is not that they have no grammar but simply that they have different grammatical rules. Non-standard dialects are not a free for all in which you can say anything; like all language they have rules which determine what is acceptable but they differ from those of Standard English. For example, in Standard English we form the past tense of *come* by changing it to *came*. So we have 'I came home yesterday'. In many non-standard dialects this verb is treated differently and people will say 'I come home yesterday'. This does not mean that there is no grammar but simply that the grammar of these dialects differs from Standard English in respect of how the past tense of *come* is formed. Notice, too, that there is a rule – you have to say 'I come home yesterday' not 'I comed home yesterday' or 'I camed home' or any other possibility.

Non-standard dialects are not 'wrong' in any meaningful sense – they are simply different from Standard English. All dialects are full language systems with coherent grammatical and lexical (vocabulary) systems; all can be adapted to any use, even if by convention some situations tend to be associated with Standard English. Trudgill (1975, p. 27) nicely illustrates this by translating a passage from an anthropology textbook into a non-standard west of England dialect:

> Social anthropology be a title used in England to designate a department of the larger subject of anthropology. On the continent a different terminology prevails. There when people speaks of anthropology, what to us is the entire study of man, they has in mind only what us calls physical anthropology, the biological study of man.

Notice again how much is shared between Standard English and the non-standard dialect but above all notice that it is possible to discuss such subjects perfectly comprehensibly in a non-standard dialect. It's just not very common to do so.

Standard English and the National Curriculum

It should be clear by now that there is a real tension between accepting non-standard dialects that can be very important to children and helping them acquire Standard English which may open many doors for them in life. The Cox Report, which provided the underpinnings of the first version of the pupils' National Curriculum for English, argues (DES, 1989, § 4.10) that

> It is important, in considering Standard English, to bear in mind the particular functions that it serves: for example, in the education system and in professional life, in public and formal uses, and in writing and particularly in print. *It is precisely because Standard English serves as a language of wider communication for such an extensive and important range of purposes that children must learn to use it competently.* (Original emphasis.)

The same report also notes, however, 'Standard English has to be treated very sensitively in schools, since dialect is so closely related to pupils' individual identity' (DES, 1989, § 4.33).

Although the curriculum that was derived from the Cox Report is now relegated to the mists of time, it is worth dwelling on it because it got the balance between Standard English and non-Standard English just about right. What the Cox Report did was to distinguish between speaking and writing in non-standard dialect:

> *The development of pupils' ability to understand written and spoken Standard English and to produce written Standard English is unquestionably a responsibility of the English curriculum.* Standard English is the variety used in the vast majority of printed and published English texts although non-Standard English is, of course, used in some imaginative literature.
>
> (DES, 1989, § 4.34, original emphasis)

This was translated into the original National Curriculum in the following terms: with regard to the speaking and listening components, pupils at level 5 (from the age of about 11 onwards) should be able to 'recognise variations in vocabulary between different regional or social groups, and relate this knowledge where appropriate to personal experience' (DES, 1990, p. 4) and at level 6 (secondary level) they should be able to 'show in discussion an awareness of grammatical differences between spoken Standard English and a non-Standard variety' (DES, 1990, p. 5). Writing is treated rather differently: at level 4 (that of a 'typical' 11-year-old) pupils should be able to 'begin to use the structures of written Standard English' (DES, 1990, p. 13) and at level 5 (from the age of about 11 onwards), they should 'demonstrate increased effectiveness in the use of Standard English (except in contexts where non-standard forms are needed for literary purposes)' (DES, 1990, p. 13). At all subsequent levels pupils up to the age of 16 are simply required to be able to use Standard English in writing with the caveat that literary purposes may be served by using non-standard dialect.

The different treatment of speaking and writing was right, in my opinion, for several reasons. In the first place, it is spoken language rather than written which carries with it the associations of home and community which we discussed earlier. Writing is very much a feature of the school and does not carry with it the affective loading of speech. Inappropriate intervention in the way children talk can lead to resentment or even inhibit pupils from talking. Imagine how you would feel about contributing to seminars if you were expected to speak in, say, a Scottish dialect and with a Scottish accent (if you are Scottish, imagine another dialect!).

Speech is complex, spontaneous and yet under control. When we speak we are organising sounds into significant patterns, creating complex grammatical structures and selecting appropriate words as well as considering such factors as the impact we want to create and the effect we are having on our listeners. We do all of this, and more, instantaneously. Try pausing for even ten seconds while you are speaking and you will see that it seems like an eternity and yet ten seconds is not long to make decisions about whether or not what you are about to say conforms to a dialect which differs from your own in ways which might seem arbitrary and confusing. In writing we can take our time and no one will ever know from the written product how long we took to wonder about an item, or look it up in a dictionary or ask for advice. There is an old story about Oscar Wilde to the effect that he was asked at dinner one night what he had done that morning. 'This morning, I put in a comma', he replied. 'And what did you do this afternoon?' 'This afternoon I took it out again.' Another argument in favour of teachers not trying to change the way in which children speak is that they are not very good at it. If teachers could eradicate non-standard forms then they would probably have done so a very long time ago.

Furthermore, people tend to change their own speech forms when they perceive it as desirable to do so. There are many speakers of English in Britain who are bi-dialectal, speaking both in the dialect of their home and in Standard English. It seems to be forgotten in National Curriculum documents that children today are exposed to Standard English to a very wide extent. Nearly all that they read will be in Standard English (another justification for treating Standard English as the language of literacy), most of what they watch on television, in the cinema and so on will also be in Standard English. We are all at least passive users of Standard English as listeners and readers.

STANDARD ENGLISH AND CONTEXT

To a great extent the tension mentioned at the start of the preceding section between accepting non-standard dialects and equipping pupils with Standard English can be countered through the notion of appropriacy. It is more appropriate to use Standard English in formal situations and in most written contexts. We have already seen that pupils have access to Standard English; part of the work of the English teacher is, as the National Curriculum for ITT (DfEE, 1998, p. 92) states, to ensure that, 'pupils [are] taught about the oral conventions that are appropriate in different situations and for different audiences, including the use of Standard English.' We all talk differently in different situations: the language we use when discussing education in the pub with our friends is not the same as that we use in a seminar. This is a question of the vocabulary we use and of the linguistic structures we employ – exactly the features which we have already established define dialects. Such variation is something children learn from an early stage in their schooling and can be extended to cover issues of dialect using approaches such as role-play (although sensitivity is always going to be required).

RESEARCH ON PUPILS' USE OF NON-STANDARD DIALECT

Our understanding of the use of non-standard dialect by British schoolchildren has been extended by three studies, one of which, Cheshire, Edwards and Whittle (1993), was based on evidence derived from a questionnaire while the others (Hudson and Holmes, 1995) and Williamson and Hardman (1997a and 1997b) were based on studies of children's actual usage.

Hudson and Holmes examined the use of non-standard dialect in speech using material gathered for the Assessment of Performance Unit (APU) in 1988 (Gorman et al., 1989). There were several reasons for using this corpus, one of the most important being that it just predated the inauguration of the National Curriculum and so could be used to give a baseline representation of the situation before any changes which might be brought about by the National Curriculum and could also therefore be used to compare findings from later studies of the impact of the National Curriculum (none of which have yet been carried out). Also, the APU tapes were part of a national survey which allowed for the study of speech from different parts of the country. Hudson and Holmes chose four widely dispersed regions – Merseyside, Tyneside, London and the south-west – and examined the speech of 11-year-olds and 15-year-olds.

One of the important findings which Hudson and Holmes report (1995, p. 9) is that 32 per cent of their sample of 350 children used nothing but Standard English. Hudson and Holmes (1995, p. 9) make the point that the figure of 62 per cent using at least one non-standard form should be taken as a minimum because of the relative formality of the test situation and because if a longer sample of speech had been provided some of the 32 per cent might have used a non-standard form. Be that as it may, it is important to note that nearly one-third of the pupils studied were capable of speaking exclusively in Standard English when the need arose. Further, of those who used non-standard dialect, 85 (24 per cent of the total sample) used only one non-standard form and only 7 per cent used more than four different non-standard forms. The sample as a whole produced a mean of 1.7 non-standard forms (Hudson and Holmes, 1995, p. 23). This suggests that even in speech, usage of non-standard dialect is quite restricted.

Williamson and Hardman (1997a) replicated Hudson and Holmes' study using the written texts from the 1988 APU survey with a sample of 362 children from the same regions and age ranges as the previous work. As might be expected, the incidence of non-standard dialect usage is less in writing than in speech.

Taken overall, just over one-third of the written sample used non-standard dialect forms although there was a range from about a quarter to a half of each of the sub-groups identified in Table 3.1 using non-standard forms. This may seem quite high but the overall figures should also be seen in the light of an analysis of the frequency with which non-standard forms were used.

Table 3.1 Percentage of scripts showing non-standard dialect features in spoken (Hudson and Holmes, 1995) and written English

Region	Age	Written English	Spoken English
Merseyside	11	23	62
	15	33	83
Tyneside	11	48	56
	15	48	72
South-west	11	26	59
	15	45	73
London	11	37	87
	15	26	80

It will be seen that no sub-group averages as many as two forms per script and it should be remembered that Table 3.2 includes only those pupils who used non-standard forms. 'Of the 127 children who used non-standard dialect 89 (70 per cent) did so on only one occasion and only 9 (7 per cent) used more than two *different* dialect features' (Williamson and Hardman, 1997b, p. 293). To set this in a wider context, Williamson and Hardman (1997b, p. 293) note that there were on average seven spelling errors per script whereas only three children out of 362 had as many as five non-standard dialect forms. In addition,

> The incidence of non-standard dialect per word of text decreased markedly between the ages of 11 and 15 [one occurrence every 381 words for the 11-year-olds, one every 569 for the 15-year-olds]. This would suggest that even before the National Curriculum introduced an element of compulsion into the business of teaching pupils to write in standard English there was a progressive decrease in the incidence of non-standard dialect features as pupils matured.
>
> (Williamson and Hardman, 1997b, p. 298)

Table 3.2 Mean number of non-standard forms for each written script containing non-standard forms

Region	Age	Forms per script
Merseyside	11	1.2
	15	1.6
Tyneside	11	1.8
	15	1.3
South-west	11	1.8
	15	1.5
London	11	1.9
	15	1.7

This study very definitely suggests that, in spite of the weight given to Standard English in the pupils' National Curriculum, there are more important considerations for teachers who wish to further their students' writing development.

Another important finding from both the studies we have been discussing is the extent to which non-standard forms seem to occur across all the regions. Table 3.3 is taken from Williamson and Hardman's data and, besides showing how widely spread some forms are, it provides an idea of some of the commonest non-standard features.

Table 3.3 Common non-standard features used by pupils in their writing

		South-west	London	Merseyside	Tyneside
1	Irregular past tense forms	I come	they seen	he give	we done
2	Plural subject with singular verb	squirrels eats	these whiskers tells	we was	they stops
3	there is/was	there is boats	there was other comics	there is others	there is some good stories
4	Adjectives used as adverbs	catch your breath as easy as before	fell asleep very quick	it went very slow	can grip very good
5	Singular subject with plural verb	it get damp			
6	Irregular past participle	[it] will have ran out	I have just came	eggs are took	Louise had drank it

Table 3.3 (continued)

	South-west	London	Merseyside	Tyneside
7 'More' plus comparative adjective	more easier	more heavier	more safer	more worse
8 Use of prepositions	down our local school	to put it off of my mind	out the telly	buy what we wanted off them
9 'Me' with subject noun phrase	me and my mum	me and Lisa	me and my family	me and John Bell
10 No plural marker on nouns of measurement or quantity	seven foot		in 12 year	I was 19 month
11 'What' as relative	the jacket what is different	a small furry animal what lives	every thing what happened	the size what you want
12 'This' as first mention	this doctor			this single cell
13 'Should of' (etc.)		he must of been	should of	
14 'Which' with human antecedent		there are 70 per cent of under sixteens which		they were only boys which
15 'Me' for 'my'			me dad	me friend
16 Periphrastic 'do'	I do get on with them			
17 'Them' as subject				them are
18 'Them' as determiner				from them diseases
19 Give it me		give me it		
20 'Sat/stood'		we saw three policemen stood		
21 Double negative		they don't know nothing		

It is noticeable that, of the ten commonest features all bar one appear in all four regions. In fact, if sample sizes were larger, we would probably find some of the blanks filled in; for example, neither Hudson and Holmes nor Williamson and Hardman found examples like 'seven foot' in London but this feature does appear in that area generally.

> **Activity 2** When you are in school, or any other appropriate setting, listen to children talking or look at their written language to identify examples of non-standard dialect. How many appear on the list in Table 3.3? Are there any specific to the part of the country you are in? For example, Scots have a pronoun 'a body' which equates to Standard English 'everyone'.

Standard English and the 'Standards'

This discussion of Standard English and other dialects should have given you the information required in the National Curriculum for secondary English in Initial Teacher Training (ITT). We have seen that Standard English is particularly important in certain situations (Standards A3c iii and A3d i); we have outlined some of the commonest ways in which Standard English differs from other dialects (Standard A3d ii) and have noted that Standard English can be spoken with different accents (Standard A3d iii). We have also considered the nature and role of Standard English in terms of its importance in our society (Standard C27b) and have come to some understanding of its place in our social and cultural milieu (Standard C28b ii).

OTHER ASPECTS OF LANGUAGE STUDY

Language variety

The National Curriculums for both pupils and trainee teachers require an awareness of some of the ways in which language varies; these include changes over time, the distinctive forms of language used in different situations, differences between speech and writing and differences which reflect the multi-ethnic nature of our society and of the range of languages spoken by English people today.

Changes over time

We cannot hope to supply a full history of the English language here, but perhaps the following might suggest something of the extent of the changes which have taken place.

Texts from the earliest period of English read to us nowadays like a foreign language. This first text is taken from a sermon produced round about the time of the last millennium (æ is a vowel symbol; some other symbols have been modernised):

> Leofan men, gecnawath thæt soth is: theos worold is on ofste and hit
> nealæcth tham ende, and thy hit is on worolde aa swa leng swa wyrse;
> and swa hit sceal nyde for folces synnanær Antecristes tocyme yfelian
> swythe, and huru hit wyrth thænne egeslic and grimlic wide on
> worolde.

If you haven't studied Old English, as this stage of English is called by academics, or
Anglo-Saxon as it is more popularly known, you could probably not do much more
than pick out a few words which have survived in the same form to the present day:
'men, is, and, on, for' and so on. Other words have survived but have changed their
form to a greater or lesser degree: 'worold' is our word 'world', 'theos' corresponds to
our 'this' and 'hit' to 'it'.

However, many of the words have disappeared altogether – 'nealæcth', 'ofste' and
'egeslic', for example, have no modern version. In addition to the relatively obvious
features of vocabulary, there are very important ways in which Old English grammar
differs from that of our period. Old English was a heavily inflected language, like
modern German, and nouns, verbs, adjectives and even the definite article had suffixes to show such features as number, gender and the function of the word in the
sentence. So, for our word 'the', Old English had 11 different forms which were used
according to whether the following noun was singular or plural; masculine, feminine
or neuter; subject or object of the verb and so on.

By the time we come to Chaucer, writing has changed considerably, as the following shows:

> Heere bigynneth the Knyghtes Tale
> Whilom, as olde stories tellen us
> Ther was a duc that highte Theseus;
> Of Athens he was lord and governour,
> And in his tyme swich a conqueror,
> That gretter was ther noon under the sonne.

Unlike the Old English text, Chaucerian English is at least broadly comprehensible
to a present day reader although obviously there are still differences from modern
English. The complexities of the suffixes marking grammatical categories has largely
disappeared although the last remnants appear at the end of words like 'bigynneth' and
'tellen'. Spelling is more like modern English, although there are still differences (and
will be for several hundred years) in words like 'heere, olde, duc (duke), governour'
and so on. Some of the words are no longer familiar – 'whilom' meaning 'once' and
'highte' for 'was called'. There are many Internet sources available which can help
you look with pupils at Old English and Middle English, as the English of Chaucer's
period is called. Some of these sites (e.g. http://www.librarius.com/cantales.htm for
Chaucer) provide texts with explanations and you can find a variety of sites listed
under 'Old English' and 'Anglo-Saxon' which will give you glossaries to help you and
your pupils work with the texts.

If we move forward another 400 years to the introduction of Jane Austen's *Northanger Abbey* we find that the differences from current English are even fewer and rather more subtle:

> No one who had ever seen Catherine Morland in her infancy would have supposed her born to be an heroine. Her situation in life, the character of her father and mother, her own person and disposition, were all equally against her. Her father was a clergyman, without being neglected, or poor, and a very respectable man, though his name was Richard – and he had never been handsome. He had a considerable independence besides two good livings – and he was not in the least addicted to locking up his daughters.

Clearly now we have a language which is very much like our own. But appearances can sometimes be deceptive: 'independence', for example, is a word we still use but here it means 'of independent means', what we would refer to as 'having a private income'. Otherwise, the main differences are those of style – the length of the sentences, for example, is longer than we would tend to expect in a twenty-first century novel.

Obviously, these three examples can only give you the merest flavour of how English has changed over the centuries but should have given you some idea of the way that language change can affect spelling, grammar and vocabulary. These can all be the subject of active approaches to teaching about language change and your focus can be on quite recent developments because language is always changing in one way or another. Let's look at some examples of the sort of work which you might like to consider, even if your knowledge of the history of English is not very great, taking categories from the pupils' National Curriculum (DfEE, 1995, p. 18).

A study of Jane Austen, as we have seen, could give us a lead into the ways in which 'usage, words and meanings change over time' (DfEE, 1995, p. 18). This could also be extended to look at ways in which new words are introduced today. Why do they appear? Many reflect developments in technology – the word 'web' is now used in a new sense, referring to the world-wide information source. 'Internet' would be another very similar example. Pupils could be asked to collect examples and see whether or not they are entered in dictionaries of different ages. Other words may have been around for longer but have changed their meaning – 'computer' now refers to something much more wide-ranging than the 'electronic calculating machine' of the 1964 edition of the *Concise Oxford Dictionary*. The whole field of technology is an interesting one but we can also find examples from other sources: one which is always interesting to young people is the vocabulary of their own age range – at the time of writing (and these are very transitory phenomena) one word used to express approval is 'mint' but over the last 30 years we have seen 'fab', 'groovy' (yes, really), 'cool' (one which recurs from time to time) and 'wicked' among many others. Another fruitful field is that of social conditions – how old is the expression 'single parent family'? Popular culture generally is a good field for investigation – even well established terms like 'reggae' and 'disco' appear in the 1995 but not the 1964 *Concise Oxford Dictionary* (Pearsall, 1999), let alone terms like 'garage', 'warehouse' and 'grunge'.

You can also look with pupils at the means by which we create new words. One common source is the adaptation of existing words: 'web' and 'chip' (in its sense of a piece of silicon used in computers) would be examples of this. Otherwise, we borrow words, or part of words, from other languages as in '*microchip*' or '*Internet*'. The meaning of some words can be guessed from their constituent parts – 'lap-top' whereas others are less accessible – 'modem' which comes from the beginnings of the two words 'modulator' and 'demodulator' (Pearsall, 1999).

Even with older texts, a great deal of investigative work can be done although you don't know all the answers yourself. For example, Shakespeare uses our present-day second person pronoun 'you' but also employs the older forms 'thou, thee, thy', etc. Their use is not random but broadly similar to the use of 'tu' and 'vous' forms in French. 'You' forms are used to superiors or between equals in formal situations. 'Thou' forms are used to inferiors or between equals in informal situations. Charting the use of these different forms in a scene or act of a play you are reading is interesting from the viewpoint of linguistic history but will also give insights into relationships within the play itself.

Another interesting activity would be to take a Chaucer text and look at the verb endings; this would offer an insight into suffixes and inflectional endings and show how language operates systematically as well as giving an insight into language change. If this is taken on with a class in a spirit of shared investigation, you don't have to know all the answers yourself, although clearly you can do a little bit of reading round the topic before you start.

As was said at the start of this section, no chapter like this can hope to give you details of the whole history of the English language or offer a comprehensive account of all the useful and interesting activities that can be done in school on this topic. However, you will have gained a sense of how much exciting work there is to be done if the topic is approached in an investigative and open-minded way. This section should help meet requirement Standard A3d iv of the National Curriculum for Secondary English in ITT (DfEE, 1998, p. 92).

Speech and writing

Another dimension of language variation with which you must be familiar is that between the written and spoken varieties of language. It is important for your work on the development of children's writing skills that you are aware that writing is not simply a direct recording in visual form of the spoken language but that, in important ways, these two modes of language differ from one another. Much of the difference arises from the spontaneous nature of spoken language where we produce (and as listeners, decode) speech instantaneously with, typically, little time to focus on patterns of organisation at different levels whereas writing is a slower, more controllable form of language use where we can take time to shape and organise our ideas and where, as readers, we can take as long as we need to reflect on what is being said.

Other differences arise because speech usually takes place within a face-to-face situation where meanings can, if necessary, be clarified and expanded whereas writing (in out of school contexts) is generally produced when one is not in direct contact with the addressee (if we *were* in contact we would speak to someone rather than write to them).

One of the main differences is what is sometimes referred to as the 'normal non-fluency' of speech. Precisely because we are engaged in such a complex process when we speak, our spoken language is full of hesitations, false starts and errors. Consider the following short extract from a TV discussion:

> [I] think it's very unfortunate that we make it a lot worst by being so rigid in our attitude to alternative or complementary medicines. We . . . in . . . the . . . because of Newton's opposite and . . . equal and opposite reactions, you naturally get another castle . . . another . . . another entire [interruption] enclosed castle arising . . . without which . . . it builds an entirely different system and I think this is very dangerous and very unhelpful to patients.
>
> (LINC, undated, p. 194)

We see here several of the features of spontaneous talk. There is a grammatical error – 'we make it a lot worst' rather than 'a lot worse'. There are false starts, which happen when we start out on a structure and then find it does not fit what we are going to say: 'We . . . in . . . the . . . because of Newton's'; and 'enclosed castle . . . without which . . . it builds an entirely different system'. The last example also exemplifies an apparent lack of logic – the speaker means the opposite of 'without which' – which characterises this type of talk.

Later in the transcript the same speaker continues:

> erm . . . I . . . find this very worrying . . . er . . . er . . . Debra who seems a delightful person has already fallen . . . got into the other camp so to speak . . . rather than um

Here, in addition to repeating some of the features already mentioned, the speaker uses hesitation phenomena like 'erm' and 'um' which we use when we want to say something but haven't quite got it formalised in our heads and silence fillers – the two instances of 'er' – which we use to retain hold of our right to speak while again we work out what to say next.

It would be very easy to think that the speaker is very inarticulate, perhaps because of nerves, but it is *very* important to realise that she is just doing what we all do when we speak spontaneously. We only notice the apparent oddity of the language because we are focusing on it in a transcribed form. This is important because, unless you are aware of the nature of this normal non-fluency, you may misjudge the speech competence of your pupils, especially when they are trying to express complex ideas.

Other differences between speech and writing are centred on the distinction between the resources available to us as either speaker/listeners or reader/writers. In speech we have a range of features such as stress and intonation which enable us to make fine distinctions of meaning: '*He* wasn't very late' (which implies someone else was) is quite different from 'He wasn't *very* late' (which aims at minimising the degree of his lateness) even though both utterances contain the same words. Very often, a shared knowledge of the situation, in conjunction with how an utterance is delivered can enable us to mean (and be understood as meaning) the exact opposite of what the words themselves seem to suggest; how often have you heard someone who has just made a hash of something being told 'That was clever'? Reinforcing features of stress and intonation are features of gesture, body language and facial expression. All of these can come together to make a major impact on what we are saying in ways that have no real equivalent in writing. The pupil sitting at the back of your class, slumped down in his (it's usually, though not always, his) chair with a scowl on his face, playing with his biro is communicating to you without even saying a word.

Partly because of what we have just been discussing, and partly because the face-to-face context of speech enables breakdown in communication to be easily repaired, there is a tendency for writing to express its meaning much more explicitly than speech which tends to leave unsaid that which it can be reasonably assumed the listener will understand. So, discussions like the following are not at all unusual:

> *Speaker A*:   Did you go?
> *Speaker B*:   Yeah!
> *Speaker A*:   What was it like?
> *Speaker B*:   Great.
> *Speaker A*:   Were they good?
> *Speaker B*:   Brilliant.

Such an interchange is perfectly comprehensible if you realise that Speakers A and B both know that B was planning to go to a concert the previous evening. There is simply no *need* for A to say 'Did you go to the concert which we were discussing the last time that we met' and so on. In fact, continually giving information in speech which is shared with your interlocutor is a pretty good way of being stigmatised as a bore! Vagueness is tolerated in speech whereas in writing we tend to feel a need to identify what we are discussing much more clearly.

Another major difference between speaking and writing is centred on the features described in the section 'Beyond the Sentence' of Chapter 4 of this book. Writing is generally much more carefully structured than speech in terms of the organisation of the discourse as a whole. Typically, conversation is random in its subject matter and wanders from topic to topic apparently haphazardly, sometimes returning to themes which have been aired minutes earlier. There are exceptions to this – lectures, for example, would normally be expected to be coherently structured (and very informal letters would be an example of writing which can be very loosely structured) – but on the whole, learning to shape and link together a text is a skill which pupils have to acquire in relation to writing and it will be part of your responsibilities to help them do this.

To sum up, statement A3d vi of the ITT National Curriculum (DfEE, 1998, p. 92) requires that you can ensure that pupils know the differences between speech and writing and it has been suggested here that the main differences are: speech is typically spontaneous whereas writing can be a more deliberate activity and so speech is likely to be replete with the features of normal non-fluency; that speech is supported by features of the voice and non-linguistic communication which play a part in the conveying of meaning that the written equivalent, punctuation, cannot fully replicate; that speech usually takes place when there is direct contact between the participants and so is more tolerant of assumptions of shared knowledge than writing, where breakdowns of communication are much more difficult to resolve; the organisation of speech into a coherent overall structure is rare although this is a feature of much writing.

MULTILINGUALISM

England is no longer a monolingual country (Scotland and Wales never were); at a conference in 1996, data from the Schools Curriculum and Assessment Authority suggested that over 200 different languages were spoken in the United Kingdom and that about 10 per cent of pupils were bilingual. These pupils present both a challenge and an opportunity for teachers of English in the secondary phase and this section seeks to introduce some of the major issues of which you should be aware.

It is important to start by pointing out that bilingualism is not unusual, even though it may seem so to British people who have been brought up in certain parts of this country. Crystal (1994, p. 360) notes

> Multilingualism is the natural way of life for hundreds of millions all over the world. There are no official statistics, but with around 5,000 languages co-existing in fewer than 200 countries it is obvious that an enormous amount of language contact is taking place; and the inevitable result of languages in contact is *multilingualism*, which is most commonly found in an individual speaker as *bilingualism*.

The term 'bilingual' is one which has a variety of definitions; in everyday speech it is sometimes used to refer to someone who has a complete mastery of two languages. In practice, this applies to very few people, if only because one language tends to be used in some situations and the other in different contexts. For example, a Bengali-speaking pupil in Britain may use Bengali at home and when talking to other members of his or her community, use English at school and when speaking to friends or even siblings and use Arabic in religious contexts. Throughout this section when we talk of 'bilinguals' we will be referring to people who use two or more languages in their everyday lives; there is no implication that they have a perfect command of both languages or that they have the same range of competence in both. In current educational jargon, bilingual children are often referred to as 'children with English as an additional language'; the term 'bilingual' is preferred in this section partly because it is more concise but more importantly because it implies a holistic and positive view of the child.

Racism and culture

It is impossible, with respect to the majority of bilingual pupils in Britain to ignore issues of race and culture. Racism is a problem at all levels in our society and we cannot entirely separate the educational system from the broader environment in which it functions. Racism ranges from relatively minor instances of insensitivity or ignorance to extremes of violence, including arson and murder. It can create both personal and psychological problems for its victims and it is important for you to be on guard at all times. Any school in which you work should have a policy on racial incidents and it is important that you find out what machinery exists in your school (and its Local Education Authority) to deal with such events. At one level, pupils can suffer abuse or violence from their peers and you can make a valuable contribution through your work in English towards developing a culture of tolerance and accept-ance of differences. Goody (1992) provides a helpful list of materials. At another level, school as institutions can be racist – make sure, for example, that pupils are not being stereotyped and doomed to failure through self-fulfilling prophecies.

It is also important to be aware of cultural differences which can be particularly important for subjects like English and History which often rely on the shared expe-rience of the white community. Texts may rely on background knowledge which is not shared by all your pupils and it may be necessary to undertake pre-reading activities which will ensure all members of the class know the starting point for the text. It is essential to bear in mind that cultural differences can also be an enriching asset in your classroom. You may have pupils who can broaden the horizons of others whose view of the world is fundamentally Eurocentric or even Anglocentric. Activ-ities which draw on experiences and understandings which bilingual pupils are willing to share can add a great deal to your pupils' understanding of the world in which they live and of our multicultural, multi-ethnic society.

Mother tongue

There is now widespread acceptance of the view that 'It is crucial for the child who speaks a minority language to see that the minority language is given status and importance outside the home' (Baker and Prys Jones, 1998, p. 491).

This is important, firstly, because, as we have seen with non-standard dialects, language is an important aspect of one's sense of community and of an individual's sense of self. Wherever possible, interest in and study of, works in community lan-guages should be encouraged. Work on a poem in Gujerati for example, if you have a Gujerati speaker in your class, could lead to investigations of the sound system, spelling and grammar as well as consideration of the themes of the text. This can be a valuable extension of language work which would be of value to all pupils as well as having the benefit of casting the Gujerati-speaking child in the role of expert.

Secondly, use of the mother tongue may be important as a cognitive tool for the bilingual child; language is a tool for thinking and if pupils feel they can best come to terms with complex new material in their first language, then encourage them to do so, either on their own or, if relevant, with peers who speak the same language. There is no need to insist on English being used all the time if to do so would lead to a double handicap of difficult material combined with difficulties in the second language. Why shouldn't the child we imagined above make rough notes in Gujerati if that helps him or her to develop an understanding of the topic in question?

Contexts

There is a great deal of variety in the situations you may encounter with bilingual pupils. Firstly, you must always remember that all the ranges of individual variation which apply to monolingual students also apply to bilinguals. There are very able bilingual children and some who have special needs. There are bilingual pupils with rich, supportive homes and others who suffer from multiple deprivation. There are bilingual pupils whose parents see education as of vital importance and others whose parents do not. As with any pupil, you should never make assumptions until you know the pupils well.

Secondly, bilingual pupils will vary considerably in terms of their command of English, which is often related to the amount of time they have spent in the English education system. The majority of bilingual pupils in secondary schools have been born in this country, have progressed through the primary phase and may come to you with a command of English which enables them to function perfectly well in your class (although be aware of the BICS/CALP distinction discussed below). Others may have come to this country at a later stage in their childhood, often as refugees, and will have different needs from the first group.

Contexts also vary in respect of the catchment area of the school in which you are teaching. Some schools have a very high proportion of bilingual pupils whereas in others there may be only one or two in each class or even in the whole school. Specialist provision varies across the country and it is difficult to generalise but in many ways the teacher in the first kind of school has certain advantages over those in the second kind. Firstly, there is more likely to be substantial specialist support including bilingual teachers, who can support the child in his or her mother tongue. Secondly, you are likely to have more access to community members who can help with matters like translating notes from the school to parents who may not be literate in English. You are also more likely to have groups of speakers of the same language in your class and can structure work so that they can support each other in their mother tongue. Finally, the ethos of the school is likely to be more supportive of work with bilingual pupils, this being manifested in terms of, for example: more multilingual displays in the school; providing a community room where parents can come and meet and feel a part of the school community; more encouragement and support for you to undertake further training in working with bilingual pupils.

Withdrawal of pupils to give them extra English work is now relatively rare except in the case of new arrivals to this country; it should always be of a limited duration and lead to a phased introduction to mainstream teaching because withdrawal is racially and socially divisive, cuts pupils off from the mainstream curriculum and reduces contact with English-speaking peers which is a crucial element in second language learning. The norm is to give support to bilingual pupils who need it in the mainstream classroom. This works best when certain conditions prevail: there should be teamwork between the mainstream and support teacher with regard to the syllabus, with the support teacher being consulted well in advance of each lesson so that appropriate activities and materials can be prepared; teaching methods must be organised in such a way that the support teacher has an opportunity to participate – a lesson of whole-class work with the mainstream teacher leading from the front may not give the support teacher a chance to make a contribution; the support teacher must have appropriate status within the classroom and a clearly understood role as an equal partner in the work of the class – one support teacher reports that mainstream teachers treated her 'like a radiator at the back of the room' (Williamson, 1989, p. 325).

Some key concepts in second language acquisition

One central component of a second language acquisition is the provision of *comprehensible input*. This means making the language your pupils are exposed to as easy to understand as possible. We make sense of language and of the world in tandem and this is much easier when the language is rooted in real experience of the context to which the language refers so that the context supports the attempt to acquire language. This is much easier in 'practical' subjects than in English – for example, in the context of a science lesson, pupils will be able to use a pipette at the same time as learning its name. In English, preparatory work may be valuable before beginning the reading of a text. This can involve activities such as brainstorming, the use of photographs and video, and drama activities such as role-play. It is helpful if you try as much as possible to identify in advance concepts, vocabulary and structures which might create difficulties and try to deal with them before problems arise. In other words, follow normal good practice for English teaching.

Next, we need to engage learners in natural communication activities; what bilingual pupils need is exposure to real English used for real purposes, not drills or exercises which do little to further the acquisition and development of communication skills. Formal language teaching is very complex; consider the following as an example (there is a variation in some English verbs in terms of whether a following verb should be in the infinitive form ('to talk') or present participle form ('talking'); some take one, some the other and some can take either):

I want to talk *but not* I want talking
I enjoy talking *but not* I enjoy to talk
I like talking *and* I like to talk

Now, unless you've studied linguistics you have probably never been aware of this little corner of English grammar – you acquired the appropriate structures through exposure to other people using these verbs and learned how to use them yourself. It *would* be possible for students to learn a list of the appropriate uses but it is far easier for them to acquire the usages through experience of hearing them used appropriately, internalising them and then producing them in the way that a first language learner would in appropriate, meaningful contexts. If you spot a linguistic need, devise an activity which will meet that need through *using* language rather than talking *about* it. For example, if a pupil is having difficulties with some of the question forms in English, rather than trying to teach these explicitly in the abstract, structure a group activity in which a questionnaire is to be devised so that question forms arise naturally and purposefully.

Another important aspect of working with bilingual pupils which is part of normal good practice is the provision of an encouraging, supportive environment in which pupils feel comfortable about using English. Creating a positive attitude to the use of English, strong motivation and self-confidence while reducing anxiety will have a beneficial effect on second language learners (Baker and Prys Jones, 1998, p. 649).

BICS and CALP

It has long been recognised (see, for example, Skutnabb-Kangas (1981) and Cummins (1984)) that there is a distinction between Basic Interpersonal Communication Skills (BICS) and Cognitive/Academic Language Proficiency (CALP). BICS refers to one's use of language in everyday communicative situations, talking to peers, relaxing with friends, discussing the events of the day and so on. This level of language competence is often quickly acquired by bilingual learners who catch up with their monolingual peers quite rapidly. This use of language is typically rooted in a supportive context of shared meanings and understandings. CALP, on the other hand, is typically a context-reduced form of language which is more abstract and less grounded in the here and now of everyday conversation. This is much slower to develop in bilingual (and many monolingual children) and can lead to difficulties, especially in secondary schools where language is generally less rooted in supportive concrete environments than is the case in primary schools. The great danger which arises from the distinction between BICS and CALP is that erroneous judgements can easily be made. You may have a child in your class who talks to you with native-speaker-like proficiency; he or she can talk about hobbies, interests, how they get to school and so on; they may well talk with a local accent. It is easy to assume, if such a child is having difficulties with the curriculum, that the problem is not one of language but rather lies in a poor attitude to work or a lack of ability. However, it may simply be that 'The child may not have the vocabulary, more advanced grammatical constructions, nor an understanding of the subtleties of meaning to grasp what is being taught' (Baker and Prys Jones, 1998, p. 93).

Summary: some pointers for English teachers

It is important to consider the following:

- You must bear in mind the cultural dimension discussed above – remember that reading depends on a knowledge of the world as well as of the language of the text; how do you follow *Cinderella* if you don't know what a pumpkin is? Try to recognise sticking-points in advance and prepare for them to avoid the pupils encountering difficulties.

- Even if a child appears to have a good command of English, there may be gaps, particularly in vocabulary. If you are going to study *A Tale of Two Cities*, you need to be sure that the children understand the word 'revolution'; if you go on to *Hard Times* you may need to be sure that they understand the difference between the French Revolution and the Industrial Revolution. Again, think these out in advance and prepare the pupils for them.

- Oral and collaborative work is vitally important because children acquire a great deal of their English from interacting with their peers; if you think of a one-hour period with 30 pupils in a class, each child can have only two minutes speaking with the teacher (even assuming all the time is spent in individual interaction, which it never is) so it follows that if a pupil is going to have the chance to *use* English much of the work has to come in peer group interaction. If you have a beginning bilingual in your class, you should be aware of the 'silent period'; in the early stages of acquiring a second language pupils often go for a long time (it can be months) without speaking. You should be aware of this and accept it; the child is busy internalising features of the language which will be turned into speech when he or she is ready.

- Writing may not reflect oral proficiency for reasons which have much to do with the difference between speech and writing dealt with above. Try to focus on specific points which seem important for further development and work on these one at a time; don't expect everything to be corrected at one go – there will always be another occasion to work on the next point of importance.

- Think about language functions and styles: are there gaps in what the children can use English *for*? Can they undertake explanatory writing, persuasive writing and so on? Structure activities which will lead to the acquisition of a range of language uses. This, again, is normal good practice and is part of the National Curriculum requirements (DfEE, 1995, p. 23).

- Do there seem to be particular grammatical difficulties for your pupils? This may range from relatively simple things like problems with English articles ('the' and 'a') to the more complex structures they may encounter in their reading: for example, 'He is nothing if not cheerful' may be taken to mean 'he is not cheerful' rather than the opposite. When you do identify problem issues devise an activity which will engage the pupils in using the problematic feature.

- As discussed above, make some of the texts you study relate to, and value, the culture and experience of life beyond our often insular, Anglocentric framework. This again is a National Curriculum requirement (DfEE, 1995, p. 19) and is of such value to *all* pupils that you should do this even if there are no ethnic minority children in your class.

A final note on multilingualism

We can only give you the briefest introduction here to working with bilingual children but you should find it among the most satisfying and productive areas of your teaching. Remember the following points, above all, and you will have the foundations for success:

- Bilingual children constitute a resource which opens up a whole range of avenues of work on language and literature not otherwise accessible to you and the rest of your pupils.
- In many ways, following normal good practice will lead to success with *all* pupils, bilingual and monolingual.
- Give the bilingual pupils the opportunity to use their English in discussion with their peers so that they can experiment and try it out.
- Respect and value the language and culture which the bilingual pupils bring to your class.
- Try to identify the demands which will be made on bilingual pupils by the lesson you are about to teach and prepare accordingly.

SOUND SYSTEM AND SPELLING SYSTEM

All languages have a sound system and all those with a written form have a spelling system. By 'system' here we mean that the sounds or letters are organised into meaningful patterns.

In relation to the sound system this involves, first of all, selection from the vast range of noises which human beings can make with their mouths; for example, in English we do not make use of the nasal vowels which can be found in French or the clicks which form part of some African languages. Next we organise the sounds which are to be used into contrastive units known as phonemes. A phoneme consists of a set of related sounds which function as a single unit within the sound system; speakers of any given language find it easy to distinguish between sounds which belong to different phonemes but often find it difficult to distinguish between sounds which belong to the same phoneme because the latter differences are not significant in their language and do not differentiate between one word and another. Some examples will make this clearer.

Say the words 'keep' and 'call' out loud (ignore the difference in spelling, we will return to that later). Is the initial 'k' sound the same in both words? If you answer 'yes', say them again and try to feel where your tongue is when you pronounce each 'k' sound. You will find that 'k' in 'keep' is made with the tongue further forward in the mouth than it is for 'call'; this is because the following vowels are made in different parts of the mouth and when we pronounce the initial 'k' we are anticipating where the tongue is going to move to next. Try to start with the 'k' you would use for 'keep' but say 'call' instead – doesn't it feel awkward? You may find it hard to hear but the different articulation of the two 'k' sounds leads to a difference in the sounds produced. The two 'k' sounds belong to the same phoneme in English; they never differentiate between words but are merely different variants (the technical term is allophones) of the phoneme /k/ (phonemes are cited between slashes) which are used in different phonetic contexts.

Now consider the pair 'keep' and 'peep'; the initial sounds again differ from each other but this time they appear in the same phonetic context and mark the distinction between two different words. What we have here is two different phonemes – /k/ and /p/ – which differentiate between a series of pairs like 'pill, kill'; 'peel, keel'; 'pick, kick' and 'cat, pat'.

Spelling

There are about 44 phonemes in English (we cannot be precise because the number of phonemes varies from accent to accent); problems with spelling arise in large measure because we have only 26 letters in the spelling system. This partly accounts for the fact that the same phoneme can be spelt in a variety of ways: the phoneme /i/ for example can be spelt as in 'feel', 'leaf', 'chief', 'people', 'Crete', 'police', 'be' and 'seize'. Other spelling difficulties arise because the spoken language has changed more than the written version: for example the 'gh' in 'knight' was pronounced at one time (like the final sound in Scots 'loch'); the pronunciation changed but the spelling did not change with it. Smith (1978, p. 54) cites a total of over 300 sound-spelling correspondences. LINC (undated, p. 143) notes that, 'Less than half the words that most commonly occur in English have a regular sound–symbol correspondence. So, a strategy that is based solely on a phonetic approach is inevitably limited and ultimately misleading.' Accurate spelling is normally rooted in a sense of the shape which a word should take.

It follows from this that there is great value in emphasising to pupils the *visual* aspect of spelling. One technique commonly used to help pupils develop their visual memory is the 'look – cover – remember – write – check' system (LINC, undated, p. 144). In this, the pupil looks at the word, covers it up, commits it to memory, then writes it and checks it with the original. The strength of this method lies in its emphasis on the visual form of the word. Other techniques can also be employed: one is to look for root words within the word to be learned and use them as a basis for correct spelling – for example, if you can spell 'road' and 'worthy' it should be easy to spell 'roadworthy'. It is also worth looking at *recurring* patterns of error in individual pupils' work: for example, do they regularly make errors with doubled letters, or with dropping a final 'e' before a present participle ('bake' and 'baking'). If you are about to introduce pupils to a new word with an unusual or irregular spelling, it is worth explicitly drawing their attention to its spelling (DfEE, 1998, p. 95). A knowledge of the spelling of common prefixes and suffixes can also help pupils with long words which they might otherwise feel reluctant to attempt: for example knowing that the suffix '-ful' is spelt with one 'l' will be helpful in a whole range of words like 'cheerful', 'joyful', 'helpful' and so on.

Punctuation

Like spelling, punctuation is a system which exists only in relation to written language and as such pupils often have difficulty with it. It is assumed here that you, as a student teacher of English, know how to use punctuation in English. If this is not the case, there are many sources you can turn to (Greenbaum, 1996, pp. 503–55; Wray and Medwell, 1997, pp. 18–20 and 39–42 and web sites such as http://cite.telecampus.com/GED/punct.html).

The teaching of punctuation is a relatively little researched area of English teaching; Beard (undated, p. 50) notes, 'Punctuation has rarely been discussed at length in literacy education publications . . . Recent investigations by Nigel Hall and Anne Robinson (1996) have highlighted how little is known about how punctuation is taught and learned'.

As a teacher of English in the secondary phase, pupils should come to you with a substantial command of the major features of punctuation: the National Curriculum for Key Stage 2 specifies that 'In punctuation, pupils should be taught to use punctuation marks correctly in their writing, including full stops, question and exclamation marks, commas, inverted commas, and apostrophes to mark possession' (DfEE, 1995, p. 15). You may find that this is a counsel of perfection and that there is a need for revision of these elements; if so, the key is to start from the pupils' own work rather than focusing on decontextualised exercises which tend not be generalised into the pupils' own writing. It is very easy to have pupils do exercises on, say, inverted commas with a very high level of success only to find they are not used when the pupils come to write. Exploring children's writing with them and showing them the ambiguity and loss of clarity which arises when punctuation is not used appropriately is a much more direct way of getting to the heart of the matter, which is the incorporation of punctuation marks into the work which the children produce. Like-wise, the more 'advanced' punctuation marks not mentioned in the Key Stage 2 programmes of study cited above – the colon and semi-colon – can be introduced in relation to children's own writing by showing them the value of these features as a means of clarifying the structure of what they have written. As Beard (undated, p. 50) suggests, knowledge of punctuation 'is likely to be best learned in a context which stresses authentic reading and writing activities'.

Answers to Activity 1   These sentences were based on a list of frequent complaints made to the BBC concerning the use of non-standard grammar. The notes below refer to Fowler (1965) and Treble and Vallins (1961), two of the major texts on prescriptive grammar, that is to say grammar which tells you how you ought to speak rather than providing a description of how people actually speak.

Purists would object to these sentences on the following grounds:

1 'Between you and I . . .' should be 'Between you and me . . .'. This 'rule' arises from the influence of Latin on early thinkers about correctness in English; Fowler (1965, p. 258) notes, '*Between you and I* is a piece of false grammar which, though often heard is not sanctioned.' Typically of writers on this subject, Fowler omits to say by whom any given usage could or should be sanctioned.

2 'I don't know why people have to constantly look for mistakes.' Purists would argue that an infinitive (the form of a verb which consists of 'to' plus the stem of the verb – 'to know, to see, to comprehend' and so on) should not be interrupted (in this case by the adverb 'constantly'). Fowler, almost unbelievably, devotes two and a half pages to this issue (pp. 579–82).

3 'None of the mistakes here are serious.' Treble and Vallins (1961, p. 123) argue 'Since *none* = "not one" logical grammar would fix it as a singular'. So, it would be argued, we should have 'None of the mistakes here is serious.'

4 Even Fowler doesn't maintain that 'It's different to speaking in a foreign language' has to be used instead of 'It's different from speaking in a foreign language' asserting that 'the principle on which [different to] is rejected (you do not say *differ to*; therefore you cannot say *different to*) involves a hasty and ill-defined generalisation'. However, some would disagree.

5 'Hopefully, we will be more tolerant in the future'; many people object to this use of 'hopefully' as a sentence adverbial, qualifying the whole sentence and feel it should only be used of people who are full of hope as in 'We travelled hopefully'.

REFERENCES

Baker, C. and Prys Jones, S. (1998) *Encyclopedia of Bilingualism and Bilingual Education*, Clevedon: Multilingual Matters

Beard, R. (undated) *National Literacy Strategy: Review of Research and Other Related Evidence*, London: DfEE

Carter, R. (1995) *Keywords in Language and Literacy*, London: Routledge

Cheshire, J., Edwards, V. and Whittle, P. (1993) 'Non-Standard English and Dialect Levelling' in J. Milroy and L. Milroy, *Real English: The Grammar of English Dialects in the British Isles*, London: Longman, pp. 53–96

Crystal, D. (1994) *The Cambridge Encyclopedia of Language*, Cambridge: CUP

Cummins, J. (1984) *Bilingualism and Special Education: Issues in Assessment and Pedagogy*, Clevedon: Multilingual Matters

DES (1989) *English for Ages 5 to 16* (The Cox Report), London: HMSO

DES (1990) *English in the National Curriculum*, London: HMSO

DfEE (1995) *English in the National Curriculum*, London: HMSO

DfEE (1998) *Teaching: High Status, High Standards; Requirements for Courses of Initial Teacher Training*, DfEE Circular 4/98

Fowler, H.W. (1965) *A Dictionary of Modern English Usage*, 2nd edn, Oxford: OUP

Goody, J. (ed.) (1992) *Multicultural Perspectives in the English Curriculum*, Sheffield: NATE

Gorman, T., White, J., Brooks, G. and English, F. (1989) *Language for Learning: A Summary Report on the 1988 APU Surveys of Language Performance*, London: SEAC

Greenbaum, S. (1996) *The Oxford English Grammar*, Oxford: OUP

Hall, N. and Robinson, A. (eds) (1996) *Learning about Punctuation*, Clevedon: Multilingual Matters

Hudson, R. and Holmes, J. (1995) *Children's Use of Spoken English*, London: SCAA

Hughes, A. and Trudgill, P. (1987) *English Accents and Dialects*, 2nd edn, London: Edward Arnold

LINC (Language in the National Curriculum) (undated) *Materials for Professional Development*, no publisher

Pearsall, J. (ed.) (1999) *The Concise Oxford Dictionary*, Oxford: Oxford University Press

Quirk, R. and Wrenn, C. L. (1963) *An Old English Grammar*, 2nd edn, London: Methuen

Skutnabb-Kangas, T. (1981) *Bilingualism or Not: The Education of Minorities*, Clevedon: Multilingual Matters

Smith, F. (1978) *Reading*, Cambridge: CUP

Treble, H.A. and Vallins, G. H. (1961) *An ABC of English Usage*, Oxford: Oxford University Press

Trudgill, P. (1975) *Accent, Dialect and the School*, London: Edward Arnold

Trudgill, P. (1983) *Sociolinguistics: An Introduction to Language and Society*, Harmondsworth: Penguin

Wardhaugh, R. (1992) *An Introduction to Sociolinguistics*, 2nd edn, Oxford: Blackwell

Williamson, J. (1989) 'An Extra Radiator? Teachers' Views of Support Teaching and Withdrawal in Developing the English of Bilingual Pupils', *Educational Studies*, 15, 3, pp. 315–26

Williamson, J. and Hardman, F. (1997a) 'To Purify the Dialect of the Tribe: Children's Use of Non-standard Dialect Grammar in Writing', *Educational Studies*, 23, 2, pp. 157–68

Williamson, J. and Hardman, F. (1997b) 'Those Terrible Marks of the Beast: Non-standard Dialect and Children's Writing', *Language and Education*, 11, 4, pp. 287–99

Wray, D. and Medwell, J. (1997) *English for Primary Teachers: An Audit and Self-Study Guide*, London: Letts Educational

4   What Do We Mean by Grammar?

JOHN WILLIAMSON

Quotation 1	Why care for grammar as long as we are good?
	Artemus Ward

Do not think we are arguing against goodness but as student English teachers you need to care for grammar because the National Curriculum for English requires that, at Key Stages 3 and 4, pupils should be given opportunities to learn about discourse structure, phrase, clause and sentence structure and words. The following sections are going to introduce you to these elements of the grammar of English, although for reasons of clarity we will change the order somewhat.

Quotation 2	I will not go down to posterity talking bad grammar.
	Benjamin Disraeli

The term grammar has a variety of meanings; Disraeli in Quotation 2 is using the term *prescriptively* – that is to say he sees grammar as telling people how they should use their language. Such grammar is prescriptive in the sense that it *prescribes* how we ought to speak. For the rest of this chapter we will be using the term 'grammar' *descriptively* – that is, to describe to us the patterns of organisation found in English. These patterns can conveniently be split into two categories – organisation up to the level of the sentence and organisation above the level of the sentence.

GRAMMAR TO SENTENCE LEVEL

There are five levels of grammar up to and including the sentence, as follows:

sentence
clause
phrase
word
morpheme

The relationship between these elements is essentially hierarchical. (The exceptions implied in the 'essentially' of the last sentence will be outlined later.) Each element consists of one or more of the elements below it until we come to the morpheme which is the lowest constituent of grammatical structure. As already mentioned, we are not going to deal with the elements of grammatical structure in the order given above.

THE MORPHEME

Crystal (1994, p. 90) offers us a version of one of the clearest definitions of this unit: 'The smallest meaningful elements into which words can be analysed are known as *morphemes*.' Let's look at what this means through some examples.

If we consider the word 'happy', we can see that it can not be segmented into any smaller *meaningful* units: it does not consist of 'ha + ppy' or 'happ + y' – there is no meaning in 'ha', 'ppy', 'happ' or 'y'. 'Happy' is therefore a word which consists of only one morpheme – 'happy'. If we now think about 'unhappy' we can see two meaningful units: one is our old friend 'happy' but the other is a new meaningful unit, 'un' which carries the meaning 'not'. 'Unhappy' is therefore a two morpheme word, consisting of 'un + happy', each element of which conveys meaning. There is a difference between 'un' and happy' in that 'happy' is a *free morpheme*, that is to say one which can stand by itself as a word, and 'un' is a *bound morpheme*, one which will normally only occur as part of a word.

Morphology, which is 'the study of the structure of words' (Greenbaum, 1996, p. 626), appears in the National Curriculum for English (DfEE, 1995, p. 7) as early as Key Stage 1 where pupils should learn about *prefixes* and *suffixes*. A prefix is a morpheme which appears at the start of a word, a suffix one which appears at the end of a word. Thus, in 'unhappiness' we have a prefix 'un' and a suffix 'ness' (don't worry about slight changes of spelling like 'happy/happi' which sometimes occur when morphemes are combined to make up words). In English, prefixes usually change the sense of words in terms of their overall meaning – so, as we have seen, 'unhappy' means 'not happy', 'rediscover' means 'discover again' and 'mis' has a meaning 'wrongly' in such words as 'misinterpret'. The meaning of suffixes, however, is typically a grammatical meaning. So, our earlier example of 'ness' has the 'meaning' of changing an adjective 'happy' into a noun 'happiness'. One of the commonest uses of suffixes is as an inflection in nouns, to indicate number and possession, and verbs, to indicate such features as person and tense. So, one of the characteristics of many nouns is that they have a set of forms like:

	Singular	*Plural*
Non-possessive	boy	boy**s**
Possessive	boy**'s**	boys**'**

Here the plurality and possession are indicated by the suffixes **s,** **'s** and **s'**.

In the case of verbs, suffixes show differences in person in the present tense: 'I/you/we/they **climb**' versus 'he/she/it **climbs**' where the third person singular forms are marked by the morpheme 's'.

Similarly, many verbs use suffixes to show whether they are in the past or present tense: 'I **climb** versus **climbed**'; and to indicate the past or present participle form: 'I have **climbed**; I was **climbing**'.

As always seems to be the case in grammar, there are exceptions to these regular patterns. Some verbs don't add a morpheme simply to show past tense or the past participle, so we have forms like:

'I **saw** him yesterday' and 'I have **seen** him'.

These are perhaps most easily thought of simply as special cases of the past tense and past participle morpheme.

Activity 1	Analyse the following words into morphemes; remember that all the parts of any word you segment have to be meaningful units:

1	talk	word
2	boyish	happening
3	elephant	disinter
4	quick	misinformed
5	quickly	dogs

The answers to all the grammar activities appear at the end of this chapter.

THE CLAUSE

We are going to go back to our hierarchy of elements now and work outward from the *clause*. The essence of the clause is that it 'typically consists minimally of a subject and a verb' (Greenbaum, 1996, p. 618). We will come to the complications implied by 'typically' later. Research by Williamson and Hardman (1995) suggested that well over 90 per cent of student teachers could identify a verb. If you suspect you are one of the remainder, please do Activity 2. If you still have problems, read the section on verbs later in this chapter.

| Activity 2 | Identify the verbs in the following sentences: |

1 I like chocolate.
2 I remember it very well.
3 I gave him some good advice.
4 I was very busy when he came to see me.
5 The doctor examined me but she found nothing wrong.

So, now we've cleared that up, the *verb* element in a clause consists of either a single verb like those we have just been identifying or a group of verbs acting as a verb phrase (see later for details of the verb phrase). We'll just use single verbs for the moment.

The other element in clause structure that we have said is central is the *subject*. The subject of a clause comes before the verb in statements and, in the present tense, the subject determines the form taken by the verb. So, for example, we have '**I** sing' but '**She** sings'. (The subject is in bold type.) The subject can either be a noun or pronoun acting on its own or it can consist of a noun phrase (see below) in which a number of words act together as a single unit as in '**The woman** was a solicitor' or '**My friend** is unhappy'.

| Activity 3 | Identify the subject in the following clauses: |

1   The bride was married on Thursday.
2   The children dressed up for the party.
3   The blackbird returned to its nest.
4   A baby cried for food.
5   Jerry Springer is a chat show host.
6   Five sealions were basking on the rocks.
7   My television is broken.
8   She wore a blue suit.
9   The dragonflies landed on the marsh.
10 Nepal is very hilly.

OBJECTS AND COMPLEMENTS

This is a more complex aspect of clause structure but the good news is that you don't absolutely need to know about this to deal with the National Curriculum. This section and the next are included to give you a complete picture of clause structure.

Some verbs require an additional element to complete their sense – look at the following sentences:

1   Everyone likes chocolate.
2   She became a student.

In both of these sentences there is an element coming after the subject and verb. They look very similar but there are some important differences between sentences 1 and 2. 'Chocolate' in 1 is an *object*, 'a student' in 2 is a *complement*. There are two main differences between these elements. An object can usually be made the subject of a *passive* clause. So, we have an *active* clause ('Everyone likes chocolate') which can be transformed into its passive equivalent 'Chocolate is liked by everyone'. In the passive, the active object becomes the subject and part of the verb 'be' is introduced to the verb phrase.

We cannot do this with sentence 2 – *'A student was become by her.' (An asterisk introduces an ungrammatical utterance.) 'A student' in sentence 2 is not an object but a complement. Complements however have a feature which is not shared by objects: in sentence 2, the subject 'she' and the complement 'a student' refer to the same person. This *co-referentiality* is characteristic of complements. A complement which is co-referential with a subject is called a *subject complement*. Another feature of complements is that they, unlike objects, can consist of adjectives: 'She became unhappy.'

| **Activity 4** | Which of the following contain objects and which contain subject complements? |

  1 The boy ate the sweets.
  2 The girl kicked the ball.
  3 The girl seemed nice.
  4 My father was a sailor.
  5 Pavarotti sang the aria.
  6 The forecast predicted rain.
  7 The bridegroom cancelled the wedding.
  8 The bride was sad.
  9 Northumbria has many coastal castles.
10 *The Full Monty* was a very popular film.

Unfortunately, the complexity of objects and complements doesn't quite end there. Consider sentences 3 and 4:

3   My father gave me the book.
4   The university made him a professor.

Again, these look very similar but again there are hidden differences. Sentence 3 contains two objects – an *indirect object* ('me') and a *direct object* ('the book'). Both 'me' and 'the book' in sentence 3 can be made the subject in a passive:

5   I was given the book by my father.
6   The book was given to me by my father.

So both are objects. Broadly speaking, if you only have one object, it's a direct object; if you have two objects, the first one is an indirect object. We can say:

7   He was made a professor by the university

so 'him' in sentence 4 is an object, but we can't say:

8   *A professor was made to/for/by him by the university.

So what do we have in sentence 4? The clue lies in co-referentiality. If we look at 'him' and 'a professor' in sentence 4 we find again that both refer to the same person; since 'him' is the object, we refer to 'a professor' as an *object complement*. (In other instances, the object and object complement may refer to the same object, creature, quality and so on – it's not always a person.) Like subject complements, object complements may consist of an adjective – in 'I like my coffee white', the object 'my coffee' and the complement 'white' are co-referential.

So far, we have the following possible patterns in clauses:

| *Subject* | *Verb* | | |
| Henrietta | dreams. | | |

| *Subject* | *Verb* | *Direct object* | |
| Ranjit | eats | chocolate. | |

| *Subject* | *Verb* | *Subject complement* | |
| John | is | a student. | |

| *Subject* | *Verb* | *Indirect object* | *Direct object* |
| Susan | sent | Henry | a message. |

| *Subject* | *Verb* | *Direct object* | *Object complement* |
| The group | elected | him | chairman. |

Now try to see if you've mastered this:

| **Activity 5** | Analyse the following sentences into subject, verb, indirect object, direct object, indirect object, subject complement and object complement. Just use the criteria we have been discussing and it shouldn't be *too* daunting. |

1 I wonder.
2 That girl gave Jane a present.
3 James adores Mabel.
4 Nobody eats spaghetti cold.
5 The police searched the room.
6 Truth is beauty.
7 The dog is an Alsatian.
8 John lent me his pen.
9 The teacher called him an idiot.
10 That was difficult.

ADVERBIALS

The final element of clause structure is the *adverbial*, which is in some ways harder to tie down in a definition than subjects, verbs, objects and complements. Greenbaum (1996, p. 615) notes only that 'An adverbial is an optional element in sentence or clause structure. There may be more than one adverbial in a sentence or clause'. Burton-Roberts (1986, p. 97) cites another feature: 'A very prominent characteristic of adverbials is that they can appear in all sorts of positions in the sentence.' So, adverbials are (usually) mobile and optional. Consider the following:

9   I read novels.
10   I read novels in the evening.
11   In the evening I read novels.

'In the evening' is a 'typical' adverbial in that, as we can see from sentence 9, it is totally optional in the sense that we have a complete grammatical clause without it. As Burton-Roberts says (1986, p. 92): '[Adverbials] give additional, though not essential, information.' Further, sentences 10 and 11 show that 'in the evening' is movable – it can appear at the start or at the end of the sentence. Neither of these criteria can be absolutely relied on, however, as we can see from the following examples:

12   I was in the park.
13   *In the park I was.

Not all contexts will permit the moving of adverbials, as sentence 13 shows. Furthermore in the case of 12 it's not easy to see how we can regard 'in the park' as non-essential information – it's not just giving additional information to the proposition 'I was.' In some ways, the easiest way to identify an adverb is by checking that it is not the subject, verb, object or complement of the clause in which it appears.

Another guideline is the kind of information given. Adverbials will often tell you things like when, where, how or why something happened:

14   I saw him on Tuesday.
15   I saw him in the dining room.
16   He writes carefully.
17   He was selected because of his good looks.

Sentences 14–17 are examples of adverbials of time, place, manner and reason. Other concepts expressed in adverbials include: condition (often introduced by 'if' – 'Your teeth will be healthy **if you brush them**'); concession (often introduced by 'though' or 'although' – 'He gave me a Mars bar **although I asked for a Twix**') and purpose – 'He stayed up late **in order to watch the game on TV**').

The next activity will help you clarify your understanding of adverbials through considering some examples.

Activity 6	Identify the adverbials in the following:

1   I watch football on Saturdays.
2   She studied in Lancaster.
3   She dances effortlessly.
4   Last week they went to Manchester.
5   I like him because he's funny.
6   Penguins eat fish every day.
7   If you're lucky you may win the lottery.
8   I watched him as he worked.
9   There was mistletoe over the door.
10 John had known Sally since 1987.

THE SENTENCE

The *sentence* is the unit above the clause in our hierarchy and consists of one or more clauses. The sentence is one of many important linguistic elements which are notoriously difficult to define – some have suggested there are 100 available definitions (Crystal, 1994, p. 94); LINC (undated) raises this to 'over 200'. But as English teachers we need something to work with since the National Curriculum (DfEE, 1995, p. 7) requires that pupils be taught about 'the way language is ordered and organised into sentences'. There are traditional definitions of the sentence, but there are serious problems with them. One approach is to relate the sentence to punctuation, but this is inevitably circular: a sentence ends where you would put a full stop in writing; but if you ask 'where do you put full stops' the only sensible answer is 'at the end of sentences'. We know where full stops go because we have a concept of the sentence which is independent of punctuation. Another traditional definition runs along the lines that a sentence contains a complete idea. Again, it is easy to show that this does not work; consider:

18   Mary came home. John made tea.

In so far as the concept of 'ideas' can be made to work, we can see sentence 18 as containing two ideas and, indeed, it consists of two sentences. But what about:

19   Mary came home and John made tea.

We have the same two 'ideas' but now we have only one sentence. We can take this even further:

20   Mary came home because John made tea.

Arguably here we have three ideas – the original two plus one, expressed in 'because', which gives a causal relationship between these two events.

This sort of difficulty arises because the sentence is a *grammatical* unit, not one that is centred on ideas. We can express as many ideas as we like in one sentence providing we meet the appropriate grammatical criteria. The essence of the *sentence* is that it consists of a single clause or more than one, provided that they are linked together. We shall see shortly that there are two forms such linkage takes – co-ordination and subordination. Greenbaum (1996, p. 618) summarises neatly: 'A set of clauses interrelated by co-ordination or subordination (or minimally one clause that is independent of any such links) constitutes a sentence.' This provides us with an explanation that we can easily use to help pupils in their understanding of what a sentence is: if you have a new subject and verb, you have a new sentence *unless you join them together*. Clearly, this presupposes they have already been taught what a subject and verb are – which should not be beyond the bounds of possibility considering that pupils even at Key Stage 1 should be 'introduced to . . . subject verb agreement' (DfEE, 1995, pp. 5 and 10).

We have then an idea of a sentence as consisting of either a single clause (in which case we have a *simple sentence*) or a series of linked clauses. Let us consider first the simpler of the two ways of linking clauses: *co-ordination* 'links items of equivalent grammatical status' (Greenbaum, 1996, p. 86) and 'typically each [clause] could be an independent sentence' (Greenbaum, 1996, p. 45). So, with co-ordination we simply tag clauses on to one another joined usually by 'and' (much the most common, especially in children's writing), 'or' or 'but'. Sentences in which clauses are joined together exclusively through co-ordination are known as *compound sentences*. What is deemed to be excessive use of co-ordination is often seen in children's writing – 'I got up and I got dressed and I had breakfast and I went to school and I . . .'

The second way in which clauses are joined together is more complex (although children at Key Stages 2, 3 and 4 (DfEE, 1995, pp. 16 and 24) should be introduced to it). *Subordination* occurs when one clause is made part of another clause. There are many forms which this can take and we have space here to consider only some of the possible patterns. Think about the following sentence:

21   I eat fish on Fridays.

We should by now be able to say that this is a clause and that we can analyse it thus:

Subject	Verb	Object	Adverbial
I	eat	fish	on Fridays.

'On Fridays' is clearly an adverbial: it could be omitted and still leave an acceptable sentence ('I eat fish'); it could be moved ('On Fridays I eat fish'); it tells us *when* the fish is eaten so is an adverbial of time. Now look at:

22   I eat fish when I feel hungry.

'When I feel hungry' meets all the criteria of an adverbial which we have just cited in respect of 'on Fridays': it is deletable, movable and tells us *when*. 'When I feel hungry' is an adverbial, just like 'on Fridays'. But there is a major difference: 'when I feel hungry' has its own subject, verb and subject complement. So it is a clause. It is a clause functioning as part of the structure of another clause and it is to precisely such a relationship that we apply the term *subordination* which 'is a non-symmetrical relation, holding between two clauses in such a way that one is a constituent or part of the other' (Quirk and Greenbaum, 1973, p. 309). Sentences in which clauses are only joined through subordination are known as *complex sentences*. (Where both co-ordination and subordination are present, we have *compound-complex sentences*.)

Activity 7	All of the following sentences contain two clauses; one consists of the whole sentence, the other is a subordinate clause. Identify the latter.

1 Jane goes to the theatre when she can.
2 As soon as the bell goes the pupils leave.
3 Surinder likes maths because she is clever.
4 If Newcastle win they will go to the top of the league.
5 I don't like him although he is nice.
6 This saw cuts wood like a knife cuts butter.
7 I saw him where the two roads meet.
8 If you take the rabbit to the vet he will cut its claws.
9 You will die unless you drink.
10 The woman had no grey hair after she visited the hairdresser.

This is perhaps the point at which to mention the exceptions to a generalisation made earlier. We have been assuming that clauses always have subjects but there are some situations in which this is not the case. One occurs in imperative sentences, in explicit commands of the type 'Shut the door' or 'Be quiet'. Omission of the subject is the defining grammatical characteristic of imperatives. Another common case of subject omission arises when two clauses in the same sentence have the same subject: we can say either 'I came home and I had tea' or 'I came home and had tea'. When the second subject repeats the first we can choose what is called 'identical subject deletion' and omit the second instance of the repeated phrase.

THE PHRASE

Phrases, you will remember, come between the clause and the word in the hierarchy of grammatical elements mentioned at the beginning of this chapter. Fowler (1974, p. 103) offers the following definition: a *phrase* 'is a sequence of words which as a group fulfils a single structural function'. Remembering that a 'sequence' can consist of a single word, this gives a clear idea of the phrase. Think about the structural functions we identified in the clause (subject, verb, object, complement and adverbial). Each of these will frequently (though not always) consist of a phrase of one or more words.

23	*Subject*	*Verb*	*Object*	*Adverbial*
	Jane	met	Margaret	weekly.

Each of the one word phrases in sentence 23 could be expanded as, for example in sentence 24:

24	*Subject*	*Verb*	*Object*	*Adverbial*
	The woman	may meet	her friend	on Tuesday.

Let's look now at the types of phrase we use in English and the ways in which they can be expanded.

NOUN PHRASES

The key element in the *noun phrase* is a noun or pronoun which acts as the *head*, by which we mean the central element around which the rest of the phrase (if any) is centred. If there is only one word in the noun phrase, as in 'Jane' or 'Margaret' from sentence 23 or 'I' from sentence 21, it will be the head, which is the only obligatory element in the noun phrase.

In addition to the head, we may also have one or more *premodifiers* that come before the head in the noun phrase. There are very many types of premodifier and we will illustrate only four of the more common ones here. Very often, the noun phrase starts with a *determiner*; the commonest determiners are the articles, 'a/an' and 'the' but we also find words like 'all', 'both', 'this', 'some' and numbers such as 'two' introducing noun phrases. The next category which we shall consider is adjectives, used either on their own ('pretty woman') or preceded by a determiner ('the pretty woman'). Also commonly used are personal pronouns in their possessive form – 'my', 'your', 'his', 'her', 'its', 'our', 'their'. Finally, for our purposes, nouns are frequently premodified by other nouns, either in their simple form or as possessives: 'paper boy' or 'Henry's son'. (For the difference between 'pretty' and 'paper' see the section later on adjectives.)

The other structural possibility in the noun phrase is that we may have *postmodifiers* which come after the head. There are two common types of postmodifier, the first of which is a *prepositional* phrase. Most frequently, prepositional phrases consist of a preposition followed by a noun phrase. This leaves open the question of what a preposition is and that is much more easily exemplified than defined. Words like 'in', 'on', 'under', 'over', 'above', 'below', 'near', 'beside', 'up', 'down', 'beside' and so on can function as prepositions. So we find noun phrases like the following:

Premodifier	*Head*	*Postmodifier*
The clever	girl	in my class.
The big	house	beside mine.
The dark	cupboard	under the stairs.
The	king	over the water.

The	man	in the iron mask.
The butter	knife	across the table.
Our	friend	from Mongolia.

Note that our hierarchy of grammatical elements has once again been violated: we have here phrases (prepositional phrases) acting as part of other phrases (noun phrases) instead of functioning directly as part of clause structure. The same kind of thing happens with the last type of postmodification which we are going to consider here.

Think again about the first of the last group of phrases:

| Premodifier | Head | Postmodifier |
| The clever | girl | in my class. |

Now, suppose we changed that to 'the girl who is in my class'. The segment 'who is in my class' is clearly functioning in the same way as 'in my class' did in the first sentence in terms of having as its purpose an extension of our understanding of which girl is being discussed. It is therefore a postmodifier in the noun phrase 'The girl who is in my class.' But there is a major difference between 'in my class' and 'who is in my class'. The latter has its own verb, 'is', and has 'who' acting as subject. So 'who is in my class' is a clause. Like the adverbial clauses we looked at earlier, 'who is in my class' is a subordinate clause because it forms part of the structure of another clause. This particular kind of clause, acting as the postmodifier in a noun phrase, is known technically as a *relative clause*.

Let's look at some more examples of relative clauses:

Premodifier	Head	Postmodifier
The	man	who shot Liberty Valance.
The	car	which is in the drive.
The	girl	I met.
The	information	that I got from the web.

All of the postmodifiers above are clauses because they all have their own subject–verb structure but are postmodifiers because they add information about the head.

Activity 8   Identify the premodifiers, heads and postmodifiers in the following phrases:

1   The ball.
2   The big ball.
3   The red ball.
4   The big red ball.
5   The big red beach ball.
6   The ball in the cupboard.
7   The red ball in the cupboard.
8   The ball I gave to Jane.
9   The ball in the cupboard which I never use.

VERB PHRASES

You will be pleased to know that structurally the *verb phrase* is much simpler than the noun phrase. It consists of a main verb that may be preceded by one or more auxiliary verbs. So, at its simplest, the verb phrase may consist simply of a single verb, as in almost all the examples we have cited up to this point: 'Jane **sings**.' It may be preceded by part of the verb 'be' in which case the main verb will take the present participle form: 'Jane **is singing**' and 'Jane **was singing**'.

Either the main verb alone or 'be' plus a main verb may be preceded by part of the verb 'have' in which case the following verb will take the past participle form: 'Jane **has sung**', 'Jane **had sung**', 'Jane **has been singing**' and 'Jane **had been singing**'.

Finally, all or any part of the above can be preceded by a *modal verb*. The modal verbs are 'can', 'could', 'may', 'might', 'shall', 'should', 'will', 'would', 'must'. These verbs have certain unique features not shared by other verbs including the lack of an infinitive form with 'to' – so we have 'to sing', 'to walk', 'to cry', 'to have', 'to be' but not 'to would' or 'to must' and so on.

The overall structure of the verb phrase looks like this, then, with brackets indicating the elements which may not always be present, although where they are present they appear in this order: (modal) (have) (be) main verb.

ADJECTIVE AND ADVERB PHRASES

Adjective and *adverb phrases* are similar enough to be dealt with together. They consist, respectively, of an adjective or adverb with the possibility of premodification and post-modification.

Both adjectives and adverbs are typically premodified by adverbs that usually indicate to what degree the head adjective or adverb applies to the situation:

Premodifier	*Adjective or adverb*
very/quite/rather/extremely/pretty/fairly	quick/quickly

Postmodification of adjective and adverb phrases is broadly similar to that of noun phrases, with prepositional phrases and clauses being among the elements acting as postmodifiers: 'I was **fond of him**' and 'I am **confident that he will do well**' where the adjectives 'fond' and 'confident' are postmodified respectively by a prepositional phrase and a clause. In the case of adverbs, we can look to examples such as '**Fortunately for us**, it is near the end of term' and 'You sing **better than I do**'.

We have now covered the five types of phrase found in English clauses and sentences – noun phrase, verb phrase, adjective phrase, adverb phrase and prepositional phrase – and noted that although generally these form parts of the structure of clauses we do find phrases used as part of other phrases and that we can find clauses being used as part of phrases. Try the following activity to see how much of this you have grasped.

Activity 9	Analyse the following sentences into phrases:

1. The table is very heavy.
2. My friend from Liverpool has been to China.
3. The train went to Birmingham very quickly.
4. The drink that I ordered was terrible.
5. The white parrot has yellow head feathers.
6. The pond was full of weeds.
7. Two men were fishing by the riverside.
8. Some people are rowing the boat.
9. A duck has landed on the village pond.
10. Your poodle may have had an ear infection.

THE WORD

The *word* has always been a problematic unit to define although one which literate speakers have found relatively simple to handle; Seiler (1964) commented that the word is an easy concept for the layman but a difficult one for the linguist. You can probably assume that you know what a word is (although we all have difficulties with some examples, especially where hyphenation is involved – do you prepare 'well-planned lessons' or 'well planned lessons', for example?). One attempt at offering a definition is to say that 'a word is any segment of a sentence . . . at which pausing is possible' (Hockett, 1958, p. 166) – but, as with pausing as a means of determining sentences, this begs the question of how we know where pausing is possible. Indivisibility has also been used as a criterion – we can add extra items between words but not within them – so, 'my friend' can become 'my best friend' but not 'my fribestend'. Also, this definition applies equally well to the morpheme – as you can see from 'friend' above. One of the best attempts to define the word was that of Bloomfield (1933); he characterised words as minimal free forms – 'the smallest units of speech that can meaningfully stand on their own'. However, many words, such as 'the', are extremely unlikely to stand on their own as sentences. None of these definitions, then, is perfect but all give some insight into the general characteristics of words.

The main interest of the National Curriculum at word level is in the parts of speech and it is to these that we will now turn.

NOUNS

Both nouns and verbs have traditional definitions which are all that many people remember of language work from their own days in primary school. These usually run along the lines that a noun refers to a person, place or thing and that a verb is a doing word or a word which refers to an action. In some ways these are quite useful notions in that they cover many nouns and verbs; you should, however, be aware that these definitions are problematic in many cases. Think about:

25   He can jump 24 feet.
26   His best jump was 24 feet.

Now, ask yourself whether 'jump' is a noun or a verb in these sentences. Your answer was probably that 'jump' was a verb in sentence 25 and a noun in sentence 26. But does the latter refer to a person, place or thing? Surely 'jump' has the same reference in both sentences; the noun 'jump' refers to an action in sentence 26, just as the verb 'jump' does in sentence 25. This phenomenon occurs with many common noun/verb pairings such as 'talk', 'walk', 'thought', 'smile' and so on. If we really want to know what a noun or a verb is, we need to look to grammatical criteria, rather than looking at the meanings conveyed. Unfortunately, as you might expect by now, there is no *simple* alternative to the traditional definitions.

We have already mentioned some of the *formal* criteria for identifying nouns and verbs in the section above on the morpheme. (Formal criteria relate to the characteristic patterns or forms adopted by the class of words in question.) So, a word that changes form to mark number and possession will be a noun:

	Singular	Plural
Non-possessive	table	table**s**
Possessive	table**'s**	tables**'**

Unfortunately, not all nouns follow this pattern – 'furniture', for example has no plural forms and neither do many nouns which refer to abstract qualities – 'honesty', 'truthfulness', 'fidelity' and so on.

Perhaps more useful for understanding nouns are *functional* criteria (which define a word class by the way it functions). Even here we need to be careful – Greenbaum (1996, p. 627) defines a noun as 'a word that (alone or with modifiers) is capable of functioning as subject . . . or direct object'. But this would include pronouns, which have very different formal properties from those of nouns. Perhaps we are better to think of a series of frames (we need a series rather than a single frame because not all nouns will occur in all contexts) like: 'The . . . was on the table.' Any word that can fill the space is a noun. Think of as many examples as you can: 'book', 'apple', 'paper', 'stripper', 'napkin' or even 'hippopotamus' (it may be being operated on by a vet) can all appear here and are all nouns. Abstract nouns may not work with that frame but we could use 'I admired his . . .' where the blank could be filled not only by a wide range of concrete nouns but also by abstract ones such as 'honesty', 'truthfulness' and 'fidelity' which did not meet our formal criteria above. The tests outlined in this paragraph may have already suggested to you one very easy way of helping pupils to develop their concept of the noun – through the use of cloze procedures in which, instead of deleting words at random you can delete only nouns (or any other part of speech); the pupils will generate words which fit into the blanks and all the teacher has to do is to attach the label 'noun' to the pupils' offerings.

Formal and functional criteria do not give an easy simple answer to the question 'what is a noun?' because the category 'noun' is a complex and varied one. As has just been suggested, pupils need to build up their understanding through experience of the different features which nouns possess. If you, as a teacher, feel the need for a definition then perhaps there is not too much harm in using the traditional ones as long as you realise that children may sometimes be confused rather than helped by them and supplement them with activities like cloze procedure.

VERBS

Formal criteria are perhaps more useful with regard to the *verb* than to the noun. A word which can change its form by adding 's' to mark third person singular ('I **seem**' versus 'he/she/it **seems**'), which has a form with 'ing' (**'speak/speaking'**), a form to show past tense (**speak/spoke**) and a past participle form which is usually used when the preceding verb is 'have' (**'speak/spoken'**) is a verb.

As with nouns, we can use functional criteria and cloze procedure as in 'I . . . the book', where the blank could be filled by 'read', 'borrowed', 'bought', 'stole', 'destroyed', 'lost', 'hated' and so on. Again, as with nouns, not all verbs will be usable in all contexts but a frame of this pattern should cover all verbs which take an object or complement. Other verbs will work with an adverbial in place of 'the book': 'I . . . quickly' would suggest verbs like 'thought', 'spoke', 'ate', 'ran', 'went', 'vomited' and so on.

ADJECTIVES

Most adjectives can be used either as the premodifier in a noun phrase or as the complement in a clause; so we can say 'the clever girl' and 'the girl is clever'. This marks the distinction between adjectives and nouns as premodifiers mentioned earlier in the section on noun phrases: we can say 'the garage mechanic' but not 'the mechanic is garage'.

Many adjectives undergo a formal change to mark the comparative and superlative forms: 'bright', 'brighter', 'brightest' and others (those containing more than one syllable) mark the same distinctions using 'more' and 'most': 'more beautiful' and 'most beautiful'. Note however that this does not apply to all adjectives: 'single' and 'dead' for example do not allow comparative and superlative forms.

ADVERBS

A great many adverbs 'are formed from adjectives by the addition of *-ly*' (Burton-Roberts, 1986, p. 61), such as 'wisely', 'neatly', 'foolishly' and so on although not all adverbs follow this pattern – 'often', 'fast', 'late', 'soon' and 'hard' (as in 'work hard'), for example.

Like adjectives, many adverbs can be made comparative or superlative, usually taking the expanded forms '**more** rapidly' and '**most** rapidly'. In functional terms, adverbs generally act as adverbials in clause structure: 'He will finish the work **quickly**' (see earlier, under 'Adverbials') or as premodifiers for adjectives: 'She was **extremely** nice' (see earlier, under 'Adjective and adverb phrase'.)

OTHER PARTS OF SPEECH

To meet the demands of the National Curriculum from Key Stage 2 onwards, you also need to have some understanding of pronouns, prepositions (these are covered earlier, in the section on noun phrases) and conjunctions.

PRONOUNS

Pronouns are a class of words that can be substituted for nouns in various contexts. Perhaps the most important group consists of *personal pronouns* that directly replace noun phrases. So for 'the girl' in 'the girl kicked the ball' we can have 'she kicked the ball' as long as the preceding context has given us some idea of to whom 'she' refers. Personal pronouns are characterised by person and number:

	Singular		*Plural*	
	As subject	*As object*	*As subject*	*As object*
First person	I	me	we	us
Second person	you	you	you	you
Third person	he/she/it	him/her/it	they	them

Each of these also has *possessive* forms: as determiners we have 'my', 'your', 'his', 'her', 'its' and 'our'; as subjects or objects we have 'mine', 'yours', 'his', 'hers' and 'ours' as in 'mine's a pint' or 'I don't think much of yours'.

Other types of pronoun include *demonstrative pronouns* ('this', 'that', 'these' and 'those'), *indefinite pronouns* ('anyone' and 'someone'), *relative pronouns* which introduce relative clauses ('who', 'which' and 'that') and *reflexive pronouns* ('myself', 'yourself', etc.).

CONJUNCTIONS

Conjunctions serve to join grammatical units together. There are two types: co-ordinating conjunctions and subordinating conjunctions. *Co-ordinating conjunctions* join two units of equal status which may be clauses, phrases or individual words. The commonest co-ordinating conjunctions are 'and', 'but' and 'or': 'I like coffee **but** I hate tea', 'toil, envy, want, the patron **or** the gaol' and 'Jack **and** Jill went up the hill'. *Subordinating conjunctions* link subordinate clauses to their main clause; examples include: 'before', 'until', 'when', while' and 'where' (showing time relationships), 'where' (place), 'if' and 'unless' (condition) 'if' and 'although' (concession), 'because' and 'since' (reason), 'to' and 'in order to' (purpose) and 'so' and 'so that' (result). (These examples are taken from LINC, undated, p. 335.)

Activity 10   Identify the parts of speech in the following sentences:

1   The magnolia was in flower.
2   Foreign investment is at a low level.
3   The elderly man bred pigeons as a hobby.
4   The church was destroyed by fire.
5   The city baths are used by children and adults.
6   They want tickets for the cup final.
7   The electricity man read the meter.
8   Her diamond and sapphire ring shone brilliantly.
9   The weather will become cooler and wetter.
10 It was very foggy at the coast.

BEYOND THE SENTENCE

We should by now have a fairly good idea of the structural patterns up to the level of the sentence. But we do not write or speak in a random collection of sentences – there are relationships between sentences in both writing and speech. Think about the following sentences, taken from a children's book on jungles (Catchpole, 1983, p. 7):

Activity 11   Put the following sentences into the correct order:

1   To stop this, some passion flowers have poison on their leaves.
2   The eggs hatch into caterpillars which then eat the leaves.
3   In the jungle, animals and plants depend upon each other a great deal.
4   The poison protects them from the birds, which learn that certain-coloured butterflies taste nasty.
5   Their caterpillars are immune to the poison, which is stored and passed over to the adult butterflies.
6   Although flowers attract insects to pollinate plants, there is a risk that butterflies will lay eggs on the leaves.
7   But certain butterflies only lay their eggs on passion flower leaves.

The original order was:

1   In the jungle, animals and plants depend upon each other a great deal.
2   Although flowers attract insects to pollinate plants, there is a risk that butterflies will lay eggs on the leaves.
3   The eggs hatch into caterpillars which then eat the leaves.
4   To stop this, some passion flowers have poison on their leaves.

5   But certain butterflies only lay their eggs on passion flower leaves.

6   Their caterpillars are immune to the poison, which is stored and passed over to the adult butterflies.

7   The poison protects them from the birds, which learn that certain-coloured butterflies taste nasty.

I assume you put the sentences into more or less the original order. But how did you *know* how to order them? Sentence 1 is a fairly typical *topic sentence* in that it serves to orientate the reader to the topic that is going to be considered in the paragraph. The rest of the sentences contain various linguistic clues as to their order. Sentence 2 contains the noun phrase 'eggs'; characteristically if we encounter a plural noun with no determiner or a singular noun premodified by 'a', we are seeing the first mention of whatever the noun refers to. Sentence 3 must therefore follow 2 because here we have 'the eggs' with 'the' implying that the eggs have been mentioned earlier. In sentence 4, 'this' must refer back to something that has been raised in an earlier sentence – here, quite clearly, it refers to the attempts of passion flowers to stop their leaves from being eaten. 'But' in sentence 5 implies a relationship of contrast between what precedes it and what follows it. (Sentences 4 and 5 could have been written as a single sentence – probably the writer was trying to avoid facing his young readers with overlong sentences.) The relationship between sentences 4 and 5 is also high-lighted by lexical repetition (*lexical* is a linguistic term derived from *lexis*, which means vocabulary); both sentences contain the words 'passion flower' and 'leaves'. Sentences 5 and 6 are linked through the relationship between 'certain butterflies' and 'their caterpillars'. Sentence 7 is related to sentence 6 through the use of the pronoun 'them', which relates back to 'the adult butterflies' of sentence 6 (we know that 'them' refers to butterflies because of the use of 'certain-coloured butterflies' later in sentence 7).

It is not intended to suggest that there is only *one* appropriate ordering of these sentences – you may like to see if you can justify your own ordering through examination of features like those mentioned in the preceding paragraph. The central point is that the sentences that make up this paragraph are linked together through the use of a range of cohesive devices. *Cohesion* 'refers to lexical and grammatical devices for linking parts of a written text or spoken discourse' (Greenbaum, 1996, p. 619). Learning to make texts function as cohesive wholes is a skill which pupils need to acquire, especially since written language tends to make more use of some cohesive devices than spoken language. Cohesion across sentences is a focus of the National Curriculum requirements both at Key Stage 2 and Key Stages 3 and 4 (DfEE, 1995, pp. 16 and 24.)

COHESIVE DEVICES

There are many ways of making texts cohesive entities and there is space here only to introduce you to some of the major ones. You will be able to spot others for yourself once you have seen the kind of feature we are looking at.

Lexical repetition is a widely used device; we saw this in the 'Jungles' paragraph where there was repetition of 'plants', 'eggs', 'leaves', 'caterpillars', 'passion flower(s)' and 'butterflies'. We often seek to discourage children from excessive repetition in their writing but a certain amount will pull the text together.

The use of *lexically related* words also functions as a cohesive device; these may be words with similar meanings – 'kill' and 'murder' or words with opposite meanings – 'live' and 'dead' or words with more subtle relationships – 'butterfly' and 'caterpillar'.

Of great importance is the use of *cataphoric* and *anaphoric* reference. 'References to what comes earlier in the text are anaphoric, whereas references to what comes afterwards are cataphoric' (Greenbaum, 1996, p. 375). We have seen several examples of anaphoric reference in 'Jungles': 'To stop **this**' where 'this' refers back to 'caterpillars who eat the leaves', '**Their** caterpillars' where 'their' refers to 'certain butterflies' in the preceding sentence and 'The poison protects **them** from birds' where 'them' refers to 'the adult butterflies'. Cataphoric expressions are probably less important in cohesion, but would include instances like: 'Have you heard **this**? Scotland won the championship.'

The use of *pronouns* is very widespread – these may be possessive as in 'Their caterpillars' or may act as substitute for whole noun phrases: 'The boy was angry. **He** had not been picked.' Words like 'this', 'these', 'that' and 'those' can serve a similar function: 'To stop *this*' from 'Jungles', for example.

The verb 'do' behaves with relation to verbs in very much the same way as pronouns do to nouns: 'I like to lie in the bath and drink Chablis. Whenever I **do** this, I feel very relaxed.'

More explicit forms of cohesion involve the use of a wide range of *connectives* which can express a variety of relationships between sentences. Place connectives relate sentences on a spatial basis: 'The police station is situated in the main road. **Nearby**, there is a pub. **Just along the road** is an off-licence.' Time connectives indicate a temporal relationship: 'Every morning I get up and shave. **Then** I get dressed. **After that** I have breakfast. **Meanwhile**, my wife is sleeping.' The co-ordinating conjunctions 'and' and 'but' are often used to indicate relationships between sentences as well as functioning within sentences: 'To stop this, some passion flowers have poison in their leaves. **But** certain butterflies only lay their eggs on passion flower leaves.' Many connectives suggest a logical link between sentences. This may simply take the form of listing, as 'first', 'second', 'third', 'in addition', 'furthermore', 'finally', 'in conclusion' and so on. Other relationships include: contrast ('on the other hand'), result ('consequently') and concession ('nevertheless', 'however' and 'in spite of that').

COHERENCE

We have exemplified some of the ways in which texts are made cohesive. Well organised texts go beyond this, however, in that they are also coherent. LINC (undated, p. 334) neatly outlines the difference between these two concepts:

For a text to be fully satisfactory to a listener or reader it needs not only appropriate grammatical links between sentences (*cohesion*) but also the concepts, propositions or events to be related to each other and to be consistent with the overall subject of the text. This semantic and propositional organisation is called *coherence*.

Greenbaum (1996, p. 386) summarises some of the main conceptual relationships which can link sentences in a paragraph or larger text:

generalization	refutation
particularization	chronological narration
exemplification	description
supporting with factual evidence	definition
supporting with argumentation	offering solution
restatement	evaluation
elaboration	contrast
qualification	comparison
concession	summarization

It is not being suggested that you teach all these types of paragraph to your pupils but the list provides a useful guide to you in developing your own understanding of some of the ways in which sentences in a paragraph can relate to each other and form a satisfying whole.

TEACHING GRAMMAR

We cannot provide here a complete guide to the teaching of grammar – that will come from experience of working with pupils in a range of contexts and from working with experienced teachers and tutors who will help you develop your skills. However, two important principles can be stated here.

First of all we would stress the importance of teaching grammar in context. When the teaching of grammar last ceased to be a central component of English (in the 1960s and 1970s) it was largely because it had become a sterile set of exercises, removed from any real world context of language use. From the Cox Report on there has been substantial agreement that good practice links the teaching of grammar to the everyday contexts of the English classroom. So, for example, work on adjectives might focus on the study of texts which use adjectives in interesting ways or work on subordinate clauses could be linked to development in the pupils' own writing. There is ample scope in the English curriculum for wandering along the byways of grammar without making the work dry or disconnected from the reality of pupils' experience with language and literature. Stubbs (1990) shows to good effect how an examination of grammar can illuminate the presuppositions in a text through a close examination of a *Daily Mail* article published at the time of Nelson Mandela's release from jail in South Africa. Stubbs' article is long and densely argued, but the following should give an idea of the kind of insights gained:

> in the *Daily Mail* article, when Blacks are reported as doing things, committing violence or issuing threats, they are in subject position, and at the beginning of the clause, e.g.:
>
> – *Mobs of Mandela's followers* ran wild and looted shops . . .
> – *Mandela's supporters* knifed a man repeatedly . . .
> – *The youths* hurled bottles and rubbish at the police
>
> (Stubbs, 1990, p. 6)

Examples like these are contrasted with the presentation of violence by whites, for example:

> There are only four examples in the text where the police are in grammatical subject position. Three put the police in the subordinate clause, thus presenting their violence as a reaction to preceding actions and not as initiated by them:
>
> – in Capetown, where *police* fired on the crowds
> – outside Durban, when *police* fired at a celebration
> – at the police, *who* immediately responded with more shotgun blasts
>
> In the fourth instance, the police are explicitly presented as responding:
>
> – *police* immediately resorted to birdshot, teargas and baton-charges.
>
> (Stubbs, 1990, p. 7)

Stubbs (1990, p. 7) goes on to address the significance of this analysis:

> The general point is as follows. The article does not anywhere say explicitly that 'the Blacks are the cause of the violence', but the grammar expresses this message. Position 1 in the clause in English expresses what the clause is about, its theme. This article is about Blacks causing violence, although this is never said in so many words. The meaning is deniable. Alternative, rather obvious interpretations, are not proposed: for example that the violence is caused by the Whites and by the system that they have set up.

Stubbs' analysis has been considered in some detail here because it serves as a model of the ways in which a consideration of grammar can interrelate with our reading of a text to show factors not immediately apparent on a cursory or superficial reading. You can probably immediately see ways in which such an analysis would help you to explore the language of advertisements, for example, or poetry.

The second principle is rooted in the fact that children come to school with con-siderable *implicit* knowledge about language. The role of the grammar teacher is to make that implicit knowledge *explicit*. So, for example, children know all there is to know about how nouns function in clauses in the sense that they use them appropri-ately every day of their lives. They may use non-standard forms (see Chapter 3 on Standard English) but they will use them in accordance with the grammatical rules with which they handle language. This is true even of people who have never heard the words 'noun' or 'clause'. What we are trying to do is to make them consciously aware of what they know implicitly and the more we build on that implicit knowledge, the easier it will be for pupils to learn grammar and the more successful they will be.

Let's look at some examples of what this might mean in practice. Consider the following cloze procedure text (the numbers in the gaps are simply to make the following discussion easier):

> The . . . 1 . . . goes to school early every . . . 2 . . . His first . . . 3 . . . is English, which he enjoys. He reads interesting . . . 4 . . . and sometimes discusses them with his . . . 5 . . . His English . . . 6 . . . is friendly and helpful and helps the boy with his . . . 7 . . .

Now, think about some of the words that could go in these spaces: 1 – boy, lad, child, pupil; 2 – morning, day, Monday; 3 – lesson, period; 4 – books, stories, things; 5 – friends, fellow-pupils; 6 – teacher; 7 – work, writing.

What all these have in common is that they are all nouns. Pupils can fill in blanks like these with nouns because of that implicit knowledge we have been discussing which tells them the kind of words that can be used. To help develop the concept 'noun' explicitly all we need do is to remind the children that the words they have been using are, in fact, nouns.

Take another, more difficult example – the *subordinate clause*. Subordinate clauses are quite difficult to pick out of texts that have already been written but are relatively easy for children to produce themselves if they are given the appropriate stimuli such as being asked to complete the following sentences.

1   I like English because . . .
2   School is good when . . .
3   You will do well at school if . . .

These could be completed with subordinate clauses like:

1   . . . it is interesting/I like my teacher/we read good books.
2   . . . we have English/the teachers help us/it's dinner time.
3   . . . you work hard/you are clever/you are a swot.

The point again is that pupils are simply doing what they do all day long -- making up sentences; all you have to do is to reinforce the point that what they have produced are subordinate clauses.

You may be saying at this point, why weren't the activities in this chapter based on the principle you have just outlined? The answer is that to work in this way you need to be able to give feedback; closed questions were used here so you could be given the answers – this is a drawback of textbooks that doesn't apply in classroom teaching.

WHY TEACH GRAMMAR?

Quotation 3	What's a' your jargon o' your schools, Your Latin names for horns and stools; If honest Nature made you fools, What sairs your grammars?
	Robert Burns

Burns is asking here the age old question 'So what?' There are many reasons for teaching grammar, some of which should be clear from what you have read in this chapter.

Quotation 4	The proper study of mankind is man.
	Alexander Pope

The first argument relates not merely to grammar but to the development of knowledge about language in all its forms. The human species has been characterised as 'The Articulate Mammal' (Aitchison, 1976, quoting Ogden Nash) because the possession of language is one of the most fundamental characteristics of humanity. Human language is richer, more complex and more widely enabling than the communication system of any other species as far as has been established hitherto. There can be no study more beneficial to our understanding of ourselves and the meanings we construct for ourselves as individuals and members of society than the study of language which must include a study of our use of grammar.

More prosaically, the possession of a shared *metalanguage* (a language for talking about language) enables teachers and pupils to discuss language in ways which are very useful for a variety of purposes: it enables teachers to discuss pupils' work in ways which allow them to explain the features which are being used and ways in which the pupils can develop; it allows for the kind of discussion of a wide range of texts illustrated in the example from Stubbs discussed above; it will help students to understand about differences between Standard English and other dialects and give them a deeper understanding of features which they will need to acquire in order to use Standard English in their speech and writing, as required by the National Curriculum; it can afford them linguistic self-respect through an understanding that their own, non-standard dialects, are fully formed grammatical systems; and it is a useful tool for the learning of foreign languages.

For teachers a knowledge of grammar is extremely useful in developing their understanding of what their pupils can and cannot accomplish in their language use. A knowledge of grammar can help teachers make judgements which go beyond the superficialities of spelling and punctuation which often provide the only yardsticks against which pupils' linguistic capabilities are measured.

Finally, of course, you need to know about grammar because it is an important part of the National Curriculums for both pupils and trainee teachers.

GRAMMAR AND THE STANDARDS

This outline of the grammar of English should have given you an understanding of the requirements of the ITT National Curriculum for grammar. Most of these are expressed in § 28, section a, of which we have covered here subsections i (morphology), ii (grammar) and iii which deals with text level organisation. We have covered the 'grammatical terms and conventions listed in the pupils' National Curriculum' (DfEE, 1998, § 15a, p. 96) and have suggested ways of teaching these and we have shown you how to 'use correctly technical terms which, in addition to those in the National Curriculum English Order, are necessary to enable trainees to be precise in their explanations to pupils, to discuss secondary English at a professional level, and to read inspections and classroom-focused research evidence with understanding' (DfEE, 1998, § 27a, p. 99).

ANSWERS TO THE ACTIVITIES

Activity 1			
	1	talk	word
	2	boy + ish	happen + ing
	3	elephant	dis + inter
	4	quick	mis + inform + ed
	5	quick + ly	dog + s

Activity 2	Identify the verbs in the following sentences:
	1 I **like** chocolate.
	2 I **remember** it very well.
	3 I **gave** him some good advice.
	4 I **was** very busy when he **came** to see me.
	5 The doctor **examined** me but she **found** nothing wrong.

Activity 3   Identify the subject in the following clauses:

1 **The bride** was married on Thursday.
2 **The children** dressed up for the party.
3 **The blackbird** returned to its nest.
4 **A baby** cried for food.
5 **Jerry Springer** is a chat show host.
6 **Five sea lions** were basking on the rocks.
7 **My television** is broken.
8 **She** wore a blue suit.
9 **The dragonflies** landed on the marsh.
10 **Nepal** is very hilly.

Activity 4   Which of the following contain objects and which contain subject complements?

1 The boy ate **the sweets** (object).
2 The girl kicked **the ball** (object).
3 The girl seemed **nice** (subject complement).
4 My father was **a sailor** (subject complement).
5 Pavarotti sang **the aria** (object).
6 The forecast predicted **rain** (object).
7 The bridegroom cancelled **the wedding** (object).
8 The bride was **sad** (subject complement).
9 Northumbria has **many coastal castles** (object).
10 *The Full Monty* was **a very popular film** (subject complement).

Activity 5 Analyse the following sentences into subject, verb, indirect object, direct object, indirect object, subject complement and object complement:

	Subject	Verb		
1	I	wonder.		

	Subject	Verb	Indirect object	Direct object
2	That girl	gave	Jane	a present.

	Subject	Verb	Direct object	
3	James	adores	Mabel.	

	Subject	Verb	Direct object	Object complement
4	Nobody	eats	spaghetti	cold.

	Subject	Verb	Direct object	
5	The police	searched	the room.	

	Subject	Verb	Subject complement	
6	Truth	is	beauty.	

	Subject	Verb	Subject complement	
7	The dog	is	an Alsatian.	

	Subject	Verb	Indirect object	Direct object
8	John	lent	me	his pen.

	Subject	Verb	Direct object	Object complement
9	The teacher	called	him	an idiot.

	Subject	Verb	Subject complement	
10	That	was	difficult.	

Activity 6 Identify the adverbials in the following:

1 I watch football **on Saturdays**.
2 She studied **in Lancaster**.
3 She dances **effortlessly**.
4 **Last week** they went **to Manchester**.
5 I like him **because he's funny**.
6 Penguins eat fish **every day**.
7 **If you're lucky** you may win the lottery.
8 I watched him **as he worked**.
9 There was mistletoe **over the door**.
10 John had known Sally **since 1987**.

Activity 7   All of the following sentences contain two clauses; one consists of the whole sentence, the other is a subordinate clause. Identify the latter.

1   Jane goes to the theatre **when she can.**
2   **As soon as the bell goes** the pupils leave.
3   Surinder likes maths **because she is clever.**
4   **If Newcastle win** they will go to the top of the league.
5   I don't like him **although he is nice.**
6   This saw cuts wood **like a knife cuts butter.**
7   I saw him **where the two roads meet.**
8   **If you take the rabbit to the vet** he will cut its claws.
9   You will die **unless you drink.**
10   The woman had no grey hair **after she visited the hairdresser.**

Activity 8   Identify the premodifiers, heads and postmodifiers in the following phrases:

	Premodifier	Head
1	The	ball.

	Premodifier	Premodifier	Head
2	The	big	ball.

	Premodifier	Premodifier	Head
3	The	red	ball.

	Premodifier	Premodifier	Premodifier	Head
4	The	big	red	ball.

	Premodifier	Premodifier	Premodifier	Premodifier	Head
5	The	big	red	beach	ball.

	Premodifier	Head	Postmodifier
6	The	ball	in the cupboard.

	Premodifier	Premodifier	Head	Postmodifier
7	The	red	ball	in the cupboard.

	Premodifier	Head	Postmodifier
8	The	ball	I gave to Jane.

	Premodifier	Head	Postmodifier	Postmodifier
9	The	ball	in the cupboard	which I never use.

Activity 9   Analyse the following sentences into phrases:

(Key: NP = noun phrase; VP = verb phrase; PP = prepositional phrase; Adj. P = adjective phrase; Adv. P = adverbial phrase. Phrases that are in bold act as part of other phrases.)

    NP   *VP* *Adj. P*
1 The table is   very heavy.

    NP   *PP*   *VP*   *PP* *NP*
2 My friend **from** **Liverpool** has been to   **China**.
    (**Liverpool** is also an NP.)

    NP   *VP*   *PP*   *Adv. P*
3 The train went **to Birmingham** very quickly.
    (**Birmingham** is also an NP.)

    NP   *NP* *VP*   *VP* *Adj. P*
4 The drink that **I**   **ordered** was terrible.

    NP   *VP* *NP*
5 The white parrot has yellow head feathers.

    NP   *VP*   *Adj. P* *PP*
6 The pond was full   **of weeds**.
    (**Weeds** is also an NP.)

    NP   *VP*   *PP* *NP*
7 Two men were fishing by **the riverside**.

    NP   *VP*   *NP*
8 Some people are rowing the boat.

    NP   *VP*   *PP* *NP*
9 A duck has landed on **the village pond**.

    NP   *VP*   *NP*
10 Your poodle may have had an ear infection.

Activity 10   Identify the parts of speech in the following sentences:

(Key: det. = determiner; prep. = preposition; con. = conjunction; pro. = pronoun.)

	det.	*noun*	*verb*	*prep.*	*noun*		
1	The	magnolia	was	in	flower.		

	adjective	*noun*	*verb*	*prep.*	*det.*	*adjective*	*noun*
2	Foreign	investment	is	at	a	low	level.

	det.	*adjective*	*noun*	*verb*	*noun*	*prep.*	*det.*	*noun*
3	The	elderly	man	bred	pigeons	as	a	hobby.

	det.	*noun*	*verb*	*verb*	*prep.*	*noun*
4	The	church	was	destroyed	by	fire.

	det.	*noun*	*noun*	*verb*	*verb*	*prep.*	*noun*	*con.*	*noun*
5	The	city	baths	are	used	by	children	and	adults.

	pro.	*verb*	*noun*	*prep.*	*det.*	*noun*	*noun*
6	They	want	tickets	for	the	cup	final.

	det.	*noun*	*noun*	*verb*	*det.*	*noun*
7	The	electricity	man	read	the	meter.

	pro.	*noun*	*con.*	*noun*	*noun*	*verb*	*adverb*
8	Her	diamond	and	sapphire	ring	shone	brilliantly.

	det.	*noun*	*verb*	*verb*	*adjective*	*con.*	*adjective*
9	The	weather	will	become	cooler	and	wetter.

	pro.	*verb*	*adverb*	*adjective*	*prep.*	*det.*	*noun*
10	It	was	very	foggy	at	the	coast.

RESOURCES

There are a number of works to which you can turn if you wish to develop further your own knowledge of the material covered in this chapter. Several of the works to which reference has been made during this chapter are helpful although you should be aware that grammarians often vary from each other in respect of their use of terminology. Probably the most accessible book, and one which is not too expensive to buy, is:

Crystal, D. (1988) *Rediscover Grammar*, London: Longman

In addition, you may find it useful to consult the following text specifically addressed to the National Curriculum which, despite its title, goes beyond the knowledge needed at primary level and contains valuable self-auditing activities which will enable you to check your knowledge:

Wray, D. and Medwell, J. (1997) *English for Primary Teachers: An Audit and Self-study Guide*, London: Letts Educational

There are now some good materials available for use in the classroom. At secondary level, the most wide ranging title is:

Bain, E. and Bain, R. (1996) *The Grammar Book*, Sheffield: NATE

You may also find the primary version of use, particularly if you are working with children who have not undertaken much work in grammar:

Bain, R. and Bridgewood, M. (1998) *The Primary Grammar Book*, Sheffield: NATE

As with any published material, neither of the above should be used uncritically but both provide a wealth of varied, stimulating ideas which can be adapted for your own purposes.

On a smaller scale, you will find useful ideas in both of the following:

Hudson, R. (1992) *Teaching Grammar*, Oxford: Blackwell
Hunt, G. (1994) *Inspirations for Grammar*, London: Scholastic Publications

REFERENCES

Aitchison, J. (1976) *The Articulate Mammal*, London: Hutchinson
Bloomfield, L. (1933) *Language*, New York: Holt
Burton-Roberts, N. (1986) *Analysing Sentences: An Introduction to English Syntax*, London: Longman
Catchpole, C. (1983) *The Living World: Jungles*, London: Walker Books
Crystal, D. (1994) *The Cambridge Encyclopedia of Language*, Cambridge: CUP
DfEE (1995) *English in the National Curriculum*, London: HMSO
DfEE (1998) *Teaching: High Status, High Standards; Requirements for Courses of Initial Teacher Training*, DfEE Circular 4/98
Fowler, R. (1974) *Understanding Language*, London: Routledge and Kegan Paul
Greenbaum, S. (1996) *The Oxford English Grammar*, Oxford: OUP

Hockett, C.F. (1958) *A Course in Modern Linguistics*, New York: Macmillan

LINC (Language in the National Curriculum) (undated) *Materials for Professional Development*, no publisher

Quirk, R. and Greenbaum, S. (1973) *A University Grammar of English*, London: Longman

Seiler, H. (1964) 'On Defining the Word' in H.G. Lunt (ed.) *Proceedings of the Ninth International Congress of Linguists*, The Hague: Mouton

Stubbs, M. (1990) *Knowledge about Language: Grammar, Ignorance and Society*, London: Institute of Education, University of London

Williamson, J. and Hardman, F. (1995) 'Time for Refilling the Bath? A Study of Primary Student Teachers' Grammatical Knowledge', *Language and Education*, 9, 2, pp. 117–34

5 What Do We Mean by Teaching Literature in Secondary English?

DAVID STEVENS

'Education is not filling a bucket but lighting a fire' said W. B. Yeats and most English teachers would agree with him in principle, if not always in practice. The reason for this practical qualification, of course, is that educational legislators over recent years seem to have been far more concerned with emphasising 'bucket filling' in schools and telling teachers what should and should not go into the bucket than with safeguarding and developing the inspirational. Perhaps this is inevitable, in that it is far easier to legislate for the tangible, but it sometimes seems as if counting and measuring the components of the curriculum have endangered our sight of the whole process and its purposes. The 'Standards' may themselves be regarded as one more example of this preoccupation. It is likely to be in the broad field of 'literature' teaching (we shall return to the contentious nature of what exactly constitutes literature) that the inspirational aspects of English teaching are likely to be most keenly felt and it is here that the philosophical distinction alluded to by Yeats often may be transformed into a struggle for supremacy.

Many prospective PGCE English students cite love of reading and a desire to transmit this love to young minds (as frequently it was fostered in themselves by an inspirational English teacher) as the primary reasons for wishing to enter the English teaching profession. Despite the increasing variation in student English teachers' degree backgrounds, the majority continue prominently to feature literature study. It is hardly surprising that it is in this area that practising and would-be English teachers feel most confident and comfortable – and, perhaps, most resentful of outside interference. Much of the most effective English teaching and planning remains literature-based with other dimensions skilfully integrated. If English teachers are to develop their inspirational qualities it is important that a way is found to use the national curricula for teacher education and for the teaching of English in schools to advantage without becoming obsessed by mere bucket filling and inevitable leaks. We need, in fact, to find a synthesis between the inclination to light fires in the hearts and minds of our pupils and the need to meet the Standards of an over-crowded literature curriculum whether at Key Stage 3, GCSE or A/AS level.

Activity 1	In pairs or individually consider the following questions:

- How do you feel your own experiences and tastes in literature will find their way into your teaching of literature?
- Is it helpful to distinguish between language and literature (as examination boards invariably do) in the teaching of English?
- What in your view constitutes literature? Consider the traditional canon and relate to more modern texts, including those from other cultures and those not normally deemed 'literary'.

THE STARTING POINT

Clearly, Year 7 pupils bring with them diverse experiences of literature on entry into the secondary school English classroom: some will have read avidly a wide range of literature both at school and at home; others will find reading difficult – impossible, occasionally – or unattractive or both. The starting point for the English teacher at secondary level is anything but a clean sheet and it certainly pays dividends to have some awareness of what exactly has been written on the sheet. Standard A1 vii asks for teachers' demonstrations that they 'understand, for their specialist subject(s), progression from the Key Stage 2 programmes of study' (p. 9), and it is this understanding which should provide the foundations for what is to follow. The results of the Standard Assessment Tests (SATs), the reading age scores and the base line tests all have their uses and English departments need to make something productive of them. A more vivid picture of Year 7 pupils' experiences, strengths and weaknesses may be gained from familiarity with what actually goes on in the partner primary schools and the possibility of conducting cross-phase 'bridging activities'. With planned cross-phase collaboration, for example, Year 6 pupils could start work on a literature-based long-term assignment which may be continued independently during the summer vacation (as a form of structured research and reading) for guided development and completion in Year 7 of the secondary school. The establishment of the National Literacy Strategy in the primary phase, further, has profound implications for the kinds of literature-based activities that in-coming pupils will have been accustomed to, including textual deconstruction, and secondary phase English teachers need to plan and teach accordingly. In practical terms, there are some positive steps that could be taken to facilitate a smooth and creative transition across the great divide.

- Regular meetings between representatives of secondary English departments and primary language co-ordinators – to discuss practical concerns such as which books are taught in which phase and precisely what sorts of reading (whole class? small group? individual?) – are encouraged and in what proportion to each other.

- ICT links between pupils and teachers could be used to report on books being read. This would be a kind of reading journal with a highly specific audience.
- Various creative literature-based events could provide opportunities for primary and secondary pupils and their teachers and parents to work together, such as poetry readings, visiting authors' workshops or playing book-based games, for example.

The key point here is to make the connections with as many people as possible who have contributed to the reading histories of the – invariably eager – new Year 7 pupils.

| **Activity 2** | • In meeting a Year 7 class for the first time, how would you set about judging the pupils' levels of engagement with and experience of literature? |

- In your opinion, what would be the 'ideal' text with which to start literature teaching with a new Year 7 mixed ability group?
- What would be your over-arching aim in teaching this text?

THE TEACHING OF POETRY

If, as I have suggested, literature continues to be central to the English teaching project, it is with the teaching of poetry, as arguably the most self-consciously 'literary' of literary modes, that the need to combine content and inspiration is often shown in sharpest focus. In DfEE Circular 4/98, Annex F (DfEE, 1998), which is the basis of the references throughout this chapter, there is frequent mention of such terms as 'texts' and 'critical readers' but specific requirements for the teaching of poetry are kept to a minimum. Perhaps this is hardly surprising given the nature of most English teachers' own degree backgrounds and it does imply that there remains considerable flexibility in the 'what' and 'how' of poetry teaching. Thus, in the tersely prescriptive language found throughout Circular 4/98, we have in Annex F, Section B7:

> Trainees must be taught how to teach poetry, including how to:
>
> involve pupils in appreciating, understanding, responding to and writing poetry, including through teachers and pupils reading poetry aloud;
>
> teach the range of poetic forms and equip pupils with the technical terms they need to discuss poems, their meanings and effects, *e.g. metre, metaphor, simile, onomatopoeia, assonance, alliteration, hyperbole, oxymoron, sonnet, ballad;*
>
> group poems to enable appreciation of theme, form, period and author's voice.

If these statements constitute the standard of English teaching to which we must aspire, there seems to be little to worry about. The difficulties start, though, when we realise that the requirements must be applied to the specified content of the National Curriculum and to the GCSE, A and AS level syllabuses in both English and English literature. Indeed, the inclusion of the list of prescribed authors and works – covering all literary genres but often most keenly felt in relation to poetry requirements – was one of the most contentious and strongly resisted elements of what has been seen as the politically motivated revision of the 'Cox' curriculum between 1993 and 1995 (see, for example, Cox, 1995). In the more recent revision of the National Curriculum for English, culminating in the present Orders (applicable from 2000), the issue has again arisen but, despite some variations from the previous version, lists of prescribed authors remain.

Issues in the teaching of poetry

Given the specificity of these requirements, it may be worthwhile to take stock of what precisely we are attempting in the teaching of poetry.

Activity 3	In terms of the teaching of poetry, what principles underlie your interpretations of:

- Circular 4/98 – in Annex A dealing with the generic *Standards for the Award of Qualified Teacher Status* and in the specifically English Annex F?
- The National Curriculum?
- Examination syllabuses' requirements at GCSE?

A useful starting point, for both teachers (whether practising or potential) and for groups of pupils, might be to consider the nature of poetry and its possible definitions. A list may include the following formulations:

- The best available words in the most effective order.
- Words grouped and used to express intensity of feeling.
- Consciously rhythmic combinations of words.
- Words grouped within a specific structure which may include elements of rhythm, rhyme and other poetic devices.
- Words chosen and grouped for emphasis on the *sound* to express meaning.
- Any group of words which is not prose.

Recent research indicates that addressing the nature of poetry with pupils, as opposed to simply studying poems 'cold', can lead to a greatly enhanced range of responses and to keener enthusiasm. Pike (2000, p. 45), for example, suggests that the purpose of poetry eludes many adolescents, and if pinning down the purpose of poetry is difficult, deciding what poetry is poses an equally inscrutable problem. Such questions have, after all, challenged the best literary minds. Yet, in an increasingly utilitarian educational climate, it is particularly important that teachers help pupils to explore such questions.

A group of student teachers grappling with the nature of poetry actually arrived at the definitions noted above and similar expressions of the essential qualities of poetry, and many convincing reasons were given. Clearly, poetry *may* have elements of several of these characteristics and there is inevitably considerable overlap. Poets themselves have offered their own versions of their art's definition and no doubt readers will have their own favourites; what matters is not so much the result of the exercise – for poetry is notoriously and fittingly elusive – but the reflective activity itself. When asked to condense a definition into three words *and* somehow to combine the above and further ideas, the group collaboratively arrived at the sense of poetry as *language working hard*.

Again, this formulation may be contentious, but as a working definition I have found it to be practically helpful in both the writing and the teaching of poetry. For if poetry can indeed be seen as language working hard, it may as well work hard for teachers of English: in an increasingly overcrowded English curriculum, both for schools and for PGCE courses, there is a great deal that may be achieved and covered through the medium of poetry. And it has several advantages in this respect: it tends to distil many of the finer points of linguistic expression; it is often short and therefore palatable; and, as we shall see, it is often attractive and accessible. Lest we find this simplicity too beguiling, however, we need to be aware of some of the issues and tensions inherent in the teaching of poetry – unless these too can be acknowledged it is unlikely that the Standards can be satisfactorily met. For example:

- English student teachers are often more used to responding to poetry written by others than writing their own and this simple fact tends to imply that school lessons are focused on the response to poems with the creation of poems coming a poor second. Further, those English teachers who are not poets frequently find it problematic to develop – to teach, in fact – the drafting and final writing of poetry with any confidence.
- The National Curriculum specifies 'poetry by four major poets published before 1914', drawn from a list of possible exponents, together with a similar expectation, from exemplified rather than prescribed poets, for post-1914 poetry. But such ideas are problematic and many teachers feel that the ideology of a relatively fixed canon is unhelpful and outdated.
- Despite the strides made in recent years towards the popularisation of poetry, not least by English teachers, it is inevitable that some stubborn resistance will be met in the classroom – especially in the light of the statutory obligation, noted above, to teach canonical poets. This may well come most strongly from pupils whom the English teacher is most keen to enthuse, such as

adolescent boys, and at the very least it is important to bear this in mind and adopt relevant strategies to counter the possible undesirable effects.

- If, however, too much emphasis is placed on making poetry accessible and public, through exclusively selecting lighter verse and performance poetry, for example, the potential power of many poems to provoke profound, often intensely personal, thoughts and feelings may be neglected. Certainly, the previous National Curriculum's requirement, implicit also in the current Orders, that we use poetry to 'extend pupils' ideas and their moral and emotional understanding' suggests a seriousness of approach where appropriate.

Tensions such as these notwithstanding we need to turn now to practical ways of covering the curriculum for poetry and meeting the Standards. One of these requirements, indeed, exhorting English teachers to seek breadth of coverage and to *teach the range of poetic forms* (Section B7b, p. 94), may provide us with the clue to effective teaching and practical resolution of some of the tensions and controversies.

Activities for the teaching of poetry

By its very nature, poetry tends towards particularity and intensity of expressive language, as several of the possible definitions and tensions noted above suggest. For this reason we need to tread carefully in recommending activities for the teaching of poems in general; sometimes it may be possible to transfer approaches and techniques from poem to poem – or from genre to genre, for that matter – but as often as not this might endanger the individual nature of the poem in question. The activities and approaches summarised below, then, are often attached to particular poems, and I leave it to the reader's judgement as to whether and to what they may be transferable. Similarly, they are intended as suggestive rather than prescriptive – it is certainly not my business here to fill buckets.

Teaching *A Martian Sends a Postcard Home* (Craig Raine)

If part of the appeal of poetry is to engender a sense of wonder in our familiar surroundings through the stretching, exploratory use of language, then this poem performs that role admirably. As the previous National Curriculum had it, 'poetry and the work of individual poets selected should include poems that . . . use language in imaginative, precise and original ways'. I have been greatly impressed by the responses of Year 7 pupils in a mixed ability class to a reading of this poem – responses which showed a depth of feeling for the strangeness and wonder of life which I and other adults present in this lesson found quite startling. Raine's poem, of course, belongs to the 'Martian' school, for whom the 'making strange' of the familiar is central. It seems a good place to start our consideration of poetry in the secondary school English lesson. An approximate teaching plan would be:

- The teacher reads the poem aloud (copies having been previously distributed to each pupil).
- The whole class discusses the nature of the poem (having been given an explanation that the poem deals with eight different everyday objects or experiences seen through the eyes of the 'Martian' visitor to earth).
- The whole class guesses as to what precisely these objects/experiences may be. Several are self-explanatory, although couched in unusual terms, such as:

> Mist is when the sky is tired of flight
> and rests its soft machine on the ground:
> then the world is dim and bookish
> like engravings under tissue paper.

Others take more discovery, which is where the fun lies. For example, the telephone:

> In homes, a haunted apparatus sleeps,
> that snores when you pick it up.
> If the ghost cries, they carry it
> To their lips and soothe it to sleep
> With sounds. And yet, they wake it up
> Deliberately, by tickling with a finger.

And the penultimate object, the lavatory, can cause much amusement – and not a little bemusement before successful guessing of the 'answer'.

> Only the adults are allowed to suffer openly.
> Adults go to a punishment room with water but nothing to eat.
> They lock the door and suffer the noises alone.
> No one is exempt and everyone's pain has a different smell.

- Small groups then discuss, note and report back to the whole class on possible subjects drawn from familiar everyday experience with a view to eventual poetic expression.
- A further variation here might be to include photographic or artistic representations of 'normal' objects seen from unusual angles, or in a new light (both literally and metaphorically), again with the possibility of awakening from the unseeing contempt so often bred by familiarity. There is in this the opportunity to develop a media-based exploration of images.
- Pupils then fashion their ideas and observations into 'Martian' poems, using the given convention of the Martian visitor trying to make sense of earthly objects, customs and ideas. Possibilities include school, money, items of furniture and articles of clothing. Illustrations might also be interesting. Volunteers then go on to read poems aloud with the class guessing the subject matter of each poem.

I include some examples of extracts from poems written by Key Stage 3 pupils following this scheme of work in order to give a fuller flavour of the possibilities:

> It lives on the ceiling
> It never moves
> But when it grows dark
> It gets angry and explodes.
>
> Kimberley, Year 9

> I lie there watching the world
> Through a television that's been switched off
> I feel so scared
> I daren't even cough.
>
> Laura, Year 7

> It's a giant snake with many mouths
> Which travels very fast
> Swallowing all its victims whole
> But people wave as their friends get eaten.
>
> Paul, Year 7

A scheme of activities such as this has the advantage of covering both reading and writing of poetry, with the latter given a clear format and expectation but enough flexibility to allow for individual expression. The first of the requirements on teaching poetry (Section B7a, p. 94) is certainly met 'including through teachers and pupils reading poetry aloud'.

Teaching *My Bus Conductor* (Roger McGough)

McGough's poem is a fitting follow up, as it deals with a bus conductor seeing his environment anew after learning that his life expectation has been sharply curtailed through kidney failure. So as not to cover the same ground, the approaches could vary, possibly along these lines:

- The pupils are given the poem as a cloze exercise. In pairs they have to work out the missing words focusing on similes, images, alliteration and rhyme. The original words may be listed or not at the teacher's discretion; the point is to lead to a discussion in which words in poetry 'work hardest' and give a poem its essential flavour. In so doing we go some way to meet Standard B7b, p. 94, dealing with 'the technical terms they need to discuss poems'.
- Finished 'versions' then can be read aloud followed by a discussion guided to consider how and why the changes in the bus conductor's perception of his life and surroundings have changed. Pupils generally participate eagerly in such a discussion and acquiring a sense of mortality is often part of growing up – at best in a liberating rather than morbid sense.

- Using McGough's format, pupils can be asked to form their own poems, perhaps again working in pairs but using a different occupation from bus conductor, such as cleaner, police officer or teacher. It may be useful to discuss beforehand the sort of things which may be noticed in following the appropriate routines.

It is important in planning and teaching literature-based work that acknowledgement is made of the likely stages of learning. In case this seems rather deterministic and mechanical, ignoring the subtle nuances of classroom relationships, we need too to keep a realistic sense that what is *taught* does not necessarily correlate in any predictable way to what may be *learned*. This important rider notwithstanding, it is useful to envisage the stages of learning in terms of

- the *descriptive* – the initial reading of the poem, for example;
- the *reflective* – which may include general or specific textual discussion and questioning;
- the *speculative* – the kinds of activity arising from textual study, such as pupils' writing their own poems, stimulated by, but possibly wandering some way from, the initial reading.

Such a formulation is particularly helpful in the planning stages in the light of research and anecdotal evidence suggesting that many boys (and not a few girls) prefer to rush headlong from the first to the third stage, thus missing out arguably the most important aspect of the study. It is essential to guide pupils towards the reflective, if for no other reason than the eventual examination success will depend on it. The timing of specific tasks within the overall scheme of work, with short-term outcomes aimed for before going on to subsequent stages, is one effective way of insisting on the reflective phase. Particular lesson plans, within the context of the over-arching scheme of work, may be based on such tasks. Clearly, the implication of reflection is as some sort of mirroring process; in itself it is not sufficient to provide a sound basis for the speculative, active, creative stage. As well as the reflective, then, we need to cater for and stimulate the *illuminative*, whereby the active begins to develop from the passive. The examples of planning given in this chapter attempt to demonstrate these stages implicitly or explicitly, although of course, as with all such things, teachers themselves will wish to reflect and illuminate: adapting and changing as appropriate.

In terms of *A Martian Sends a Postcard Home* and *My Bus Conductor*, both poems suggest it is possible to find in everyday experience exciting scope for observation, description, reflection and illumination, not least through empathetic consideration of the 'narrative voice'. Further, there is a sense that everyday language works through metaphor (as in filling buckets and lighting fires) and an opportunity arises for an exploration of the nature of figurative colloquial language: again, poetry, as language working hard, can provide a springboard into diverse aspects of English study.

Activity 4   Consider further some of the teaching approaches described above for the Raine and McGough poems, and then try to adapt them for other poems you find appropriate for classroom use, paying careful attention to the nature of the pupils (such as age range and their ability) in question.

Teaching *The Rime of the Ancient Mariner* (Samuel Taylor Coleridge) and traditional ballads

The Rime of the Ancient Mariner is interesting and appropriate to teach on several counts. Significantly, it provides a ready opportunity to exemplify and teach about 'the historical spread of . . . poetry . . . including key authors from the English literary heritage' (Standard C28c v, p. 101) although its study does not, of course, preclude a questioning of the nature and composition of such a 'heritage' – indeed, it may occasion it. In the light of the above introductory discussion on the nature of poetry, there may also be a further opportunity to look at Coleridge's own views on the relationship between poetic form and content in the context of his philosophy of organic growth. As a prompt note to an 1812 lecture, he wrote

> The Spirit of Poetry like all other living Powers, must of necessity circumscribe itself by Rules, were it only to unite Power with Beauty. It must embody in order to reveal itself; but a living body is of necessity an organized one – & what is organization but the connection of Parts to the whole, so that each Part is at once End and Means! This is no discovery of criticism – it is a necessity of the human mind – and all nations have felt and obeyed it, in the invention of metre, & measured Sounds, as the vehicle and Involucrum of Poetry itself, a fellow growth from the same Life, even as the Bark is to a living Tree.
>
> (from *Literary Lectures*, quoted in Holmes, 1998, p. 321)

This passage deserves, and would repay, careful study in itself – quite something for a mere prompt note. Its insights, formulated a considerable time after the writing of *The Ancient Mariner*, seem particularly apposite to the teaching of this poem.

A scheme of study, further, could make good use of some of the following areas and general principles:

- The poem's appeal is on several levels and successful teaching can occur from early primary school days to A level – certainly at Key Stages 3 or 4. Presentation of the poem in a form suitable for young children, for example, could draw on this wide appeal.
- It provides a good example of pre-1914 verse, insisted on in the National Curriculum, and admirably fits the last of the Standards on poetry, enabling 'appreciation of theme, form, period and author's voice'.

- It is a fine vehicle for teaching about poetic terms and techniques, not least because Coleridge himself adopted and adapted the archaic ballad form and, as we have just seen, was acutely conscious of the fusion of form and content in verse.
- For similar reasons, the poem lends itself to the exploration of language change over time with the possibility of contemporary versions and equivalent voyages of discovery using, for example, the genre of science fiction.
- The imagery is vividly pictorial and there are useful resources to emphasise this, such as the illustrative engravings by Gustav Doré and Mervyn Peake and the excellent BBC educational video with accompanying booklet. The opportunities to illustrate, display and adapt for various media are endless.
- The poem provides ready opportunities for lively 'performance readings' and dramatic interpretations, including mime, thought tracking and tableaux.
- It may also lead to a consideration of the oral tradition, such as the nature of traditional ballads and possible modern equivalents like 'urban myths' and jokes.
- Following this point, the similarities between poetry and music may be further explored through listening and musical performance with scope for bringing in traditional and contemporary ballads (and, of course, Iron Maiden's version of *The Rime* which may appeal to some).
- Empathetic writing may usefully arise, exploring, for instance, the viewpoint of the hapless wedding guest or other stranger creatures and presences who populate the poem.
- The story of the poem's original context, including its place in the *Lyrical Ballads* with the famous *Preface* dealing with poetic language and purpose, and the nature of Coleridge's imagination, opium fed or otherwise, offers fertile ground for the cultural contextualisation of literature — now an important feature of GCSE and A level syllabus requirements.

Several of the above possibilities hinge on the ballad form of *The Rime* and here there is vast scope for varied teaching ideas — some of which I have explored elsewhere in relation to teaching English within the National Curriculum (Fleming and Stevens, 1998, pp. 6–9). The point here concerns the nature of the relationship between poetry and music: reluctant readers of or listeners to poetry invariably find pleasure in music — indeed I have yet to find the person who dislikes *all* music. This is a useful starting point in working towards the primary Standard regarding poetry teaching involving 'pupils in appreciating . . . poetry', without which very little may be achieved. Thus exploration of rhythm, sound, form and lyrics in songs (and rhythmic chants, incidentally) may prefigure study of poetry itself.

English teachers will wish to adapt and add to the teaching ideas noted above for their own purposes arriving at coherent schemes of work for the study of Coleridge's poem. One effective way of planning work, which attempts to address the issue of differentiation, is to envisage the scheme of study in both linear and lateral ways. Thus the central activities are for the whole class, while at every appropriate stage there could be integrated further or 'extension' tasks for those pupils who have completed the set work. Such tasks should be rather different in nature from the main activity, partly to make them attractive to more able pupils who may otherwise simply work more slowly rather than finish early only to be set onerous further work. Possibilities here include research, audio-visual presentations, illustration or dramatic role-play, each of which may imply a degree of teacher–pupil trust. Several of the Standards refer to the variety of activities, assessment opportunities and differentiation requirements vital for the effective teaching of literature. For example, in the context of the outlined plans here, teachers would be 'providing a range of resources which are likely to appeal to and develop pupils' different interests' (Section B5b, p. 93), while simultaneously adopting 'different critical approaches which emphasise different ways of reading texts depending on whether the focus is on the reader, the writer, the context or the text alone' (Standard C28c vi, p. 101). Clearly there is considerable overlap here and the key to covering the National Curriculum and Circular 4/98 is to be found in the inventive variety of approaches. In conceiving plans, teachers may also wish to consider some of the more generic ideas for meeting the Standards in teaching poetry outlined below.

Further active approaches to the teaching of poetry

There are numerous adventurous ideas for poetry teaching, many of which have been usefully summarised (see, for example, Cliff-Hodges, 1998, pp. 255–6) and Fleming and Stevens (1998, pp. 73–6) and there is no need to repeat them here. However, the following approaches may be useful additions.

Anthologies

The aim here is the creation of pupils' and teachers' anthologies of poetry with periodic presentations of the collected verse to the class. The form may be a straightforward 'scrapbook' or it may involve recording of readings, displays or use of ICT. This strategy may be used successfully for any age group and the presentations may be subsequently refined to require pupils to look at similarities and contrasts between poems using a range of criteria and, as needed, guidance from the teacher. Thus the ability to 'group poems to enable appreciation of theme, form, period and author's voice' (Section B7c, p. 94) may be met by both teacher and pupils (the requirement in question is unclear about which is meant, but it seems valid for both). Suitable poems may be sought from published anthologies, peer recommendations, CD-Rom and Internet sources, libraries and recordings: the range of possible sources implies sharpening of research skills, another important aspect of the English curriculum.

Adaptations

The adaptation of poems for broader, specified purposes is a useful line to pursue. Poetry among its many qualities offers the chance to express ideas succinctly and vividly and extracts or whole poems could be used for a range of broader functions:

- Using poems as the basis for the creation of brochures, advertising or persuasive literature of one sort or another.
- Subtitling narrative or other types of writing with poetic quotations.
- Making short video adaptations of poems such as Wordsworth's *Lucy* poems.
- Asking pupils to write poems from the point of view of characters in a book being studied, exploring personal emotional responses.
- Using the representation of poetry in pictorial or diagrammatic form, such as poetry trees, animals or human figures, with the possibility of display.

Conversely, objects, pictures and the like may be transformed into appropriate poems, building up gradually from questions that a pupil may put to, say, a sea-shell (the willing suspension of disbelief operates here) or to a character depicted on a postcard, into the teacher-directed form of a poem itself. Indeed, poetry and pictorial art go well together, as poets like Blake well knew, and there are now excellent publications (for example, *Double Vision*, Benton, 1990) as aids in developing this fruitful relationship.

Teaching the poetry of William Blake

The mention of Blake leads on to a consideration of his work; for me, his qualities make him indispensable in any English curriculum and he comfortably takes the Standards in his stride. Recent research (Stevens, 2000) has enhanced my sense of Blake's value in the classroom. When introducing his selected works for school use (Blake, ed. D. Stevens, 1995) I wrote of my enthusiasm for teaching Blake as founded on two premises: 'his work is accessible, and it is robust . . . such is the stature of the man's work that you can do almost anything to it, even irreverently, and it will still bounce back, all the better for the exercise'. This still holds true. Further, his symbolic language seems to me a fitting antidote to the literalness so prevalent in contemporary culture, while being accessible to a youthful audience. Blake takes the literalness out of literacy and we need figures like that. I shall focus here on two contrasting yet complementary poems from *The Songs of Innocence and of Experience* – *The Chimney Sweeper* from *Innocence* and his identically titled counterpart from *Experience* – in the context of the general study of a number of poems from this collection. In planning a sequence of lessons, for these and any other poems, it is important to keep in mind the primacy of the verse itself. Activities may well lead away from the poetry, exploring all sorts of interesting avenues, but there is a basic question to ask in conceiving a scheme of work: how will a sense of enhanced understanding of the original text result from the activity?

This question implies a guiding principle for effective literature teaching and perhaps the most fundamental role for the English teacher in guiding the process of learning. We need, too, to ask:

- What are the over-arching aims of the sequence in the context of a planned curriculum?

- How will more limited short-term lesson objectives relate to these aims?
- What other contextual considerations, such as syllabus requirements, are there?
- How will the work be differentiated to cater for differing aptitudes, interests and abilities?
- How will we know that learning has taken place?

Keeping these questions firmly in mind, let us consider a sequence of approaches as taught to an upper-ability Year 10 GCSE English class following the NEAB syllabus. The specified objectives in the NEAB syllabus for 1998 are:

- Respond to texts critically, sensitively and in detail using textual evidence as appropriate.
- Explore how language, structure and forms contribute to the meaning of texts, considering the different approaches to texts and alternative interpretations.
- Explore the relationships and comparisons between texts, selecting and evaluating the relevant material.

The scheme of activities is designed to cover all these objectives within the broader aim of sharpening and communicating responses to literature in context. Differentiation comes partly through the subtle guidance, sometimes transformed into overt direction, offered by the teacher as to which tasks are undertaken by which pupils. It is also partly achieved by outcome, with the tasks specifically designed to be broad enough to allow for a variety of responses. Following the reading and general class discussion of the poems, the full list of possible activities is presented in worksheet form to each pupil, with the explicit instruction to complete one individually written task on each poem and one small group-based task on either or both poems which may be orally presented.

The worksheet for *The Chimney Sweeper* from *Innocence* could include the following activities:

- Discuss the presentation and symbolic meaning of light and darkness in the poem, comparing it to another poem by Blake, such as *The Little Black Boy*.
- Explain why Blake included the poem in *Songs of Innocence*, given its harrowing subject matter; contrast to a more obviously 'innocent' poem such as *Laughing Song*.
- Present reasoned arguments advocating the poem as either a revolutionary call to action or a plea to make the best of a bad job and accept the suffering inflicted by society.
- Write a dialogue between the chimney sweep and the little black boy of that poem showing how their experiences and solutions might relate to each other.

The worksheet for *The Chimney Sweeper* from *Experience* could include the following activities:

- Write the script of an interview with the father and mother of the poem facing probing, possibly hostile, questions.
- Write out the words of the prayer uttered by the parents.
- Imagine the *Innocence* poem to be the youthful thoughts of the now older, more cynical chimney sweep of the *Experience* poem, then script the conversation between him and a young, frightened 'recruit'.
- Research and describe the nature of child labour in Blake's time, and show how this social context relates to the poems.

Some of the tasks outlined here may seem rather daunting for lower-ability pupils and there may need to be significant adjustments, additions and omissions to tailor the work to the needs of particular classes. Nevertheless, there are important general considerations here. Firstly, even in lower-ability or mixed-ability classes – perhaps especially here in the light of the temptations to do the opposite – it is incumbent upon English teachers to 'aim high' in setting up activities. Secondly, it is precisely the teacher's role here to *teach* pupils to extend their capabilities, without of course setting unrealistic targets which are likely to build in a sense of failure. This is the balancing act of teaching and no meaningful standards or Standards are likely to be met without an intelligent awareness of the tension involved.

In terms of evaluating the pupils' success in completing the activities – and the success of the scheme of work itself, for evaluation is perhaps the most important aspect of planning in teaching – we need to be sensitive to the nature of the original poetry studied. At the highest level, then, we must be prepared for a degree of originality in interpretation of the activities. We need to look for a sense of the metaphorical, non-literal quality of the verse – the ability, in E.M. Forster's famous phrase, to 'only connect'. The connections may be made in various ways – on the personal level, for example, or the social, cultural or generic level – with the important provision that they are based on a demonstrably close reading of the texts themselves. Syllabuses at GCSE and A levels are increasingly seeking this kind of contextualisation and whether it can be achieved is an important factor in the evaluation of the scheme of work. Lower down the scale of achievement, understanding of the verse is likely to be of a more 'basic' kind, more literal and less able to open up imaginative connections.

Teaching *Telephone Conversation* (Wole Soyinka) and *The Telephone* (Robert Frost)

Conveniently, both these poems are to be found in the tried and tested *Voices III* compilation (Summerfield, 1968) and are also anthologised widely elsewhere. Using a Nigerian and an American poet in juxtaposition, linked by a similar theme, opens

up fascinating possibilities. The Standards (reflecting the National Curriculum requirements) have English teachers introducing to their pupils 'a range of texts from different cultures' (Standard C28c v, p. 101), and the two poems in question fit the bill
admirably. The Standards also refer specifically to A level teaching and, again, the
need to demonstrate ability to 'reflect on their own response to texts and consider
other readers' interpretations' and to 'use their detailed knowledge and understanding
of individual texts to explore comparisons and connections between them' (Standard
C29a ii and iii, p. 101) is relevant here. It is also relevant, of course, to any of the
poems we have looked at in this survey and it is important to realise that A level
English teaching need not be qualitatively different from any other English – specifically literature – teaching. The careful fostering of a 'workshop' approach, with a full
range of activities, learning styles and teaching methods catered for, is the key to
effective English teaching throughout the 11–18 age range.

The requirement of Standard B6d (p. 93), for which teachers have to 'decide how
and by whom the text will be read' poses interesting possibilities for all poetry
teaching, as we have already seen. The two poems in question here are both short,
but quite challenging to read aloud. It may be appropriate to arrive at an initial
acquaintance through 'reading aloud by the teacher to bring out the qualities of the
text, followed by group reading of the same text for close study of the language', as
suggested in the possible examples of good practice following Standard B6d. However, it would perhaps be more stimulating to start activities by focusing on the nature
of telephone conversations – their opportunities and limitations – before coming to
the poems themselves. Ideas here include:

- Listening to some of the radio sketches of the American comedian Bob
  Newhart, such as 'Bringing Tobacco to England' or 'The Driving Instructor',
  as stimuli for pupils to invent one half of a conversation implying the other
  speaker's words. In effect, this reflects the widespread experience of hearing
  one side of a telephone conversation. The results can be impressive, either
  humorous or serious, especially if pupils are given a dramatic context within
  which to work. A telephone as a prop (preferably unconnected) adds to the
  performance.
- Exploring, through drama, discussion or writing (or a combination of all
  three), the difficulties facing an 'outsider' in any community trying to secure
  accommodation – as in *Telephone Conversation* – or something similar. Again,
  the context and possible setting should be suggested by the teacher.
- Perhaps using again the *Martian Sends a Postcard Home* poem, in which one
  of the riddles refers to a telephone, exploring the imagery – unexpected, as
  in Frost's poem, or otherwise – associated with telephones. This might be
  particularly fertile ground in the light of the popularity of mobile and car
  phones with all the attendant image projection and prejudices.

The subsequent study of the poems, following reading and initial discussion, could
concentrate on comparison and contrast along the lines of:

- The conversational nature of *Telephone Conversation* and *The Telephone* (pre-twentieth century verse, such as Coleridge's conversation poems, may add a further dimension here).
- The communicative limits and potential of telephone conversation as presented in both poems.
- The cultural contexts and how they affect both poems in terms of both content and style, focusing on pupil-chosen examples from the texts.
- Written assignments highlighting the similarities and differences of both poems following group discussion.
- Pupil-formulated 'comprehension questions' on the poems, with the opportunity to pose various types of questions based on close reading.
- Displayed collage work revolving around images of telephones (and other images as appropriate) combined with the words and phrases of the poems.
- Oral or dramatic performances/presentations of the verse, possibly using a range of art forms.

In the end, pupils' understanding of and response to literature is most commonly assessed through their writing, either as a coursework assignment or by final examination. Several of the teaching ideas mentioned here for these poems and for the others result – or may result with some adaptation – in writing, and it is certainly part of the English teacher's function to foster the written response. Partly, of course, this is to prepare for the world of competitive examinations; it is also, however, an important tool for thought, reflection and development of a considered response. The framing of appropriate written questions and titles, then, is a vital aspect of the English teacher's role and must take into account issues such as

- the nature of the texts studied;
- the range of possible responses;
- the syllabus/scheme of work context;
- the ability range catered for;
- the relationship to preparatory speaking and listening, and to reading;
- the process, including possible collaboration, drafting and ICT;
- the balance between different written responses, such as the discursive and empathetic.

Titles for written assignments on *Telephone Conversation* and *The Telephone* may, for example, look something like this:

- Contrast the two poems, using carefully selected quotations and comments, to show how each presents the central image of the telephone in different ways, both positive and negative.
- Both poems present a telephone conversation from the 'poet's' viewpoint; imagine yourself to be the other person of one or both poems and write about your thoughts and feelings. Refer closely to the actual words of the original text(s).

Activity 5   In the same way that many of the approaches outlined in this chapter could be adapted or transferred from one poem to another, in the hands of a teacher sensitive to the particularity of each poem there are opportunities for cross-genre transposition of teaching strategies. We can go further than this: all the poems we have looked at could be adventurously taught in conjunction with prose, drama or media texts. Indeed, such is the increasingly crowded nature of the secondary school English curriculum that it would often be something of a missed chance not to do so.

In the light of this suggestion, consider which non-poetic texts could be fruitfully used alongside any of the poems already mentioned or any other verse of your own choice.

It is important to bear this sense of cross–fertilisation in mind as we go on to look at the teaching of prose literature. (Examination of the teaching of drama and media texts is covered in Chapters 6 and 7 respectively.)

THE TEACHING OF FICTION TEXTS

Activity 6   • From your own reading, which novels and short stories do you think are particularly apt for teaching in the secondary school?
   • Do you consider the distinction made between literature and other fiction, such as children's fiction, to be a helpful one in the teaching of English?
   • How important is it in your view to *teach* and *assess* fiction/literature, as opposed to simply read it with pupils?

Teaching Gothic literature

Activity 7   Consider the following introduction to the teaching of the Gothic – specifically the various reasons put forward for its teaching. Then re-order the list in terms of priority, deciding which are particularly relevant – or inappropriate – in your own experience.

Some of the possible advantages of teaching Gothic texts as central to any literature course, whether it be for Key Stage 3, GCSE or A level, are:

   • They have a wide appeal, thus including reluctant readers who may be boys.
   • Many of them (for example *Dracula* and *Frankenstein*) have been adapted for a range of ages and reading abilities.
   • There are many media education and cross-genre opportunities in them.
   • Many are pre-1914 and thus appropriate to National Curriculum (and Standards) requirements.
   • The dangers of contemporary irrelevance may be avoided as the Gothic tradition is alive and thriving now.
   • Several have arisen from other cultures, for example Edgar Allan Poe's *Tales of Mystery and Imagination*, which I examine below.

As a general introduction, pitched here to the needs of an A level English literature group, the following quite detailed approaches may be helpful. Formulation and teaching of activities such as these aim at stimulating further reading together with promoting the beginning of a sense of cultural contextualisation. Effectively undertaking this kind of teaching strongly implies that the teacher meets Standard C29a i (p. 101) having 'the breadth and depth of knowledge, understanding and skills required for a post-16 course in literary study'.

1 Through interviews, surveys, text- and ICT-based research, investigate exactly what is meant by the term Gothic in today's world. To help you explore this topic, you may find the following areas helpful:

- trends in fashion and appearance;
- horror fiction and horror films, and reasons for their continuing popularity;
- aspects of modern music – who are the Gothic bands of the moment?
- why exactly the Gothic continues to fascinate so many people.

In presenting your findings from this research, a particularly vivid way might be to construct a collage in which various images of the contemporary Gothic idiom are represented in both pictures and words. To extend or vary the emphasis of this project, you could also take images from the eighteenth and nineteenth century Gothic tradition and, in your collage, juxtapose these images with the modern ones. What sort of similarities and contrasts did you notice from this juxtaposition?

2 By means of role-playing, explore the continuities and contrasts between historical and contemporary Gothic fiction (which may, for this purpose, include film). In small groups, consider and make a list of possible questions that selected authors, film directors, and characters, from both written and filmed texts, might wish to debate. You could focus on the following areas:

- the *content* and *themes* of the Gothic;
- the *characters* likely to be found in the genre;
- the *settings* most chosen by authors and directors;
- the sort of *audience* likely to be appealed to;
- the differences and similarities between historical and modern wider *contexts*.

The resulting debate could be presented 'live' or by video to an audience of fellow students.

3 Carefully selecting your materials, build up a scrapbook collection of quotations from both historical and contemporary Gothic sources (the photocopier could be useful here). This should give you a vivid 'flavour' of the Gothic.

You could follow this up by 'cutting and pasting' portions of text, perhaps using IT to assist, achieving an 'inter-textuality' through which both historical and modern expressions of the Gothic are compared and contrasted. Again, some sort of collage of words might be appropriate, using the photocopier's enlarging facility to achieve the right effect for display if necessary.

4 Having no doubt experienced something of the horror film genre's conventions, try taking one of the historical Gothic texts studied and consider how it could be re-presented as a modern Gothic horror film. Your presentation of your ideas could take the form of:

- director's notes, including casting, music, setting and 'mood' creation;
- storyboarding specific scenes or, briefly, the whole story;
- writing the script, remembering that descriptive passages from the original will need to be either deleted, re-presented pictorially or re-presented through the dialogue.

5 For future students of the Gothic tradition, aim to write, collaboratively in small groups, an introductory handbook entitled *The Student's Guide to the Gothic* (or another title of your choice). It may be best here to divide the group into those undertaking specific tasks and themes, such as:

- historical and contemporary manifestations of the Gothic: comparisons;
- the artistic presentation of the Gothic;
- selected quotations with your own annotations;
- the social and political contexts;
- the sorts of audience which could feature real-life lovers of the Gothic horror genre;
- biographical sketches of the key authors and others involved in the Gothic tradition.

Teaching *Frankenstein* (Mary Shelley)

Some texts generally considered as 'Gothic' clearly transcend the genre and it is important, especially at A level, that genre limitations as well as potential characteristics are studied. In the case of Mary Shelley's *Frankenstein* (Shelley, ed. D. Stevens, 1998), for example, there are many exciting 'ways in' which it may have some Gothic implications but go well beyond them too. The novel's relationship to the Prometheus myth offers cross-genre possibilities of an unusual kind, as suggested in these approaches:

- Consider the subtitle of the novel, *The Modern Prometheus*, and research further the nature of the Prometheus myths.
- How do these myths relate to Mary Shelley's novel?
- Does the Prometheus figure stand for Frankenstein, his creature or, somehow, both?
- Trace the main points of similarity between the myths and the novel by making a diagrammatic representation of both *Frankenstein*'s and the myths' plots, using an appropriate symbol to denote points of contact.

- If possible, look also at Percy Bysshe Shelley's *Prometheus Unbound* (Shelley, ed. E.B. Murray, 1993) which he was working on while Mary was writing her novel.
- The young couple certainly discussed each other's work; is there any evidence of mutual influences?
- How does your study of the Prometheus stories illuminate your understanding of *Frankenstein*?
- Was Mary Shelley right to entitle her novel *Frankenstein* rather than *The Modern Prometheus*? Can you think of other appropriate titles?

These approaches are adapted from the Cambridge University Press edition of *Frankenstein* (Shelley, ed. D. Stevens, 1998) and follow the general ethos of the *Cambridge Literature* series in promoting active, wide-ranging approaches to literature. The fundamental questions posed in each volume in this series serve as useful guidelines for English teachers intent on exploring textual and contextual possibilities. They are:

- Who has written this text and why?
- How was this text produced?
- What type of text is it?
- How does the text present its subject?
- Who reads this text and how do they interpret it?

In effect, these questions, properly debated and resolved in the planning of work and in classroom teaching, address many of the points made in Standard C28c (pp. 100–1), dealing with:

> Knowledge about texts and critical approaches to them, including
>
> i   identification of the conventions associated with different types of text and how they are used and changed for effect;
>
> ii how ideas are presented, depending on point of view, context, purpose and audience;
>
> iii different critical approaches which emphasise different ways of reading texts depending on whether the focus is on the reader, the writer, the context or the text alone.

Teaching *The Black Cat* (Edgar Allan Poe)

This particular story (from *Tales of Mystery and Imagination*) is short enough to be covered fairly swiftly in an overcrowded English curriculum and has the added advantages of being generally attractive to older pupils, dating from before 1914 and being of another culture (American). Inclusion of this story here, however, does raise important questions about the suitability of texts with the corollary of what amounts to teachers' censorship of pupils' reading. This issue is likely to surface particularly with regard to pupils' personal reading, time for which is widely given (if, unfortunately, often withdrawn when the pressure mounts) within the English curriculum. Indeed, the previous National Curriculum (DfEE, 1995) insisted that 'pupils should be . . . encouraged to read widely and independently solely for enjoyment' (Standard 1a, p. 19) and the present version states that through English 'pupils learn to become enthusiastic and critical readers' (Standard 1a, p. 14). These sentiments are reinforced in DfEE Circular 4/98 which exhorts teachers 'to encourage individuals to read, through encouraging pupils' regular, individual, private reading' (Section B5a, p. 93). Certainly, however, some reading matter could not be tolerated during lesson time, and each teacher or department – and, for that matter, school, including the library – must draw the line somewhere. The difficulties, though, are several: no English teacher wishes to seem intrusive or judgemental or to discourage reluctant readers from reading texts which at least inspire some enthusiasm. Such issues should be openly discussed within each class in the context of debate about the whole nature of reading and the development of reading habits. In terms of texts chosen by the teacher for class study – including, possibly, *The Black Cat* – we must perhaps be even more careful, as our choice may be taken to mean unqualified approval. Any text may offend some member of the class and we must be mindful of this possibility. The important point is to plan a coherent and varied reading curriculum that may include books dealing explicitly with violence or other potentially controversial themes. The violence in Poe's story, in fact, is not more lurid or disturbing than that found in *Macbeth* or *King Lear* and it certainly raises significant relevant issues about the world in which young people are growing up.

Nevertheless, a good English teacher must introduce the story carefully and sensitively. As it is only seven pages long, the story would probably benefit from a thoroughly prepared 'performance' reading by the teacher, especially as, despite its several advantages, the story poses significant difficulties for pupils in terms of accessibility of language. There are many good reasons for making plans for textual study explicit and clear to pupils from the start. The teacher (and pupils, for that matter) may wish to deviate from the plan and there should always be scope for improvisation in the English curriculum; if necessary, this sense of flexibility may itself need careful stating and may involve a degree of negotiation with pupils. If one of the overarching aims of any good teaching is to foster a sense of responsibility for learning in pupils themselves – a requirement which surely finds expression in Standard 4k xii (p. 13) for which the teacher should be 'exploiting opportunities to contribute to the quality of pupils' wider educational development' – then this sort of negotiation can only be positive. A scheme of work for *The Black Cat*, then, for a Year 10 mixed ability group may look something like that given below, although the pre-reading activities, for obvious reasons, may be better addressed separately from the main body of the worksheet. Clearly, the English teacher will need to organise the activities appropriately to the needs of a particular group in terms of balance of activity and different ways of learning and in the context of the overall English curriculum.

Based on a study of *The Black Cat* (Edgar Allan Poe) the following activities are suggested:

1   Before reading the story, pupils could examine the story's title, then:
- The whole class could report back and display the resulting ideas and impressions through a guided discussion on the connotations of key words – especially controversial senses of the word 'black'.

2   While reading the story and gaining first impressions, pupils could:
- Go over the text again (in pairs or small groups) and consider key questions. They could note down words and phrases which are difficult to understand, thinking of modern English equivalents for some of these. Would they prefer a 'modern version' by, say, Stephen King?

3   Further activities (by individuals, pairs or small groups) could be:
- Develop the last activity further to come up with a series of comprehension questions on the story which should focus on the areas of language, plot, character and style of writing. These can then be collated and discussed by the whole class or exchanged with another pair or group for consideration and 'answering'.
- Research and collect into an anthology other texts which relate in some way to *The Black Cat*, including poems and other stories (including, possibly, others by Poe), audio and video materials and pictures. Pupils should be prepared to present their collection to the rest of the group, pointing out how it affects their understanding of the original story.
- Explore the question of the viewpoint in the story, focusing on the narrative voice, its placing in the third person and the possibility of other viewpoints which remain silent in the story itself. The narrator's wife, for example, may have an interesting story to tell, perhaps in the form of a diary which was hidden until she died.
- Make other 'empathetic' explorations, for example: the final police report, detailing the investigation and arrest; the narrator's own final statement and confession; and the report of the American equivalent of the Cats' Protection League.
- Rewrite the story in the form of a ballad, for which it is very suitable: it has macabre and supernatural elements, a sense of tragic decline and disintegration of love and an atmosphere of dark sensationalism. In terms of the apparently motiveless taking of life leading to a train of self-destruction, the story may relate to *The Rime of the Ancient Mariner*.
- Explore other kinds of adaptation, for example, the story could be made into a short film, storyboarded and scripted, or into a dramatic interpretation, perhaps using mime and music to create the right sort of atmosphere; or artwork could be done, possibly for the cover of a new edition or to advertise the film just mentioned.
- Consider what may have occurred before the start of the story and write a 'prequel', concentrating on the psychology of the central character.

Teaching *Staying Up* (Robert Swindells)

Some of the points we considered in relation to *The Black Cat* apply also to this novel. Like some other stories written by Swindells – notably *Stone Cold* – it deals with some difficult and sensitive socially realistic issues, such as the effects of unemployment, class differences in a youthful relationship and the conflict between peer pressure and commitment to academic progress in an adolescent boy. The narrative voice, however, is shared between this boy, Brian, and a teenage girl, Debbie, and it is in fact her story which is the closer to the bone as it deals with a rapist. So again we have a story to which some may object – although Swindells deals sensitively and responsibly with these issues, all of which come up in the ever-popular teenage soaps on television. Certainly, alone among the texts we have examined so far, it falls within the category of 'texts written specifically for pupils of secondary school age' (Standard C28c v, p. 101) and is arguably a fine example of this genre. The novel also works well as a story on several levels and the seriousness of the social realism is well integrated with the plot and characterisation. The 'staying up' of the title refers on one level to the desperate need of the local football club to avoid relegation – a need matched by the desperate support given to the club; more profoundly, though, it suggests a general need to survive against the odds. The metaphorical interplay is well worth investigating in itself as part of the English curriculum.

We have already looked at a range of approaches to literature in the teaching of English, many of which, clearly, could be transferable to *Staying Up*. We must, however, at the same time be aware of the dangers in swamping the enjoyment of a good read of an entertaining book through the overkill of approaches, however imaginatively creative. English teachers need to be aware of the pitfalls of over-study, murdering in order to dissect as Wordsworth warned two centuries ago. There sometimes seems little opportunity for pupils simply to enjoy a book during school time, either individually or communally. Calthrop (1971, p. 23) recounted the experience of English teachers testifying to the sheer enjoyment of a class reading a book for pleasure; teachers who

> felt that the shared experience of reading a common book was something of great value to themselves and to their classes. They . . . took the view that the feeling of sharing something worth while, the common sense of enjoyment, and the resulting sense of community was a deeply educative process . . . a reciprocal process . . . akin to the experience of a theatre audience.

It is all the more important some 30 years on, with far greater pressures on both pupils and their English teachers at every stage of the secondary curriculum (and, of course, the primary), to safeguard and develop this sort of collaborative feeling within English lessons. And it can be done. The secret lies in tuning in to the needs of the audience – the pupils – as any performer must do. Teaching in this sense is performance and the principal prop so often will be some form of literature.

This warning amounts to a statement that there is a need to keep a sense of perspective. If enjoyment of reading is paramount – and I can think of two or three occasions when the kind of shared whole-class enjoyment alluded to by Calthrop applied to a reading of *Staying Up* – it need not preclude further activities. But if the reading is not enjoyed on one level or another, then following it is not likely to be very fruitful for either teacher or pupils. One could take any of the numerous empathetic approaches to literature which have enlivened English classrooms (many of which are helpfully listed in an appendix to the Cox version of the National Curriculum – *Approaches to the Class Novel*) and apply them to *Staying Up*. My own preference here, not just because I am beginning to exhaust my literature teaching repertoire for this, the final fictional work in this chapter, is to limit approaches to a few. They may include:

- A pre-reading activity, whereby pupils are given several elements of the plot (for example, a struggling football team, the closure of a local factory and an adolescent boy–girl relationship) and asked to weave them into their own story. It is interesting and enjoyable to compare pupils' narrative ideas with Swindells' own.
- The same sort of interest may stem from prediction exercises taken at various times in the unfolding plot, either quickly written down and shared, or given more dramatic form through thought-tracking.
- Ideas of prediction and varying the plot could take fuller expression still in converting the entire story into some sort of 'choice novel' in which readers choose at various points between a range of courses of action, each one leading to a different point in the ensuing story. An alternative to conscious choosing is to shake dice, thus making the whole enterprise into a kind of game. Either way, the project is quite ambitious and is best undertaken by small groups, possibly using ICT to shift text around.

All three of these activities focus on the plot and aim to encourage readers to take an active role in interpretation: playing with the elements of narrative, in essence. This is a fitting conclusion to thoughts on fictional literature, which could be said to rely by definition on plot.

THE TEACHING OF NON-FICTION

The concept of literature is a problematic one. The very word suggests to most people some sort of venerable writing, the best of which constitutes a *literary tradition*. But we also speak of 'reading the literature' when deciding which car or hi-fi to buy and, to avoid arguments of definition, it may be best to broaden the scope of inclusion. Certainly, for teaching purposes, this aspiration towards inclusiveness seems appropriate: in the reality of the classroom, comparisons across genres, periods, authors and texts can usefully illuminate our responses to either fiction or non-fiction. In terms of the latter, many of the most contemporary and imaginative stimuli may be found under the umbrella title of 'media-based texts' which are examined in Chapter 7. There are, however, also many good examples of printed non-fiction, and educational publishers have been quick to anthologise and present relevant texts, taking in, for instance, travel literature, journals, biography and polemical writing. In the rather brusque terms of Annex F (Section B9, p. 94) we are told:

> Trainees must be taught how to teach non-fiction, through:
>
> providing for systematic, structured reading of non-fiction texts using a range of texts using a range of techniques . . .;
> teaching pupils how to analyse the organisational and linguistic features of non-fiction and use these features in their own writing . . .

This sort of instruction is unlikely to inspire the imaginative teaching and learning which make the best English classrooms such invigorating places in which to work. We can perhaps infer from these terse words that the non-fiction referred to is that purely to be read for informative purposes rather than any kind of aesthetic pleasure. Certainly, pupils need to know how to read for information (the examples quoted refer to *skimming* and *scanning*), but it would be a shame to limit the reading of non-fiction to this purpose only. In this chapter, we are concerned with the literary; our definition is inclusively broad and more focused on the mode of reading than with quibbles about what is read. In a sense, if the reader reads for some sort of aesthetic pleasure, than what is read may be termed literature. The two texts we look at here are quite different from each other but each can be successfully taught as an example of non-fictional literature and each demands an essentially aesthetic response not qualitatively unlike that given to the poems and fiction we have looked at previously.

Teaching *The Diary of Anne Frank*

The Diary of Anne Frank (Frank, 1995) has long been widely read by secondary school age youngsters – perhaps more often as an individually read text than as a class reader – but nevertheless it has a distinctive place in the English curriculum. Despite its painfully harrowing subject matter – or possibly to some extent because of it – the evocative, yet matter-of-fact, narrative of the trapped Jewish girl in Nazi-occupied wartime Holland speaks intimately across the divide of time, culture and personal experience. There is a growing sub-genre of literature portraying the Holocaust: fictional texts such as *Friedrich* (Richter, 1991) and *The Devil in Vienna* (Orgel, 1991), both of which are appropriate to 11–16-year-olds, or *Fugitive Pieces* (Michaels, 1998), *Captain Corelli's Mandolin* (de Bernières, 1998), *The Reader* (Schlink, 1998) and *Time's Arrow* (Amis, 1992), all of which are suitable for an adult or A level readership. Ian McEwan's picture book, movingly illustrated by Innocenti, *Rose Blanche* (McEwan, 1985), cuts right across the age range here and adds a further reading dimension in the combination of words with pictures. Effective teaching could focus creatively on cross-genre fertilisation here, comparing, say, our emotional responses to fiction and non-fiction and going on to tease out the differences between them. Under which category, for instance, does *Schindler's Ark* (Kenneally, 1982) fall? Similarly, good use could be made of the inter-disciplinary dimension of the curriculum, all too easily forgotten and ignored in the understandable concentration on the subject-based National Curriculum structure. Many pupils study the Holocaust through history and religious education lessons and there is an excellent opportunity here for cross-curricular research and learning. With these considerations in mind, the possibilities for teaching *The Diary of Anne Frank* include:

- Using the 'jigsaw' technique, groups of four could be asked to research, discuss and report back on the historical context or a particular specified aspect of the *Diary*. Each of the four pupils in the group would be allotted a different area to research or discuss and would then get together with the individuals from the other groups who fulfil the same role. Subsequently, each of the original 'home' groups would then reconvene to hear the findings and eventually feed this information into a general class discussion or presentation. Clearly, good teaching for this activity needs to include appropriate resourcing for the research, using the library service and the potential of other curriculum areas. This general approach may take place usefully before, during or after the reading of the *Diary*.

- A consideration of the genre of diary or journal writing could be made, thus focusing on the *form* of this text in relation to other pertinent examples, including, if appropriate, pupils' own writing. Instances are many and wide-ranging, from the light-hearted fictional *The Secret Diary of Adrian Mole* (Townsend, 1992) and the more recent sequel, *Adrian Mole: The Cappuccino Years* (Townsend, 1999), through the moving account of a teenager growing up in contemporary war-torn Bosnia, *Zlata's Diary: A Child's Life in Sarajevo* (Filipovic, 1994), to more traditionally literary works such as Daniel Defoe's *Journal of the Plague Year* (Defoe, ed. L. Landa, 1990) or Dorothy Wordsworth's *Journal* (Wordsworth, ed. M. Moorman, 1971). Activities may highlight the comparison of texts in terms of *purpose* and *audience*, both of which are interestingly problematic in this context and could lead to lively discussion.

- Taking ideas on the form of diary writing a little further, the teaching could concentrate on the uses many writers have made of the genre within broader works of fiction. Useful examples include several Gothic-influenced classics, such as *Frankenstein* (Shelley, ed. D. Stevens, 1998), *Dracula* (Stoker, ed. D. Rogers, 1993) or *Wuthering Heights* (Brontë, ed. R. Hoyes, 1997), and more contemporary publications like *The Color Purple* (Walker, 1983) or, specifically for a youthful readership, *Dear Nobody* (Doherty, 1991). The consideration of journals as some kind of 'framing device' for narrative could then creatively inform pupils' own writing, conceivably at any level. And, of course, there is the tried and tested (and perhaps over used, for some texts) approach of asking pupils to write the diary of a character featured in whichever fictional work is being studied.

Teaching *Ways of Seeing* (John Berger)

Ways of Seeing, John Berger's series of pertinently illustrated essays on the nature of our perceptions of the world we inhabit, is a rather different type of text. It is perhaps more suitable for post-16 students conceivably following media studies, communications or even art courses as well as those centring on English literature or language and as such its potential strength may well lie in its multi-faceted possibilities. The book's fundamental thesis is of particular and controversial interest to English teachers: 'Seeing comes before words. The child looks and recognizes before it can speak . . . It is seeing which establishes our place in the surrounding world; we explain that world with words, but words can never undo the fact that we are surrounded by it' (Berger, 1972, p. 1). The essays go on to elaborate on this idea, using examples from traditional and modern art, and from the mass media. In the sense that this text echoes Blake's words 'As a man is, so he sees' (letter to Reverend Trusler, 1799 – Blake, ed. D. Stevens, 1995), it is part of a continuing debate concerning the relations between subjective and objective and that debate often centres on the place of language – even if dismissive of its pre-eminence. In this general context, students could be asked to carry out a range of creative tasks, such as:

- Seeking and presenting materials to illustrate the arguments of specific sections of the book, particularly drawing on knowledge and understanding of the media.
- Creating collages of pictorial images to surround and exemplify carefully chosen quotations from the text.
- Writing a reasoned reply – illustrated if possible – to one or more of the more contentious arguments featured.
- Writing the parallel script – either expository or for the three purely pictorial essays in the book which are 'intended to raise as many questions as the verbal essays'.
- Creating the storyboard and script of a television version of the book, bearing in mind that it was originally conceived as the accompaniment to a BBC television series of the same name.

The last text looked at in this chapter, especially, is an apt reminder that traditional assumptions about the nature of literature and its teaching within the English curriculum are changing fast. The introduction to Annex F (p. 90) affirms this observation in its expectation that teachers will develop and adapt their art: 'It is expected that, throughout their careers, teachers will . . . keep up to date with the subject and its pedagogy'. This sense of change is in itself nothing new, of course, and change is a – perhaps *the* – vital ingredient of any successful teaching. As one of the central informants of this chapter, William Blake, had it: 'Expect poison from the standing water.' The danger in setting standards or Standards is that they become set in stone rather than being seen as guiding principles. In this chapter, I have tried to demonstrate that the statutory requirements may be met without the English teacher's style becoming cramped. Perhaps we could use some poetic licence here. In terms of the teaching of literature, it may be fitting to envisage the Standards as fellow guests at a rather eclectic – maybe fancy-dress – party. It is wise to meet these Standards, make their acquaintance and then move on to more interesting company. They are unlikely to be too offended.

REFERENCES

Amis, M. (1992) *Time's Arrow*, London: Penguin

Benton, M. and Benton, P. (1990) *Double Vision*, London: Hodder and Stoughton

Berger, J. (1972) *Ways of Seeing*, London: Penguin

de Bernières, L. (1998) *Captain Corelli's Mandolin*, Vintage

Blake, W. (ed. D. Stevens, 1995) *Selected Works*, Cambridge: Cambridge University Press

Brontë, E. (ed. R. Hoyes, 1997) *Wuthering Heights*, Cambridge: Cambridge University Press

Calthrop, K. (1971) *Reading Together: An Investigation into the Use of the Class Reader*, London: Heinemann

Cliff-Hodges, G. (1998) 'Possibilities with Poetry' in Davison, J. and Dowson, J. (eds) *Learning to Teach English in the Secondary School*, London: Routledge

Cox, B. (1995) *Cox on the Battle for the English Curriculum*, London: Hodder and Stoughton

Defoe, D. (ed. L. Landa, 1990) *Journal of the Plague Year*, Oxford: Oxford University Press

DfEE (1995) *English in the National Curriculum*, London: HMSO

DfEE (1998) *Teaching: High Status, High Standards; Requirements for Courses of Initial Teacher Training*, DfEE Circular 4/98

Doherty, B. (1991) *Dear Nobody*, Orchard

Filipovic, Z. (1994) *Zlata's Diary: A Child's Life in Sarajevo*, London: Penguin

Fleming, M. and Stevens, D. (1998) *English Teaching in the Secondary School*, London: Fulton

Frank, A. (1995) *The Diary of Anne Frank*, Basingstoke: Macmillan

Holmes, R. (1998) *Coleridge: Darker Reflections*, London: Harper Collins

Kenneally, T. (1982) *Schindler's Ark*, Hodder and Stoughton

McEwan, I. (1985) *Rose Blanche*, London: Jonathan Cape

Michaels, A. (1998) *Fugitive Pieces*, London: Bloomsbury

Orgel D. (1991) *The Devil in Vienna*, London: Heinemann

Pike, M. (2000) 'Pupils' Poetics', *Changing English*, 7, 1, pp. 45–54

Richter, H. (1991) *Friedrich*, London: Heinemann

Schlink, B. (1998) *The Reader*, Phoenix

Shelley, (ed. E.B. Murray, 1993) *Works of Percy Bysshe Shelley*, Oxford: Clarendon Press

Shelley, M. (ed. D. Stevens, 1998) *Frankenstein*, Cambridge: Cambridge University Press

Stevens, D. (2000) 'William Blake in Education: A Poet for our Times?' *Changing English*, 7, 1, pp. 55–63

Stoker, B. (ed. D. Rogers, 1993) *Dracula*, London: Wordsworth Classics

Summerfield, G. (ed.) (1968) *Voices III*, London: Penguin

Townsend, S. (1992) *The Secret Diary of Adrian Mole*, London: Penguin

Townsend, S. (1999) *Adrian Mole: The Cappuccino Years*, London: Penguin

Walker, A. (1983) *The Color Purple*, London: Women's Press

Wordsworth, D. (ed. M. Moorman, 1971) *The Journals of Dorothy Wordsworth*, Oxford: Oxford University Press

6 What Do We Mean by Teaching Drama?

MICHAEL FLEMING

Drama has a much more significant presence in the English National Curriculum than is often assumed and its place has been strengthened in the 2000 version. It is not uncommon to hear the claim that drama only occupies a fairly minor role in the speaking and listening attainment targets and that the proportion of time allocated to it in an English scheme of work is likely to be fairly limited. This view arises because 'drama' is often taken simply to refer to active forms of improvised role-play and play-making rather than including, as well, the study of literary texts and the writing of scripts. If the wider view of the subject is taken, it could be argued that drama has occupied a prominent and very secure place within all versions of the English National Curriculum. Shakespeare is compulsory at Key Stage 3 as well as at Key Stage 4. In addition other varied drama texts have to be read which extend pupils 'moral and emotional understanding' as well as their understanding of drama in performance. Pupils' writing at both key stages should include dialogues, scripts of plays and screen-plays, using their experience of reading, performing and watching plays. Within the speaking and listening attainment targets, there are explicit references to drama activities, including role-play, the performance of scripted plays and the response to drama. Drama can also be used as a way of introducing or exploring the meaning of a poem, short story or novel. Seen in this way, it can be argued that drama occupies a major role within the English curriculum.

> **Activity 1** Read through the programmes of study for Key Stages 3 and 4 and either underline or list all the explicit references to drama in all its forms. Can you think of different ways of categorising the different references to drama in the National Curriculum?

The different views arise because the term 'drama' and the way it is used in education is not entirely straightforward. In order to understand why this is the case it is helpful to have a brief overview of how the teaching of the subject has developed in the last

40 years. This discussion will then provide a framework for examining the drama content of the National Curriculum for Initial Teacher Training in English.

WHAT IS MEANT BY DRAMA?

Outside the context of education the term 'drama' traditionally has had two related meanings: the study of plays (drama as a literary discipline) or the performing and watching of plays in a theatre. Within education the term has for many people meant something rather different. Ideas which developed in the 1950s and 1960s meant that for many teachers drama was emphatically *not* to do with theatre or the study of texts of plays but more concerned with spontaneous dramatic playing. Young children naturally engage in make-believe play when they are young and the approach to drama developed by Slade in the 1950s was based on a recognition of the value of what he called 'child drama'. The romantic language and idealised claims in the following quotation are typical:

> Play associated continually with beauty, and with the treasure of
> knowledge through the agency of an understanding adult mind, leads to
> better creation, more joy, has a marked effect on behaviour and results in
> the more discernible phenomenon of an Art Form.
>
> (Slade, 1954, p. 342)

His view that child drama was a separate art form meant that young pupils were not encouraged to perform or work from scripts of plays nor was responding to dramatic performances a primary objective. This distinction between 'theatre' and 'drama' was made even more strongly by Way (1967) when he argued that theatre was largely concerned with communication between actors and an audience whereas 'drama' was largely concerned with experience by the participants. His work tended to be more structured and introduced a wider range of teacher-led games and exercises into the classroom but was also based on what seem now to be rather vague notions of individual creativity and self-expression.

Theatre was rejected by many writers and teachers as inappropriate for young people because it seemed to promote stilted, unnatural performances. It was thought that there was too much emphasis on getting the actions to look right at the expense of any understanding of content. There was little concern with developing pupils' knowledge of theatre craft (acting, design of scenery, lighting, etc.) and more emphasis on the personal development of the pupils. Ideas in drama at the time reflected wider educational thinking which valued spontaneous, creative, self-expression as a contrast to the mechanical acquisition of knowledge or skills which had preoccupied previous generations. The natural dramatic play of children was seen to have more potential for pupil development than performance to an audience which seemed to require repetitive rehearsing and the mindless repetition of lines written by others.

In the 1970s and 1980s drama teaching developed considerably, particularly under the influence of Heathcote and Bolton who intervened more significantly in the work of the pupils using aspects of theatre form to shape the drama. Instead of having pupils act out their own invented plays in small groups or engage in individual exercises, the teacher took more control of the drama to create work of more seriousness and depth. The work was largely improvised and techniques like having a teacher take a major role were used to create drama which had considerable power to engage the pupils. The following description of part of a lesson taught by Heathcote at the time illustrates the kind of intensity which was not untypical. The class is beginning a play about a ship at sea in 1610 and the teacher asks the pupils to voice their thoughts.

> 'This ship is as strong as the people in it. This ship doesn't exist as a ship; it exists as people. Right! May we just hear what people were thinking as the ship was towed away?'
>
> 'I'm afraid I'll never get off this ship.'
>
> 'It is strange to look at the figurehead up there because he seems to represent the whole crew.'
>
> 'It's so great . . . You have such pride. You're a part of all this – so proud of what you helped to create – so close to everyone. You can take part in this dream . . .'
>
> (Wagner, 1976, p. 18)

This type of 'process' work contrasted greatly with what was seen as the rather more artificial drama which was orientated towards 'product'. The division between theatre and drama persisted quite strongly even into the 1980s with some commentators expressing dissatisfaction with what they saw as a lack of any real attention to drama as a discipline in much of the creative, improvised work which was taking place in schools.

One of the ways in which the drama lesson might have satisfied those critics who felt it was losing any sense of a proper identity as a subject would have been to include more work on scripted plays. It is not surprising that this did not happen, however, because the study of plays was seen more as an aspect of literature studies, and as something which happened in a rather passive way in the classroom. In the context of school, as elsewhere, plays tended to be studied from behind desks and were considered part of English rather than the drama curriculum.

> In most academic institutions drama has, until relatively recently, been taught as a branch of literary studies, as dramatic literature and hence as divorced from the theatrical process. Such approaches to reading a play as were generally on offer did not significantly differ from the ways in which students were called upon to read a poem or a work of prose fiction i.e. as literary objects. At best a student might be invited to become an armchair critic or to imagine a theatrical space in her or his 'mind's eye'. Rarely, however, did drama leave the written page.
>
> (Aston and Savona, 1991, p. 2)

> **Activity 2** Talk to teachers in your school and try to establish what 'teaching a drama
> lesson' means. You might, for example, ask them to describe a typical drama
> lesson.

The summary given here of the development of drama teaching is very sketchy (more detailed histories can be found in the References/Suggestions for further reading) but it is possible nevertheless to see three major uses of the term 'drama' being used:

- as a literary discipline;
- as theatre;
- as dramatic play.

It is also possible to see why these categories are not really adequate for describing drama provision in school. Plays were written to be performed and watched rather than to be studied only as literary texts; viewing drama simply as a 'literary discipline' is very narrow and results in confining the study of plays to their themes and characters rather than extending consideration to how meaning is actually created in the performances. The concept of theatre used in this categorisation was based on a very traditional model, assuming that the roles of playwright, actor, producer and audience had to be separate and static. It was also assumed that the audience was a passive receiver of meaning, a view which modern reception theory has challenged. Finally, to describe all improvised approaches to drama as 'dramatic playing' is misleading because in the approaches to improvised drama which developed in the 1970s and 1980s drama had far more aesthetic and theatrical form.

One way of describing most recent developments in the subject is to see these three ways of conceptualising drama as merging and enriching each other, drawing on the strengths of each of them, as well as recognising their weaknesses. Many teachers in schools assume that teaching a drama lesson necessarily means engaging in forms of improvised work. It is not uncommon to hear teachers say that they do not like teaching drama because they find that trying to sustain creative improvisation every lesson with a class of 30 is very challenging. But teaching a drama lesson could just as easily mean working with a text of a play or watching a performance; in fact many lessons are likely to embody a mixture of these elements. It should also be remembered that undue emphasis on aspects of performance with insufficient attention to content can lead to the kind of empty experiences which were rejected by early advocates of creative approaches to drama. It is quite possible for pupils to get carried away with theatre craft (by dressing up, playing with lighting boards, colouring in stage diagrams and scenery) without thinking about meaning.

Table 6.1 summarises some of the weaknesses and strengths of each method of conceptualising drama. A balanced English curriculum needs to retain the strengths of each approach.

Table 6.1 An overview of drama teaching

Drama as	Weakness	Strength
Literary discipline	Drama was written to be watched and performed, not studied passively from behind desks.	Places emphasis on content and gives balance to an approach that overemphasises stagecraft at the expense of meaning.
Theatre	Danger of emphasis on empty experiences for pupils where the focus on acting, lighting, scenery does not take enough account of content.	Restores drama as a cultural, communal activity with its own distinct subject content. Emphasises responding to drama as well as performing.
Dramatic play	Lack of sufficient subject discipline means that it is often difficult to know what learning is going on. It is difficult to assess or determine progression.	Pupils tend to be involved and engaged because the work is accessible.

We are now in a position to examine the content of the National Curriculum for Initial Teacher Training in the light of this brief history. According to Circular 4/98 trainees must be taught how to introduce pupils to drama through:

> utilising drama techniques e.g. small group playmaking; teaching in-role; tableaux, to involve pupils in examining themes, issues and meanings;

> using performance of texts to develop pupils' understanding and appreciation of language, dramatic form, character and performance;

> using role play, script writing, writing in-role and a range of stimuli to develop pupils' reading, writing, speaking and listening;

> requiring pupils to reflect upon and evaluate features of their own and others' performance in order to develop their understanding of techniques for conveying meaning.

| Activity 3 | Examine both the English National Curriculum and the National Curriculum for Initial Teacher Training. In your view is the drama content appropriately balanced? |

An English scheme of work needs to contain elements of all aspects of drama but it is not necessary always to cover these separately. It is possible to combine different approaches in one sequence of activities. The following brief project uses very basic drama techniques in a highly structured way in order to explore an extract from *Romeo and Juliet* (Act 3, Scene 5, lines 68–204). It demonstrates how the various drama elements can combine and enrich each other.

1 The class gathers in a circle and plays a simple game of 'killer'. One pupil as 'detective' sits in the middle and tries to guess who is doing the killing. It is the job of the killer (who has been selected secretly by the teacher) to wink at people in order to kill them without being noticed by the detective. When people are killed they fold their arms.

A simple warm-up game can help settle the class, improve group cohesion and get everyone concentrating. It should not last very long and it is important to resist the pupils' requests to keep it going.

2 The class is divided into pairs and given a simple role-play exercise. Pupil A tries (and eventually succeeds) to persuade pupil B, a close friend, to go somewhere (such as holiday, concert or football match). Pupil B is at first reluctant because parents are unlikely to approve but eventually agrees.

This activity is very tightly structured with a defined outcome and is thus fairly straightforward for pupils because it draws on familiar experience. They are given an element of decision-making so that they have some ownership. The activity should be introduced as a simple warm-up exercise. If some of the dialogues are shared this should be done briefly and without too much emphasis on polished performance.

3 Pupil A now becomes Pupil B's parent who is informing Pupil A of an important family gathering that happens to coincide with the previously arranged outing. The parent is at first extremely enthusiastic about the family gathering but the tone changes when Pupil B is reluctant to cancel arrangements in order to attend. The pupils are to freeze the action at the point when a row is developing when the parent says something he or she will later regret.

The pupils are again invited to fill in details but the content is highly prescribed. Notice, however, that the activity is a little more demanding because the pupils are required to think about the shape and form of the work, the change in tone and the movement towards a climax. The simple constraint of freezing the action acts both as a control measure (to avoid an unproductive slanging match) and to provide more aesthetic shape to the work. The pupils are also asked to think about the relationships involved by creating the final line. This work could be developed by asking pupils to script the exchange.

4 Pupils now combine to create groups of four, ideally mixing boys and girls. The extract from *Romeo and Juliet* is distributed. They are to read it through and work out (a) what it is making the father angry (b) what clues there are in the language which tells the father how he should act.

The pupils need to become familiar with the scene but unless they are very experienced in drama they should not simply be told to act it out. This is more likely to distract from the content and result in some awkward, flat reading with minimal action. The nurse's spoken part is very small but her positioning will be significant in the subsequent activities.

5 Groups of four pupils are asked to create three tableaux with appropriate positioning and expressions to show exactly where the actors would be standing when the following lines are delivered: 'What still in tears? Evermore show'ring?'; 'I would the fool were married to her grave!' 'You are to blame, my lord, to rate her so.'

This activity gives balanced attention to both content and form. The pupils need to understand what is happening in the scene in order to work out how it might be staged. They should be encouraged to experiment with different positions and expressions. The tableaux can be shared and the lines read to accompany them. As a follow-up the groups could be asked to try the exercise again creating slightly more unexpected ways of staging them. It may be necessary for the teacher to discuss the scene with the pupils, explaining some of the words and meaning before they embark on this activity.

6 The pupils are asked to select and underline six or so lines which include all the characters and which convey the essence of the scene. They commit these to memory and bring them to life through action. An example of lines might be as follows:

Father:	Evermore show'ring?
Mother:	She will none.
Father:	I will drag thee there on a hurdle hither.
Juliet:	Good father.
Father:	My fingers itch.
Nurse:	You are to blame, my lord.

Pupils may need to be helped to see how the lines will be brought to life and the meaning filled in through the action that accompanies them. They can perform the brief scenes to each other and compare the selected lines and approaches. Do different lines and performances give a different view of the characters? Which is more representative of the scene as a whole?

7 The teacher and pupils discuss the different ways in which the nature of the performance of the scene as a whole can convey different interpretations and meanings. How close are the mother and father to Juliet? What does the line 'I would the fool were married to her grave' tell us about Juliet's mother? How can the line be delivered differently to convey firstly, that this is being said in the heat of the moment or, secondly, that Juliet's mother is very cold and lacks feeling towards her?

If the pupils already have a wide knowledge of the play they can relate this scene to what has happened elsewhere. They could be reminded of their own earlier drama work and asked to compare the scene in Romeo and Juliet *by considering the cultural differences between then and now. One obvious difference is the arranged marriage. They could also consider the reactions of the teenage daughter.*

8 The pupils watch a video version of the scene and analyse the way it has been staged, comparing it to their ideas. If they can compare two different versions, all the better.

They could be reminded of their own drama work and the way they created a scene that escalated in intensity and changed in tone. Does the video performance convey the development to a climax successfully? What was the most impressive aspect of the performance? What was the least helpful? A contrast in styles of dress and setting in two different video versions will also promote useful discussion.

In following this suggested project the pupils will have created drama work of their own, examined the meaning of the Shakespeare extract and considered ways in which it might be staged and how this will affect the meaning.

DRAMA CONVENTIONS

The sequence of drama activities described above was structured very tightly in order to give the teacher maximum security. Sometimes teachers are reluctant to engage in active drama work with pupils because the risks seem too high. The noisy, chaotic lessons in which pupils were simply told to get into groups and prepare a play without sufficient guidance put many teachers off. This is not surprising. Although young children naturally engage in make-believe play, the creation of a structured drama needs more skill and experience. The sophisticated approach developed in the 1970s had far more structure and was extremely impressive when it worked but it was difficult to sustain on a regular basis in the normal classroom. Many of the impressive lessons and projects described by Bolton (1992) and Wagner (1976) were taught as one-off demonstrations and tended to rely on the expertise of the teacher rather than on the acquired skills of the pupils. Drama teaching was made far more accessible in schools by the employment of drama conventions or techniques that made the whole approach to creating drama less mysterious and more practicable. They can also be viewed as drama skills which pupils can acquire to inform their own play-making and responding.

The term 'convention' in the context of the theatre is used more usually to refer to particular customs (e.g. that a tragedy should be in five acts) or to the acceptance of the make-believe context (we accept the convention that time can be telescoped during a play). In drama teaching the term has been used differently to embrace a wide range of dramatic techniques as well as ancillary activities which might take place in the drama lesson (such as related writing and preparatory work). Many of the drama conventions are largely derived from non-naturalistic theatre and it is important that pupils learn how to use them in order to provide more variety to their work than simply creating linear, realistic narratives. The following conventions are ones that are most useful in the early stages of drama with a class.

Tableau, freeze-frame or *still image* is probably one of the most commonly used techniques because it is accessible and culminates in silence and stillness. It can be used as in the example given above to explore aspects of performance of texts without placing too many acting demands on the pupils. It can also be used to help make concrete central themes in the literature which is being studied, for example, when studying Doris Lessing's short story, *Through the Tunnel*, the class was asked in groups to represent an image in which a young boy is excluded from a friendship group. The results were then juxtaposed against the words from the text to give it universal impact. After reading *Dr Faustus* a sixth-form class was asked to create an image which summed up the meaning of the play as a whole. Using still images based on particular lines from a poem or speech can help as it renders them into concrete form. The technique is most successful when the task set has an element of challenge and depth, for example, instead of 'create a still image of a moment from the character's early life' pupils might be asked to 'create a still image from the character's early life which has an ironic relationship to what happens later'.

Questioning in role in which members of the class ask questions of the teacher or a pupil in a role as a fictitious character can be used to explore motives, intentions and private thoughts. This technique tends to concentrate on content and gives less attention to dramatic form but it can be combined with monologues, small group improvisations and active approaches to texts of plays to slow the action down and create more depth. If a pupil is to be questioned as a character from a play or novel it should be remembered that this requires a considerable amount of knowledge of the text if the activity is to be worthwhile for all concerned; often it is a good idea if the teacher takes the role. It should also be remembered that the activity does not always have to be conducted spontaneously; if groups are given the task to prepare and present a questioning in role sequence they will have time to research their questions and answers.

Thought-tracking involves voicing aloud the inner thoughts of a character and can be used in a number of ways. It can externalise inner conflict as, for example, when two pupils give expression to Hamlet's dilemma at a particular point in the play or when someone is facing a major decision in improvised work (such as a teenager deciding whether or not to leave home). A form of thought-tracking can also be used with improvised drama or scripted plays to articulate the subtext. Here one pupil speaks the line and someone else, as their 'shadow' or 'alter ego', articulates their private thoughts. Another form of subtext occurs when pupils articulate the intended meaning as opposed to the words actually spoken.

Time-shift involves any departure from a chronological depiction of events. Examples of plays which deliberately experiment with time include *Betrayal* by Harold Pinter (events are presented in reverse order), *Our Town* by Thornton Wilder (in which one of the characters is able to return to a former period of her life) and *Death of a Salesman* by Arthur Miller (in which the dramatic action suddenly shifts to former events as recalled by the main character). In each case there is a departure from the normal unfolding of events through cause and effect and the technique helps to take pupils away from a preoccupation with narrative development in their own drama work towards the exploration of situations in greater depth. Simple examples in pupils' drama occur when they are encouraged to change the order in which they prepared the work. Techniques such as thought-tracking actually slow down the action so that the time unfolds at a slower pace than it would in real life. This is useful for exploring hidden intentions, attitudes and motives.

Beginnings and endings: when pupils are creating their own dramas they often find it difficult to know how to get started and how to finish. Small group improvisations can go on interminably and lose any sense of aesthetic focus or unity. One way to develop this skill is to examine the way in which playwrights begin and end their plays. Study of plays in performance then feeds into the pupils' own drama work. A useful project is for the teacher to photocopy the opening and closing scenes of a number of plays for the pupils to analyse. This has the further value of introducing a range of authors and encouraging pupils to do their own reading or to watch out for performances in the theatre, on film or television. Useful examples for beginnings include: Shakespeare (the use of prologues and the use of dialogue about the protagon- ist who enters in a later scene), Peter Shaffer's *Amadeus* (in which the main character is on stage as he will appear again at the end of the play) and Nigel Williams' *Class Enemy* (which begins in the middle of a conversation). Useful endings include Timberlake Wertenbaker's *Our Country's Good* (which ends with the start of the performance of a play), Alan Ayckbourn's *Sisterly Feelings* (which uses the idea of alternative endings) and Oscar Wilde's *Lady Windermere's Fan* (which leaves aspects of the play unresolved).

Activity 4	Collect a range of different play beginnings and endings for use in school with pupils. Annotate your list to show what particular dramatic techniques are exem- plified by the extracts.

Other techniques such as *forum theatre* (the 'audience' can stop the drama and make suggestions as to how it should develop), *narration* (one of the participants introduces or links scenes through narrative), *monologues* (one character speaks directly to the audience), *incongruity* (the deliberate use of anachronisms as in the film *Shakespeare in Love*) and *soundtracking* (where sounds are made to create the atmosphere of a place) can be used by teacher and pupils when creating drama. They also provide an awareness of how theatre works which will enhance their own appreciation of plays in performance.

The following random list demonstrates how conventions can be used with almost any theme or piece of text. A poem like Alfred Noyes' *The Highwayman* may seem at first not to lend itself to an approach to drama; asking a Year 7 to act out the poem in small groups is likely to be too difficult and to lead to chaos. The following suggestions illustrate how an oblique approach works; the ideas can be used on their own or woven together in order to create an extended drama project.

- A meeting in role of King George's senior officers in order to discuss ways in which the increasing problem of highwaymen robbing travellers might be tackled.
- A contemporary television documentary in which past victims of the highwaymen describe their experiences.
- Tim the ostler who appears as a minor character is questioned in role before and after the events described in the poem. He is asked about his relationship with Bess the landlord's daughter, what he has overheard and witnessed.
- The pupils are asked to imagine that the events described in the poem will be the beginning of a play. Their task is to complete some initial sketches for a possible set. They will need to consider how to present both the outside of the inn and the inside of the bedroom. Will they use different heights? They might look at some examples of descriptions of sets from published plays, for example, Arthur Miller's *Death of a Salesman*.
- From the description given in the poem pupils design sketches for the costume of either the highwayman or Bess.
- Groups of three create Bess's inner thoughts after she has been bound by the soldiers. She is torn between different courses of action represented by two interior voices.
- Small groups create tableaux of the scene in the inn when the soldiers are waiting for the highwayman's return.
- Pairs improvise some or all of the following scenes: the moment when the highwayman arrives at the inn for the first time and speaks to the landlord, the first meeting with Bess, Bess informing her friends about the highwayman just after meeting him, and a meeting between Bess and one of her parents who is suspicious and worried about her friendship with the highwayman.
- Small groups create tableau of a typical scene in the inn at night just before the highwayman arrives and add a soundtrack to create the appropriate atmosphere. (They should read the poem for ideas – galloping hooves, wind in the trees, feet clattering over the cobbles, etc.)
- A group of modern day publishers meet to discuss whether the poem should be published in an anthology for junior school pupils; some argue that it is too violent, others that it is not. They support their arguments by reading extracts from the poem.
- Investigators arrives at the inn after the soldiers have left to find the body of the landlord's daughter. Small groups improvise the scene which shows them conducting their investigation.
- The poem does not make it clear what happens to the landlord while the soldiers are at the inn. His story can be presented as a brief monologue.
- Group improvisation showing how the soldiers (the redcoats) knew that the highwayman would be returning to the inn. Ask the pupils to read the poem and say whether this is clear or left ambiguous.
- Alternatively the pupils act out what happened to the landlord in small groups – for example, he rides away, he stays in his room, he goes down to

the cellar and he collaborates with the soldiers, bringing them drinks and food. The landlord is then questioned in role to reveal his feelings – does he now feel guilty?

- A modern day family who have just moved into the same inn are told the tale of the highwayman by some locals (the pupils are encouraged to use phrases from the poem to tell the tale). That night one of the family imagines that a ghostly scene appears – depicted in tableau form.
- Years later a modern day version of the same incident occurs in the same inn. How would the highwayman translate into a modern context? Small groups invent the modern day equivalent and act out just one scene for the rest of the class. Their drama does not have to involve death.
- Imagine that the poem was written soon after the incident and has lain undiscovered and disintegrating for many years in the inn. Fragments are discovered and small groups of pupils as expert historians try to work out what it might be about. In order to prepare for this activity the teacher must tear the poem into selected fragments. They can be charred in an oven to create the image of old parchments.
- The class creates a tableau of what it imagines the scene at the daughter's graveside might have looked like at the time of the burial. Each pupil is given a phrase or a line from the poem to remember and speak aloud in order as if the tale is being summarised at the end of a film.
- Afterwards the soldiers invent a version of events so that they can hide what they have done. Their superior officers question them separately to test the truth of their story. This exercise could be undertaken in groups of four with two pupils taking the part of soldiers and two the part of questioners.
- Small groups rewrite the poem as the script of a play or (less ambitiously) they work out how a written play would be structured into scenes.

Work on *The Highwayman* can also lend itself to various related non-drama activities:

- writing newspaper headlines and articles describing the incident;
- analysing the similes and metaphors in the poem and their effect: 'the moon as a ghostly galleon', 'the road was a ribbon of moonlight', 'his hair like mouldy hay', etc.;
- writing the secret diary of Bess, the landlord's daughter;
- researching the historical background – in what period were highwaymen common in England?;
- reading the extract from Frank McCourt's *Angela's Ashes* in which the young Frank hears the poem while in hospital;
- considering those words which are not in common usage now, for example, 'ostler', 'harry' and 'stable-wicket' and which words we still use but not quite in the same way or not quite as commonly, for example, 'press', 'refrain', 'priming' and 'blanched';
- writing a verse imitating the style, rhythm and rhyme of the original;

- identifying the direct speech in the poem and saying what this adds to its impact;
- considering the notion of 'genre' and saying whether this is more of a romance or an adventure tale (this could be approached by asking the pupils what section of anthology should it appear in or whether they think the tale is realistic) and whether the image of the woman letting down her long hair is familiar from other stories or fairy tales;
- examining the use of repetition in the poem and the effect this has;
- writing a different possible ending either in prose or, for the more ambitious, in the same ballad form.

THE STUDY OF SHAKESPEARE

Active approaches to teaching Shakespeare embody the type of inclusive approach to drama teaching which is being recommended in this chapter. Techniques drawn from voice training, rehearsal work in the theatre, drama in education conventions and literature teaching can combine to provide an imaginative and enjoyable way of introducing and studying Shakespeare plays. Newcomers to teaching English some-times feel that here is a conflict between such active approaches and the more formal requirements of examinations at Key Stages 3 and 4. It is often thought that to succeed in the latter requires desk-bound analysis, note-taking and practice essay writing. The common answer to this objection that the activities are intended to complement rather than replace more formal approaches is only partly helpful because this answer tends to reaffirm the view that active approaches to Shakespeare provide a light-hearted alternative to the business of serious study. Active approaches and more traditional analyses of language, characters and themes should be seen as having equal value.

Increasingly GCSE and SAT questions ask pupils to demonstrate that they have an understanding of the plays in performance. This aspect of the study of Shakespeare plays has traditionally been fulfilled by getting the class to watch a film or video version of the play at the end of a period of reading and analysis. However a more integrated approach will include an awareness of the play in performance throughout the period of study. The National Curriculum for Initial Teacher Training stresses the importance of exploring Shakespeare plays as texts for performance as well as helping pupils to appreciate the impact of the language.

Activity 5	Examine the drama questions in past SAT and GCSE papers. How many of these explicitly ask pupils to draw on their knowledge of plays in performance?

What is given here is just a small sample of the types of activities which can be used in the classroom. Because many of the activities are designed to familiarise pupils with the text and the rhythms prior to close reading they can be equally helpful for introducing poetry. The Cambridge editions of Shakespeare plays provide excellent sources of ideas; each page of text is accompanied not only by traditional textual notes but also by suggestions for classroom activities. Previous conventions discussed can of course be applied successfully to Shakespeare plays. Using tableaux as in the example from *Romeo and Juliet* is an accessible way of getting pupils to think about the presentation of scenes and the semiotics of performance (physical positioning, gesture, etc.) without asking for these to be acted in their entirety. In the early stages of working with a play, questioning in role can be usefully applied to minor or invented characters because this format requires less knowledge of the play; the servants who were at the feast when Banquo appeared to Macbeth may have a somewhat flawed view of what happened which can be checked against the actual text.

Choral reading

A variety of voice exercises can be used to help to familiarise pupils with the language prior to analysis. The intention here is for pupils not to worry about the meaning but rather to enjoy the sounds and rhythm of the poetry, as well as exploring the dramatic impact. A long speech can be split up and distributed so that pupils can familiarise themselves with just a few lines before it is put together. Juliet's speech in Act 4, Scene 3, lines 16–54, lends itself to treatment of this kind.

> *Juliet*: Farewell! God knows when we shall meet again. I have a faint cold fear thrills through my veins.

A typical sequence might take the following form:

1   After one or two warm-up activities the pupils are each given one or two lines of the speech.

2   They become familiar with their own lines, reading them aloud in different ways and with different intonations: loud, soft, angry, joking, etc.

3   They assemble in a circle and read the lines in sequence in an appropriate way.

4   In order to probe the language more closely, they create tableaux based on the vivid images in the speech. (It is a good idea to have the speech broken into longer extracts which can be distributed to groups.)

5   The speech is read again, this time with atmospheric background music faded in.

6   The teacher asks the class what impression the speech gives of Juliet's character and whether it adds anything to what has already been learned about her. If necessary the discussion can be facilitated by giving a list of words from which to choose.

7   In groups the class discusses how the speech might be staged and then how different ways of presenting it might convey different impressions of Juliet's character.

Presenting scenes

Asking pupils to act out scenes from Shakespeare can easily backfire; lack of confidence can easily be covered up by sending the material up. Not all pupils have the experience in drama or technical skill to know what is required; books get in the way and the result is often a rather dull, lifeless performance. In fact preparing a good reading of a scene is often more fruitful than having pupils try to act it out but such an approach does not focus on the performance elements. The example given above from *Romeo and Juliet* shows an alternative approach to reading but scene enactment does not have to be discounted entirely. The choice of extract is important – the mechanicals' play from *Midsummer Night's Dream* lends itself to an exaggerated, comic style and is a good one for pupils to attempt. Short pieces of dialogue which can be easily remembered are often more practical and can allow greater attention to interpretation than trying to enact a lengthy extract.

Improvising around the play's theme

The example given above from *Romeo and Juliet* introduced the theme of parent/child conflict prior to reading the relevant scene from the play. Modern day situations can also be used to parallel *Macbeth* in which an individual aspires to a higher position (in a company, gang, school or friendship group) and is being encouraged to do anything to secure it. The modern version does not have to be represented through naturalistic improvisation; the internal dilemma of the main character can be presented by having two pupils voice their inner thoughts and dilemmas.

Director's notes

Director's notes for scenes is another alternative to a fully fledged performance but requires the same sort of thinking. Here the pupils makes notes on stage movements, setting, reading of lines, use of props, etc. This is a useful way of examining Shakespeare in its historical context because stage directions were rarely given. Sections of text can be examined to ascertain the implied physical context (for example, Duncan's speech outside the castle in Act 1, Scene 6) or implied actions (for example, in Act 2, Scene 1, of *Taming of the Shrew*, when the language indicates what actions are required). This activity is best linked with a comparison of two stage or film performances of the same extract.

Use of mime

The term 'mime' sometimes refers to the use of actions alone to convey meaning. It is also used to refer to gesture as one of the sign systems of drama which accompanies the language. One of the differences between a literary and dramatic text is that there is a sense in which the latter is not 'complete' until it has been realised in performance; the verbal and visual need to combine to create meaning. Mime has been underused in drama teaching. It tends to be associated with pupils miming actions to accompany teacher narrative with little sense of purpose. However mime can be used more effectively if it is associated with meaning. Pupils can experiment with the way actions required for a particular scene can change the effect from sinister and threatening to lighthearted and comic (the opening scene of *Macbeth* lends itself to this treatment). Creating a mime (not the actor's actions but simply an enactment of the images) to go with a sequence of text such as the Queen Mab speech from *Romeo and Juliet* draws attention to the details of the language.

Other approaches which usefully can be used to explore Shakespeare plays include: deciding how a play might be cast using well known actors (pupils should be asked to justify their choices on the basis of their knowledge of the play as this can easily become a superficial exercise); tape-recording scenes with sound effects (noting that Elizabethan actors did not have this facility); articulating the unspoken thoughts of characters during a dialogue (the convention of the soliloquy can be used to introduce this idea); and making diagrams of suggested staging, costumes and props (which could be based on a modern version).

WRITING PLAYS

Writing plays is an activity which pupils enjoy in the classroom but which has only received fairly minor discussion or analysis in most books on English teaching. The emphasis on individual creativity and self-expression in the 1960s meant that there was a tendency to minimise the role of the teacher and celebrate originality at the expense of teaching technique and form. Subsequent approaches to writing which placed far more emphasis on process, drafting, writing for different purposes and in different forms tended to focus more on non-fiction and narrative poetry, rather than on the writing of plays. There is still a tendency to see a script as merely the recording of direct speech with insufficient attention to the conscious craft and shaping needed in order to write the text of a play. Writing plays is often seen as a convenient and popular way of practising writing rather than as an aspect of drama education and as a way of helping pupils to gain more understanding of the genre and of informing their responses to dramatic texts. Producing scripts or dialogue is also a useful writing activity (pupils often find it easier to write lines of dialogue than extended prose) but there is no reason why it should not fulfil both objectives.

When working on writing plays in the classroom it is important to be aware of the wide variety of approaches possible. It is not necessary to think always in terms of complete products; short scenes and extracts are often more manageable and achievable. As with other forms of drama, it is a good idea to experiment with different groupings; working in pairs often provides more opportunities for involvement than working in larger groups. Work on script does not have to be totally separate from improvised approaches and the study of published play texts. It is also not necessary to think only in terms of written dialogue in order to record drama: written scenarios or even diagrams can provide the text which forms the basis for improvisation. Above all, it is important to be aware of the areas which can be the subject of specific teaching and learning. The following list provides some examples of questions which usefully might be considered when pupils are working with script. Published texts of plays can be used as examples to inform the pupils' own writing and thinking about these questions.

- What type of audience 'framing' is required for the play? What information needs to be given before the opening and what form should that take (such as title, introductory information, set and action on stage before opening lines)? Plays from different times, for example, Miller's *The Crucible* and Shakespeare's *Julius Caesar*, would be used to demonstrate very different approaches.

- How will necessary information be given to the audience? Will this be contained in the dialogue or is there a danger that this will appear false and artificial? The beginning of Tom Stoppard's *The Real Inspector Hound* parodies badly handled exposition in an amusing way.

- Does the written script need to specify a particular setting or set design? Should this be included in the stage directions or should it be left to interpretation? Is a particular size and type of space implied? Why, for example, is such a minimal set required for *Waiting for Godot?*

- Should the required actions and expressions be stated explicitly or is it enough for these to be implied in the dialogue? For example, if a word like 'angrily' is not included in brackets in the text does this leave too much licence for interpretation by actors and director?

- How is information conveyed differently in written dialogue from narrative? What challenges does this bring for the playwright? How do playwrights give us access to people's motivation, intention and thoughts? We need to see Iago plotting before the scene in which he tricks Othello, otherwise we would not understand his motive; a novelist can achieve this through the prose description.

- What structural aspects need to be taken into account when writing plays? Examples include dividing into scenes, constructing a dramatic plot from a narrative, experimenting with time (flashbacks and non-linear narratives), using devices for creating dramatic tension and using dramatic irony.

- What dramatic techniques which pupils may have used in their improvised drama can be used in scripted work? Examples of these include direct address to the audience, asides, moving in and out of the role, the use of chorus and the expression of inner thoughts.

- How does the language of drama differ from everyday speech? Pupils often assume that a dramatic script is simply recorded conversation but in fact it generally has less redundancy, is more ordered and tends to carry more information.

The following practical activities illustrate a variety of approaches to play-writing and provide examples of related activities:

● Pupils can be asked to produce dialogue from other written sources, for example, novels, letters and diaries.

Near the beginning of Jane Austen's *Sense and Sensibility* Mr Dashwood is near death and asks that his son John is sent for. The opening sequence of the film version of the book opens with the following dialogue:

Mr Dashwood:	John, John, you'll find out soon enough from my will that the Estate of Norland was left to me in such a way which prevents me from dividing it between my two families.
John:	Calm yourself, father. This cannot be good for you.
Mr Dashwood:	Norland in its entirety is therefore yours by law and I am happy for you and Fanny. But your stepmother, my wife, and daughters are left only £500 a year, barely enough to live on. Nothing for the girls' dowries.

The dialogue condenses several pages of the novel's background information into these lines. It establishes that the father is ill, that John lives in London and that he will inherit the estate. The details of why the estate cannot be divided are omitted because they are not essential but the dialogue includes the important information that the daughters will now have no marriage dowries which will be essential to the development of the plot.

● Script and improvised drama can be combined using a 'play within a play' approach. If the class has been asked to produce a documentary programme called 'the homeless' or 'teenage runaways' they might choose to script the linking commentary and the 'filmed' exchange between a teenage runaway and a policeman but improvise a studio discussion on the theme. As an exercise, a few scripted lines can be given to pupils to continue in improvised form or for them to incorporate into a piece of improvisation.
● It is also possible for improvised drama to be used as the basis for scripted work as in the following sequence which provides an introduction to Act 1, Scene 7, of *Macbeth*.

1   The class is divided into pairs, A and B, and asked to think of a situation in which A is trying to persuade B to do something but B is reluctant. The pupils improvise the scene without much other prior planning. It only lasts for a short time and then the class is called to attention.
2   The teacher asks the pairs to reverse roles, using the same situation but this time B is now trying to persuade A in much stronger terms. Again, the class is called to attention after a brief exchange.

3   For the final stage the pairs again switch roles but then B is using even stronger persuasive arguments than either of the two previous situations.

4   Having experimented with improvised dialogue, the pairs are now asked to script an exchange based on their improvised work starting with a low level of persuasion but gradually escalating the force of the argument.

5   Dialogues are exchanged with another pair who each decide how the script should be acted. The performances are reviewed to see if these matched the intentions of the writers.

6   Act 1, Scene 7, lines 29–59, is distributed for the pupils to read in pairs. They are asked to try to identify the ways in which Lady Macbeth places pressure on Macbeth. After discussion with the teacher, the pairs can decide how the script might be performed.

• Pupils can be given the opening lines of an exchange of dialogue to get them started. The following suggestion is described in more detail and with variations in Simner (1994). The teacher invents a series of simple two-line dialogues between A and B as in the examples below. They are cut into individual A and B lines and distributed to the pupils. Each A finds a B at random and tries out the lines. They keep experimenting until all As are paired with a B in such a way that they are comfortable with the lines (this may not be as they were originally written). They then try speaking the lines in different ways and write extra lines of script to go with the context.

   A: I think we should arrive there fairly soon before it gets dark.
   B: I don't think we will if you keep going as slowly as this.
   A: It's not usually a good idea to hit it quite as hard as that.
   B: Well you have a go then if you think you can do better.

• The use of writing frames particularly for non-fiction has become popular in recent years as a way of supporting pupils who find it rather daunting to have to start with a blank page. The writing of plays can similarly be enabled by providing structures within which pupils can work. Without constraints pupils may not know how to begin or may find that they are not able to realise their overambitious ideas; they may invent elaborate plots but not know how to translate these into dramatic form. The following examples specify a context and provide the central ideas from which the pupils can develop their script.

Example 1

Place: A train carriage.
Characters: A parent and young child, two soldiers in uniform, a business man and a teenager.

Situation: The train has been stationary for some time because of a fault. One by one the others in the carriage try to get the businessman to let them use his mobile phone. As he is finally persuaded the train starts to move and he changes his mind.

Opening line: 'You'd think they would make an announcement and let us know how much longer we are going to be delayed'.

Example 2

Place: A fairly large lift in an office block.

Characters: The managing director, the supervisor, other workers, secretaries and junior members of office staff.

Situation: The lift gets stuck and the characters start to panic.

Central idea: The most junior member of staff is the one who keeps calm and manages the situation.

Opening line: 'Could you press the button? We have stopped and we are not at a floor yet.'

Other play-writing activities include the following: the teacher provides a setting and information from which the pupils have to write the opening lines of dialogue which convey the necessary background; pupils create a tableau and, when it comes to life, work on the five lines of dialogue which are spoken; pupils take lines from a play or a script which they have written and intersperse these with the characters' thoughts; and groups write a brief scene which includes dialogue but no information about the context – they then swop with another group who enact each other's scenes and compare interpretations.

RESPONDING TO DRAMA

The National Curriculum for Initial Teacher Training requires that trainee teachers should be able 'to help pupils reflect upon and evaluate features of their own and others' performance'. This is a more complex requirement than it first seems because it is not always easy to keep a balance between aspects of form and content when pursuing this objective. A pupil who is able to speak technically about the type of lights used in a performance may do so without appreciating what the play meant or how the lights contributed to the overall aesthetic effect. Reflection upon performance needs to derive from the experience of the play and not from the mechanical application of a set of criteria. On the other hand, it helps for pupils to be given tools which can facilitate their analysis and enhance their enjoyment.

All too often pupils are simply asked to provide a summative evaluation of each other's drama work by a casual 'what did you think of it?' which invites merely a grunt of approval or more alarmingly a stinging dismissal. The challenge is to find ways of allowing pupils to talk about what they have seen (both their own work and that of professional theatre companies) in a way which is informed but not lacking in authenticity. There are parallels with the teaching of poetry. It is not enough for pupils to be able to spot examples of alliteration, litotes, similes and other devices unless there is some understanding of how these contribute to the overall effect and aesthetic meaning of the poem and unless these relate to how it is experienced. Whereas this view is well established in the teaching of poetry, theatre semiotics is, relatively speaking, a fairly new 'science' and it is easy to become overly preoccupied with the mechanics of performance at the expense of attention to meaning.

A number of writers have attempted systematic descriptions of the factors that should be taken into account when 'reading' a performance. Kowzan (quoted in Esslin 1987) identified 13 systems: words, delivery of the text, facial expression, gesture, movement, make-up, hairstyle, costume, props, sets, lighting, music and sound-effects. Esslin in *The Field of Drama* made additions to this list drawing attention to the omission of such elements as the importance of framing and preparatory indicators (the information we are given prior to a performance). Elam (1988) identified broad categories or codes as follows: kinesic (gesture, movement and expression), proxemic (use of space), vestimentary (use of costume), cosmetic (make-up), pictorial (scenes), musical and architectural (stage and playhouse). Pavis (1992) produced a questionnaire designed to draw attention to important aspects which should be considered when studying a performance. Publications like these can provide useful check lists to which teachers can refer as a reminder of the wide range of factors which make up the sign system of the theatre. They should be used with caution because they do not always distinguish between those factors which might be considered less central (how the production was advertised) and those which are key aspects of a play's meaning. Helping pupils to respond to performance is not a simple matter of providing them with a systematic list.

The starting point when responding to a piece of theatre should be the work itself rather than a universal list imposed on every play. Different performances whether in the theatre or by pupils themselves will have distinctive characteristics. For example one notable performance of *Taming of the Shrew* began with what appeared to be a genuine altercation in the theatre before the lights went down. It gradually became apparent that this was part of the start of the play when it dawned on the audience that the drunken male who had been waving a bottle and shouting at his partner in the auditorium was in fact Sly in the opening scene of the play. This was obviously the central talking point, even at the end of the performance. It would have been unhelpful for the teacher to try to force pupils prematurely into answering the type of questions found in lists drawn up by theatre semioticians: 'what was the design of the theatre?' and 'what was the gathering in the foyer prior to the performance like?' The teacher's role should be to allow pupils to air their impressions but to seek to extend and probe their responses. For example in the play quoted, they might be asked whether the strong impact of the beginning of the play distracted them from concentrating on the opening scenes and whether it helped to make the play relevant to a modern audience.

The natural reactions of pupils that may at first seem not to resemble the rather complex terminology of semioticians should not be dismissed but rather accepted and extended. As Lyas (1997) has rightly argued, the tendency to elevate 'artistic' over more humble expressions is one of the reasons why aesthetics and the arts are sometimes thought of as 'an "aristocratic club" to which humble folks are denied entry'. It is important that pupils are not unwittingly given the idea that their own concerns and preferences have no place, whether in relation to the style and presentation of the drama or its content. If too severe a distinction is made between 'artistic' and 'ordinary' expressions, it is tempting to think 'that what happens in art is unconnected with what happens in ordinary life'. This is not, on the other hand, an argument in favour of indulging pupils' reactions without teacher intervention; it is no contradiction to say that pupils' responses should be respected but that they need also to be developed and informed as a way of enhancing their enjoyment.

For example, if a Shakespeare play is performed in modern dress that is almost certainly to be the main talking point and it would be a mistake to try to impose an artificial set of broader concerns prematurely. But this is an opportunity to relate the interpretation to the central theme: whether the *Merchant of Venice* does lend itself to a setting in a modern city of financial dealings with sharp suits and mobile phones. Pupils often react in a very immediate way to the actors in a production – whether they liked them, found them attractive, remembered them from the television, etc. But this again opens the way for a consideration of whether the casting and style of acting was successful and whether the actors matched the pupils' prior impressions of character.

Helping pupils respond to drama is not something which just happens after a performance but will be assisted by preparatory work. The types of activities already described in this chapter, by focusing on how drama is constructed and crafted, provide examples of how pupils can be prepared for performance through practical workshops. In addition to the ideas already suggested pupils might be asked to:

- take the opening scene of the play and attempt to sketch an appropriate set – the pupils' efforts can be retained for comparison after the performance;
- examine stage directions and decide what needs to be done at different stages in the production;
- take specific key moments in the play and decide what symbolic action might be appropriate (for example, does *King Lear* tear the map when he is dividing his kingdom?) – the moments can be selected more effectively if the teacher has seen the performance in advance;
- try performing different short extracts using different furniture (such as two chairs either side of a table as opposed to a long couch);
- decide how the ending of the play should be staged (considering the use of curtains, lights, music and the position of actors);
- decide how a scene could be played differently in order to emphasise or minimise the humour;
- use stylised props (for example, a piece of card saying 'money') to see what effect this has;
- invent an unusual performance for an extract.

It should also be remembered that opportunities for helping pupils respond to drama will arise not just when pupils are watching performances or acting as audience for each other's work but when engaged in their own play-making. When creating a tableau it may help pupils to have their attention drawn explicitly to the use of the relative heights of the characters or the physical distance between them to denote aspects of their relationship. Some writers might choose to call this 'an aspect of the proxemic cultural code within a systemic system of encoding theatrical conventions' but the technical language is hardly necessary to make the point.

DRAMA AND LANGUAGE

It has long been recognised that active participation in drama has the potential for developing language because it gives pupils the opportunity to engage in fictitious contexts which require a variety of uses of language. When pupils are adopting roles in different formal and informal situations they tend to adapt their speech accordingly which means that the teacher can exploit the drama to extend the language registers employed. This was the argument which was advanced in the 1970s when there was considerable emphasis on naturalistic improvisation in which pupils 'lived through' dramatic situations which sought as far as possible to resemble real life. This view of the relationship between drama and English still has some force but changes of emphasis in the way both drama and the development of language are conceived means that the relationship needs to be redefined and extended.

In recent years there has been more emphasis on the importance of pupils' acquiring explicit knowledge about language rather than simply participating in contexts of language use. In teaching drama there has been an equivalent emphasis on conscious crafting of drama using a variety of non-naturalistic techniques. There is a parallel here between the development of thinking about language development and the teaching of drama; in the latter context there will be frequent opportunities to focus very explicitly on language whether in the context of improvisation, work on script or responding to a performance. Operating within a fictitious context also means that pupils are not subject to the same pressures which real-life situations bring. The fact that drama is not real means that pupils can find protection and security in the roles they adopt rather than have their 'own' linguistic ability and persona subject to scrutiny.

Drama works paradoxically. It brings us closer to human experiences because it allows us to focus on situations selectively in the safety of a fictitious context. However there is also distancing involved which means that the language used can be subject to more conscious control and scrutiny.

Almost all practical involvement in drama is likely to involve some specific attention to language use. Table 6.2 can be used as a template and adapted using a variety of different starting points and situations. The central dramatic element is to explore a situation from a variety of different perspectives that in turn results in an exploration of different language registers.

Table 6.2 Planning template

	Example
A warm-up activity.	Pupils assemble in a circle and play the 'adverb' game – one chosen individual has to guess each adverb from the actions of the rest of the group.
Presentation of stimulus, e.g. a newspaper headline and article; a letter or a public notice that has wide repercussions within the community.	A newspaper headline and brief article is read out giving details of a mysterious infectious disease that has broken out in an area affecting the local school in particular. Pupils should briefly discuss the possible causes and consequences.
Tableaux performed in groups that represent a moment from the past or future suggested by the stimulus.	The various tableaux might show the family's reaction, the news being heard in school, the activity in the local hospital, etc.
Brainstorm (in groups) the variety of people who might have been affected or involved in the incident.	The different tableaux present an initial list which is extended to include, for example: the reaction of the media, the involvement of health officials, the police and the local factory which has come under suspicion for dumping toxic waste.
A teacher-led meeting where the class (as a whole group) enacts a meeting in order to establish the truth.	A press conference is called in which the health officials are questioned about aspects of the incident.
Small group enactment of different situations.	The small group situations highlight the way in which language uses change from context to context, from informal to formal situations. The possibilities include: friends discussing the incident, a family being interviewed, a formal inquiry and a mother complaining on the telephone.
Presentation and reflection.	The presentations are viewed and the different language uses are discussed.

CONCLUSION

As suggested earlier in this chapter the teaching of drama is sometimes avoided by experienced as well as beginning teachers because of the apparent risks involved. This chapter has argued for an approach to planning drama which is not just inclusive but also integrated. An inclusive approach is one which does not just rely on one form of activity (whether this be spontaneous improvisation or working from scripts) but uses a wide-ranging approach within a scheme of work (incorporating exercises, process drama, rehearsal, performance, watching plays, etc.). The idea of an integrated approach to teaching drama will seek to combine various types of activity within one project or lesson. There are theoretical as well as practical reasons for making this recommendation.

The great strength of drama as it developed in the 1960s under the influence of writers like Slade was that it was very child-centred – pupils were highly involved and committed to the work. This of course was also paradoxically its weakness; because the drama was so heavily centred on the child, it was difficult to justify the work on the basis of objective criteria in order to judge what pupils were learning. One of the challenges of teaching drama is to retain a high level of pupil engagement while providing purposeful learning and progression. From a more pragmatic point of view the type of lesson which combines the use of play-making with scripted work and the use of video tapes of performance makes for a more varied, structured and secure lesson plan.

REFERENCES/SUGGESTIONS FOR FURTHER READING

Aston, E. and Savona, G. (1991) *Theatre as Sign-system*, London: Routledge
Bolton, G. (1992) *New Perspectives on Classroom Drama*, Hemel Hempstead: Simon and Schuster
Elam, K. (1988) *The Semiotics of Theatre and Drama*, London: Routledge
Esslin, M. (1987) *The Field of Drama*, London: Methuen
Fleming, M. (1994) *Starting Drama Teaching*, London: David Fulton Publishers
Fleming, M. (1994) *The Art of Drama Teaching*, London: David Fulton Publishers
Lyas, C. (1997) *Aesthetics*, Lancaster: UCL Press
Pavis, P. (1992) *Theatre at the Crossroads of Culture*, London and New York: Routledge
Simner, B. (1994) *Can We Write It as a Play?*, London: Hodder and Stoughton
Slade, P. (1954) *Child Drama*, London: University of London Press
Wagner, B.J. (1976) *Dorothy Heathcote: Drama as a Learning Medium*, Washington DC: National Education Association
Way, B. (1967) *Development Through Drama*, London: Longman

7 What Do We Mean by Media Education in English?

FRANK HARDMAN

This chapter will explore the developing relationship between English and media education that has occurred since the 1930s before going on to consider the practical applications of the relationship for the teaching of the National Curriculum secondary English in Initial Teacher Training (DfEE, 1999). Teaching about the media in English resulted from a position originally put forward by Leavis and Thompson in their book *Culture and Environment* published in 1933. The book was made up of practical examples from advertisements, newspapers and journals and since the 1930s has been steadily extended to include film, television, radio and popular music. In defending the nation's culture, Leavis and Thompson (1933) argued that children would need protecting from the corrupting influence of the mass media by being exposed to the best literature so as to develop discrimination against the mass media. The literary canon therefore was seen as providing a standard against which the mass media could be compared. As we saw in Chapter 2, this position of high moral purpose still finds echoes in the contemporary debate about English teaching.

By the 1960s, teaching about the media had become an established part of the English curriculum alongside fiction, poetry, creative writing, etc., and by the 1970s separate courses in Film Studies and Media Studies at A level began to gain ground. Today all English GCSE syllabuses now include components dealing with the media and Media Studies is taught as a separate subject at GCSE as well as at A level and in a variety of vocational courses. Academic study of the media is also firmly established in higher education and some teachers will have developed an expertise at this level.

The first version of National Curriculum English (DES, 1990) also offered significant potential for media education reflecting the growing influence of the cultural analysis view of English teaching. Because of its inclusive notion of 'text' which went beyond written texts to include visual and audio texts, the 1990 curriculum provided many opportunities for media teaching in its own right and in other areas such as knowledge about language. The Non-Statutory Guidance (NCC, 1990) that accompanied the English Orders was also rich in examples of media education, both critical and practical. The fundamental principles were adapted into three approaches:

- *Media language*: How do we make sense of a media text? What conventions are at work in it? How do we categorise it in relation to other texts?
- *Representation*: Is this text supposed to be like real life? Do you find the characters and setting convincing? What roles are there for different groups (e.g. women) in this story?
- *Producers and audiences*: Who produced this text and why? For whom is it made and how will it reach them? What will they think of it?

However in the 1995 version of the curriculum, aside from one or two passing references, media education was reduced to one paragraph in the curriculum for Reading at Key Stages 3 and 4. This states that students should be given 'opportunities to analyse and evaluate [media] material, which should be of high quality and represent a range of forms and purposes, and different structural and presentational devices'.

Activity 1	Read through the programmes of study for Key Stages 3 and 4 and either underline or list all the explicit references to media in all its forms.

To critics like Davies (1996) the 1995 English curriculum represented a return to conventional notions of cultural value. Despite the constraints imposed by national policy, however, evidence from English teachers (see Chapter 2) suggests that they have continued to incorporate aspects of the media into their teaching and that they perceive media education as a key dimension to their work. The proposed 2000 curriculum also offers more scope for the study of the media alongside developments in the teaching of Information and Communications Technology. Under Reading Range (2 c) it states that it should include 'media and moving image texts, e.g. newspapers, magazines, advertisements, brochures, television, films, video', and under skills (8 a–d) it states that for pupils to develop their understanding and appreciation of media and moving image texts they should be taught 'how meaning is conveyed in texts which include print, images and sometimes sounds; how choice of form, layout and presentation contribute to effect; how the nature and purpose of media products influence content and meaning; how audiences and readers choose and respond to media'. Similarly, the ITT secondary English curriculum (DfEE, 1998) states that trainees must introduce pupils to the analysis and composition of the media through activities which demonstrate ways in which meaning is presented by the media; consider how form, layout and presentation contribute to impact and persuasion; teach about the institutions that produce media and require pupils to evaluate the messages and values communicated by the media; and require pupils to consider the ways in which audiences and readers choose and respond to media.

Before looking in more detail at the relationship between the teaching of English and media education, we will consider what we mean by the media. The media is said to consist of all the organised systems through which meanings are made and which reach numbers of people. However, the term 'the media' is generally used to refer to mass media such as television, cinema, newspapers and radio. It can be extended to include all public forms of expression and communication including books, magazines, e-mail and the Internet. Sometimes people use the term 'the media' to mean only media technologies, but the media cannot be understood merely by looking at its technologies: an understanding has to include concepts concerned with who has made the meaning, how, why and for whom.

THE AIMS OF MEDIA EDUCATION

As children acquire spoken language it gives them the ability to communicate, to relate to their environment and to construct their knowledge of the world. They then learn about written language which extends their powers of communication and understanding and simultaneously they are also learning about the languages of all the different media they are encountering. Children therefore come to school having already experienced different forms of media and with a range of audio-visual under-standings such as knowledge of media conventions which schools can acknowledge and build on to ensure that children know how, and why, they know what they know.

On one level a major main aim of media education is to deal with media technolo-gies such as computers, video, photography, film, sound recording or printing. On another level, however, it also means dealing with the fact that media technologies are not neutral because they are taken up by media institutions such as television, maga-zines, cinema, radio, newspaper and book publishing. According to this view, pupils should learn to understand the new 'mass media', such as television, in much the same way as they learn to understand print. One of the aims of full print literacy is to bring different meanings to a given text, to recognise what kind of text it is, predict how it will work, relate it to other texts in appropriate ways, to understand it critically and to read between and beyond the lines. Media education wants to extend this approach to print literacy to all the media so that every medium can be thought of as a language, having its own ways of organising meaning which we need to learn to 'read', bringing our own understandings to it and extending our own experience throughout. It therefore attempts to produce more competent consumers who can understand and appreciate the contents of the media and also the processes involved in their production and reception. Media education also aims to produce more active and critical media users who will demand and perhaps contribute to a wider range of media products.

MEDIA EDUCATION ENTITLEMENT

When engaging with media 'texts' we need to consider the following five questions:

- Who is communicating and why?
- What type of text is it?
- How do we know what it means?
- Who receives it and what do they understand?
- How does it present its subject to us?

In dealing with each of the above five questions, students will engage in critical analysis of:

- Media agencies: dealing with who produces the text and how this shapes part of the content of the message; roles in production process; media institutions; economics and ideology; and intentions and results;
- Media categories: different media (such as television, radio, cinema, etc.); forms (such as documentary, advertising, etc.); genre (such as science fiction, soap opera, etc.); other ways of categorising texts; and how categorisation relates to understanding;
- Media technology: what kinds of technologies are available to whom, how to use them; and the differences they make to the production processes as well as the final product;
- Media languages: how the media produce meanings; codes and conventions; and narrative structures;
- Media audiences: how audiences are identified, constructed, addressed and reached; and how audiences find, choose, consume and respond to texts;
- Media representations: the relation between media texts and actual places, people, events, ideas; and stereotyping and its consequences.

The above areas of knowledge and understanding represent a broad consensus about the areas that media education should cover and they are found with some variation in all GCSE and A level Media Studies syllabuses.

The areas of knowledge and understanding are interrelated and must be taught about in terms of how they relate to each other. The five questions can be applied to any text. Let us, for example, apply them to a book jacket and identify the areas of knowledge and understanding they cover. We could ask:

- Who made the book cover and why (i.e. the agencies)?
- What type of book it is (i.e. the categories)?
- Who the book is intended for, who will read it, when they will read it, how did it get there (i.e. the audiences)?
- How do we understand the information on the jacket, how are we able to do this, what do we expect to find inside, why do we expect this, are we surprised when we look inside, did the jacket give us a good idea of what to expect (i.e. the languages used)?
- What is shown (i.e. people, places, objects, colours, words, pictures and other information) and what associations do these things hold for us (i.e. the representation)?
- How did the book get from manuscript to reader (i.e. the technologies)?

| **Activity 2** | Select a class text that you are going to teach and apply the above questions. How much of it could be used as an introductory activity to the shared text? |

THE RELATIONSHIP BETWEEN ENGLISH AND MEDIA EDUCATION

The above exercise raises interesting questions about the relationship between English and Media Studies. Traditionally, English teaching has been concerned with written texts, particularly with books, chosen almost exclusively from a received canon of literary works and the individual reader's personal response to the individual writer's personal vision. The term 'media', on the other hand, is rarely seen to include books because of its focus on visual and audio-visual texts. However books, like any other media texts, clearly do 'mediate' the world in particular ways. Book publishing is also an industry that is heavily dependent upon mass reproduction and electronic technology and many books reach much larger audiences than many television programmes or films. It is also a major industry in which the financial profit motive plays a significant part and in which publishers act as 'gatekeepers' by determining what we are able to read and – through advertising, marketing and promotion – significantly influencing the ways in which we read it. English teaching has often neglected these aspects in its reading of texts and implicitly adopted an idealised, asocial view of cultural production in which the individual author is abstracted from social, historical and economic relationships. In the next section we will consider some of the broader issues raised by the relationship between English and Media Studies before going on to consider ways in which the two areas can be practically integrated in the classroom.

As we saw in Chapter 2, secondary English teachers have been keen to incorporate media education into their work. However, according to some commentators (see Davies, 1996) its place in the English curriculum is still a contested area. This raises many questions about the extent to which media education will remain a 'bolt-on' component or promote a more fundamental reshaping of the English curriculum.

As we have already seen with the book jacket example, it is difficult to maintain a clear-cut distinction between the way a text can be studied in an English or media lesson. We might make the distinction in terms of the medium of a text where English is seen as being predominantly concerned with written texts, whereas a study of the media is primarily concerned with visual and audio texts. However, in practice these distinctions are arbitrary and often a result of a division between approved forms of 'high culture' and 'popular culture' with the teaching of English focusing almost exclusively on a received canon of literary texts. This division has also led to different assumptions about the influence of such forms of culture on the reader and about how they should be read. Reading 'quality' literature is generally seen as having a humanising effect on the reader by encouraging the development of sensitivity to language, culture and human relationships, whereas the media is often seen as having a predominantly negative effect by manipulating, deceiving and promoting false values which the reader is powerless to resist.

These assumptions have led to differences in the way teachers approach the reading process in the two areas. Reading literature is seen as a process of developing pupils' receptiveness and responsiveness to something that is regarded as being morally educative whereas reading the media is about encouraging pupils to resist or see through the deception in the texts. This has led to different notions of the relationship between readers and texts and to differences in teaching approaches. English is therefore defined in terms of a set of practices (i.e. speaking, listening, reading and writing) and is concerned with the development of pupils' skills in these four areas, whereas media education is defined in terms of concepts such as audience, language and representation and is concerned with developing pupils' theoretical understanding of the way in which media texts are constructed and read.

Although English in the National Curriculum is mainly defined in terms of skills rather than of concepts, the practices of reading and writing clearly involve pupils in considering such things as 'forms and conventions' and 'audience'. There is, therefore, a great deal of common ground between English and media education as shown in Table 7.1.

Table 7.1 English and media education: common ground

	Skills	Concepts	Areas of knowledge
Common to both	speaking	convention	
	listening	authorship/agency	
	reading	language	
			audiences
	writing	audience	
	collaborative group work	representation	
			genres
	problem-solving	genre	
	critical analysis	narrative	
	planning/drafting	fact/fiction/bias	
	revising/editing	stereotyping	
	scripting/storyboarding	construction/ de-construction	
			conditions of reception
		ideology	
	framing		production technologies
		ownership/control	
			different media forms
			economics of production
More specific to media education?			media institutions

From Table 7.1 it seems there are a number of concepts which would feature in a study of the media which traditionally have had no obvious equivalent in secondary English teaching, although recent literary theory in higher education has increasingly drawn on socio-cultural concepts. For example, 'institutions' (or 'industry') drawing on sociological theory is a major concept in many media studies syllabuses where students are required to study aspects such as ownership and control of media industries, the economics of media production, the role of advertising, the processes by which media texts are distributed and circulated, and the relationships between the media and the state. These kinds of questions are also related to other aspects of media: for example, forms and conventions of media texts, the ways in which the media represents different social groups, and the ways in which audiences make sense of them. In contrast to this, traditional literary criticism has adopted an idealised, asocial view of cultural production where the focus has been on the individual author, abstracted from the social, historical and economic context.

Similar contrasts can also be seen in the way the two areas of study have dealt with the concept of 'audience'. In English teaching, the focus is on the individual's 'understanding' and 'appreciation' and developing a 'personal response' to what is read. In more traditional text-orientated criticism this has taken the form of the reader recovering the meanings from the text. However, the more recent influence of 'reader response criticism' has assigned a more active role to the reader because of the more unpredictable nature of each particular reader's experiences as they interact with the text. Reference is also made to the writer's sense of audience and awareness of the way in which language is used for different purposes and contexts.

In media education, the audience is usually regarded as a collection of diverse social groupings and the focus of study is on the different ways the different groups will use and make sense of texts. In studying and creating media texts, pupils are asked to consider the ways in which audiences are targeted and addressed. Therefore much more emphasis is placed on social accounts of the ways in which social texts are produced and read in contrast to English's traditional concerns with the individual reader's personal response.

The different conceptions of the two subjects has led to differences in pedagogical practices. If we examine the terminology of English and Media Studies syllabuses, differences in their notions of 'reading' and 'writing' become apparent. In English, in their reading, pupils are required to 'understand' and 'evaluate', to 'respond imaginatively', to 'enjoy' and 'appreciate' what they read. In writing, they are expected to 'communicate effectively' and to 'articulate experience and express what is felt and imagined'. In Media Studies syllabuses, the emphasis is very much on developing 'critical analysis' of the ways in which media texts are 'constructed' so that pupils become competent consumers of the media by learning to read visual images, codes, conventions and grammar. The concept of the constructed nature of media products in which everything is a mediated view is therefore fundamental to media education.

Media Studies at GCSE and A level has always placed a great deal of emphasis on the formal study of media language so that in their theoretical coursework and practical work students are expected to demonstrate the meaning and relevance of basic concepts such as denotation, connotation, sign, symbols, codes, signification and structure derived from the study of semiotics. Media language is therefore taught as a rule-governed system which can be analysed into its component parts. There has also been a greater emphasis on the explicit study of grammatical and conventions of written language and specialist terminology in English syllabuses following the 1995 curriculum and the National Literacy Strategy (NLS), and this is likely to continue following the 2000 version. Prior to this, the emphasis had been on language as a vehicle for understanding and communication, students were not expected to demonstrate any abstract theoretical knowledge of the formal properties of language.

Similarly in reading, more emphasis has been placed on the critical appreciation of literary texts and on the study of different structures, forms and styles. However, issues of 'representation', 'bias' and 'stereotyping' in which students are expected to identify and question ideological meanings are mainly focused on in media texts. It can be seen, therefore, that differences of emphasis remain: English places a central emphasis on writing as a form of self-expression and values reading as a personal response, whereas media education is concerned to promote a more self-conscious construction and deconstruction of meaning. Both areas of study would, however, benefit from each other by paying more attention to the interactive nature of reading which acknowledges and builds upon what students already know about the media and by acknowledging more of the social production of reading in English.

TOWARDS INTEGRATION

Despite the lack of explicit reference to media education in the recent National Curriculum documents, surveys of English teachers' attitudes (see Goodwyn and Findlay, 1999) toward media education show that it should be firmly located in English because it is dealing with fundamental questions about language and literacy that are appropriate to our time. The research also shows that the conceptual framework of media education has taken root in the English classroom. It therefore seems that media education has become integral to, and inseparable from, English and that the application of media concepts to the practice of English has been transformative in the way texts are approached. For example, many teachers report that the 'reading' skills required in media work do have a direct impact on literary study in particular, particularly in bringing a more cultural-historical approach to texts studied.

The 2000 English curriculum states that pupils should be introduced to a wide range of media texts including magazines, newspapers, radio, television and film, and the current ITT secondary English curriculum states that trainees must be taught how to introduce pupils to the analysis and composition of the media including teaching about audiences, institutions and media language. Clearly, there is scope for a wide range of media teaching which draws upon pupils' own media uses and preferences.

Teaching about language offers considerable potential for connecting English teaching with media education. Media education is concerned with developing a systematic knowledge about media language and codes and conventions and it provides a major resource for studying language, particularly spoken language. The media makes available a wide range of accents and dialects and forms of language use which provide rich data for study including the self-conscious language play of comedy programmes, advertising and tabloid headlines. It also plays a crucial role in defining and regulating the kinds of language use which is deemed to be socially acceptable in a range of contexts. The emphasis is on developing knowledge of the way language functions in such contexts through talking about the way people use language, how language is constructed and considering the effects of alternatives. Studying language in this way therefore ensures it is rooted in language use and the acquisition of a specialist terminology takes place in the context of specific activities and purposes. It also points to the importance of integrating practical work with theory and analysis and reflects the considerable potential of practical media production for speaking, listening, reading and writing activities, for example, through writing television and radio scripts, editorial columns and news broadcasts or compiling a news programme or performing a story in a radio programme format.

PLANNING FOR MEDIA EDUCATION IN ENGLISH

In planning for progression in media education, age-related texts that enable pupils to develop critical distance will be crucial. Media education must begin by acknowledging what pupils already know about media language. They have knowledge about visual conventions and the older they are the more likely it is that they have knowledge about systems of circulation (e.g. know where they might have seen an advertisement such as the one you show them). Once they know that this 'everyday knowledge' is valid and that they are being encouraged to articulate it, they will rapidly improve their powers of reflection and critical analysis of media texts.

There follows an outline of the range of opportunities for media education work which can be integrated into the English curriculum at Key Stages 3 and 4. By the end of Key Stage 4 pupils should have had the opportunity, using appropriate age-related texts, to:

- talk and write about their own media consumption and give an account of their preferences;
- describe visual representations, such as photographs, book covers and posters, making reference not only to *what* is shown but also to *how* it is shown;
- organise, through photo-play exercises, sequences of pictures to explore the construction of different narrative structures and to explain this;
- storyboard different media texts, either for the planning of a video production or as an activity in its own right;
- recognise different points of view in the media;
- use a video and cassette recorder for practical media productions;
- use a still camera to take a sequence of pictures which tell a story or give an account of a process, event, etc.;
- explore narrative structure in forms of fiction and non-fiction;
- investigate how different points of view shape argument and discussion in the media;

- understand the production and marketing of media products and how they can be used differently by different audiences;
- assess the worth of media representations of individuals, social groups or debates;
- sequence of words, sounds and images, for example, in video and radio production;
- use the World Wide Web for practical and analytical work.

The above list is not exhaustive but it provides a framework within which to start thinking about your planning for media education work within the English curriculum. Many of the areas of study are covered in commercially produced resources and in an excellent range of materials distributed from the London-based *English and Media Centre* by the National Association for the Teaching of English (NATE) – see the list of resources at the end of this chapter.

Given that many media texts date quickly, you can adapt the approaches to contemporary texts which you or the pupils bring into the classroom. You will build up a range of critical and practical approaches to media texts that are of interest to and appropriate to the age range of the pupils. You will also be able to apply many of these practical and critical approaches to the literary texts studied by the pupils. For example, one way of getting pupils to visualise the characters and setting and to explore the themes and social and moral issues of the book they are reading is through storyboarding. The pupils will be familiar with film and television adaptations of literary works of literature and you could explore how texts are changed when they are adapted to different media as well as a range of media concepts to do with construction, selection and representation. This can be achieved through a simple storyboard as set out in Figure 7.1. Using photocopies of the story, pupils draw the camera shots and angles in the picture box. These are described in note form along with camera angles and timings of the shots in the description box, and the dialogue and/or sound effects are described in the sound box. Figure 7.2 can be used to introduce the pupils to the media language of camera shots and angles used by television and film-makers.

READING MOVING IMAGE TEXTS

Building on this work, pupils can start to analyse film/television extracts, using the grid shown in Figure 7.3 as a critical framework. The grid introduces them to a wider range of media language and is designed to get them to critically analyse and reflect on the important aspects of the film/television extract by considering *how* it gets across its message. The use of a video player with a pause button which enables them to freeze frame images would greatly enhance this type of work, as would removing the sound and colour from the pictures. The opening sequences to films and television programmes provide excellent material for this kind of analysis: for example, the pupils could consider why the opening sequences to television 'soaps' are so important in introducing the programmes.

Figure 7.1 A storyboard template

Storyboard: _____		Sheet number: _____
Title: _____		

Picture	Description	Sound

Figure 7.2 Media language: camera shots and angles (*The Media Student's Book*, G. Branston and R. Stafford, Routledge)

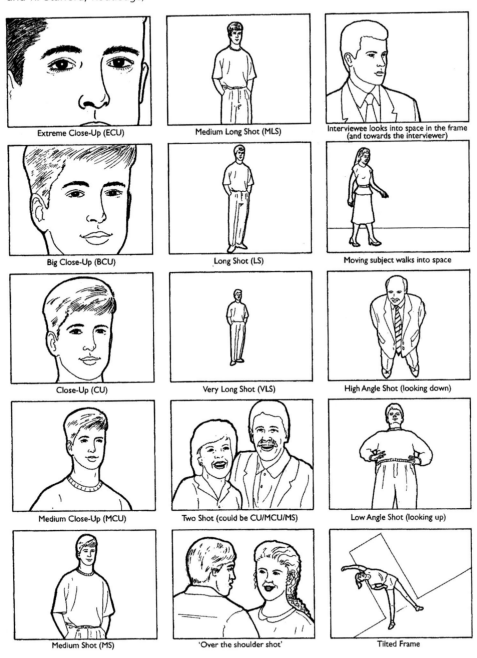

Figure 7.3 Analytical framework for reading moving images

Media language	Notes
Framing: Why has the director composed the image in this way? What is the balance of LS, MS and CU? Are there any BCUs?	
Location: What can we tell about the sequence from the place in which it is set?	
Camera angle and movement: Why has this camera angle been chosen or moved in this way?	
Lighting: What effect does the lighting have on the mood or tone of the sequence?	
Colour: Which colours stand out in the sequence? How does this affect us?	
Music: What effect does the music have on our response to the sequence?	
Sound effects: What did you hear and why were the sound effects present?	
Graphics: If there are title graphics, what style are they? Why was that style chosen?	
Costume and make-up: How do these add to our reading of the character(s)?	
Editing: How long is each shot held for? Why have the shots been sequenced in this order?	

NEWSPAPERS

Newspapers obviously provide a rich source of material for the study of the media and for language work in English (see Chapter 4). Getting the pupils to construct their own newspaper stories based on a real or imaginary event from a class reader can be a very useful exercise.

Newspaper writing frame

A writing frame, modelling the writing of a news story will provide helpful scaffolding for the pupils. It should show the layout of a newspaper story, including a headline, followed by an introduction. The introduction is usually a brief paragraph of one or two short sentences which tries to capture the essence of the story. The following paragraphs should include evidence that corroborates the assertions made in the introduction and should include details of where and when the event took place and quotes from *primary sources* – eyewitnesses to the events or the main characters involved. In longer stories this is followed by more background information and evidence or commentary from *secondary sources* – people with relevant or expert knowledge who can help the reader to understand the significance of what has happened. The writing frame should show how a well written news story answers the questions *who, what, when, where and why* early on.

An important teaching point is to show pupils how journalists are trained in the technique of writing newspaper stories so that all the important information, and the evidence that backs it up, is in the first quarter of the story. This is because in contemporary newspaper production a story will be cut back paragraph by paragraph from the bottom to make room for a late advertisement, story or picture. If a really good late story comes in at the last minute, the original story may be reduced to one or two paragraphs. This is called 'news in brief' (NIB) and it must still make sense.

A good way of demonstrating how a news story is written like an inverted triangle, with the latest information at the top followed by supporting evidence and background information, is to select a story from a newspaper and cut it back paragraph by paragraph starting at the end. The purpose of the exercise is to explore how far it can be cut without losing the key message. A similar exercise can be carried out with the pupils' own news stories to reinforce the writing technique.

Newspaper headlines

By formal comparisons the language of the tabloids is 'simpler' than that of the broadsheets: in the broadsheets, the lead stories are at least three times longer, with twice as many sentences per paragraph and, on average, the sentences are one-third longer, containing twice as many subordinate clauses, while noun phrases contain three times as many relative clauses. All newspapers, however, make use of shortened sentences in their headlines and making sense of deliberately cryptic headlines, particularly in the tabloids, demands considerable cultural knowledge and awareness of colloquial and dialect uses, together with interpretive skills. The headlines in tabloids assume knowledge of specialised, connotational or metaphorical meaning and these can be explored by pupils, together with the constant use of punning or playfulness with language.

Other ideas for working with newspapers include:

- A comparison of tabloid and broadsheet coverage of a 'newsworthy' item. This might include issues of bias and the expression of strong political opinion and moralistic comment on broader social and international issues and how tabloids are often insular in their approach, focusing on national concerns, sex scandals, the private lives of the famous or trivial (if bizarre) events. This topic could be developed to include a contrast of newspaper and television presentation of 'news' items.
- A detailed step-by-step analysis of a newspaper picture, starting with one small portion and then building up to the 'whole' picture, asking how the inclusion of more detail alters the interpretation and understanding of the picture. The original caption can also be analysed along with its function as an anchor for the meaning to be read into the picture (see the British Film Institute's *Reading Pictures* material (BFI, 1981) for further suggestions).
- Research into the ownership of newspapers, their circulation figures and readership, and how advertisers target their products at specific audiences who buy the newspapers.
- Discursive use of newspapers, for example, press intrusion and the exploitation of women in tabloid newspapers.

POP MUSIC

Pop music in all its various sub-genres provides a wealth of material for studying the media. Activities include analysing the visual imagery associated with genre, looking at the production methods of pop music, studying the wider business aspects of the medium and researching the different audiences for different genres. The 'Selling Sounds' simulation from the English and Media Centre *Production Practices* pack, involving the repackaging and rerelease of an old artist, provides an excellent starting point for this type of work. Studying videos of pop music that include a range of both musical and visual styles, such as *Top of the Pops* and *The Chart Show*, will provide a rich source of material for exploring the way in which star image is established by the style of performance as well as by the iconography and narrative meanings offered by the text. There is also a wealth of writing styles in magazines such as *Smash Hits* and *Melody Maker* that can be analysed and used as models for producing critical reviews.

DIGITAL TECHNOLOGIES

In teaching about the media it is crucial that teachers accommodate new media forms and developments like computer games and the World Wide Web. Computer games are among the most important cultural experiences now available to young people. The software and consoles for such games now make up a global market that equals the size and scope of Hollywood. While the opportunities for pupils to engage in media production on computer games are technically limited beyond the generation of ideas, sketches and scenarios for new games, their knowledge of graphics, codes and conventions can be used for critical discussion and reflection on the culture of computer games.

Clearly there is widespread public realisation of the potential of the World Wide Web as an instrument of communication which many see as creating an electronic global village which will have a major impact on our lives, our teaching and our pupils. In this information age the Internet makes available, at a keystroke, libraries, schools and peoples of the world. However a recent article in *New Internationalist* (1996), draws our attention to the fact that the Internet is now completely owned and operated by private enterprise and argues:

> the World Wide Web is primarily an advertising medium. The main information kids will find on it is advertising. All the search engines used to find anything are rigged with advertising. The main reason enthusiasts want it in schools is to deliver advertising.

While the article is probably overstating the case, it is an issue and media education in English should help pupils in becoming more adept at critically reading the persuasive advertising put out on the World Wide Web. The Internet, however, and the other forms of communication it brings us (for example, e-mail), offers great potential for publishing pupils' work. For example, work can be published on web sites like *Treasure Island* or *KidPub* or you can create your own class web site. Other kinds of Internet activities to try out are news simulations through web sites such as the British Press Association which publishes news on line as it breaks. This enables pupils to create a front page which they can compare with the national papers the next day. Only when pupils have been taught to evaluate on-screen information will they be able to deal critically with the vast amount of information found on the World Wide Web.

In terms of practical media production, digital technology offers pupils the opportunity to communicate with global audiences and to become media producers. Digital technologies dramatically lower the threshold of access to media production. This is already happening in the music industry and in print publishing and is now possible in audio-visual media. With a comparatively cheap piece of software it is possible to link a camcorder to a computer so as to assemble and edit a whole range of video material. Before the advent of such low cost software, many schools could not afford expensive editing suites. Therefore, while pupils experienced the planning and shooting of video material, many lost out on the experience of editing their work which in professional production is the most important stage of the process of making a television programme or film.

In conclusion, this chapter has set out to show how the English curriculum can provide systematic opportunities for study of the media so that young people can cope with the modern world and its extraordinary and exploding communication demands which come to us from every possible direction. Media study in English provides a crucial opportunity for developing young people's consciousness of how the technologies of communication and culture influence their lives. Media study, however, is not just about modern media or popular texts. Books should also be included in any study of the media including works of literature. As we have seen, digital technology is making the detailed and analytical study of all kinds of media texts feasible in schools. While none of this is explicitly stated in the National Curriculum, it is crucial that such areas are addressed in a modern and relevant English curriculum.

RESOURCES

The English and Media Centre produces the following media resources all available through the National Association for the Teaching of English (NATE): *Making Junk, Picture Power, Picture Power* CD-ROM, *Picture Power II, the Upgrade, The Advertising Pack, The News Pack, The Soap Pack* and *Production Practices.*

NATE also distributes *Media Education: Activities for Ages 11–14* by Carol Dahl which explores the key issues, concepts and skills of media education and has an impressive range of photocopiable resources for Key Stage 3 (published by Falmer Press).

Other general introductions include *Media Studies: An Introduction* by B. Dutton (Longman) and *Media Studies for GCSE* by P. Wall and P. Walker (Collins).

ICT resources

Treasure Island can be reached at: www.ukoln.ac.uk/service/treasure
KidPub can be reached at: www.kidpub.org/kidpub
A good e-pals advertising site is: www.iglou.com/xchange/ece/index.html
Reviews of CD-ROMS for English are available at: vtc.ngfl.gov.uk/vtc/index.html

REFERENCES

BFI (1981) *Reading Pictures*, London: British Film Institute
Davies, C. (1996) *What is English Teaching?*, Buckingham: Open University Press
DES (1990) *English in the National Curriculum*, London: HMSO
DfEE (1998) *Teaching: High Status, High Standards: Requirements for Courses of Initial Teacher Training*, London: HMSO
DfEE (1999) *English: The National Curriculum for England*, London: HMSO
Goodwyn, A. and Findlay, K. (1999) 'The Cox Models Revisited: English Teachers' Views of their Subject and the National Curriculum', *English in Education*, 33, 2, pp. 19–31
Leavis, F.R. and Thompson, D. (1933) *Culture and Environment*, London: Chatto and Windus
New Internationalist (1996) 'Controlling the Web', May

8 Assessment
MICHAEL FLEMING

Assessment, which is potentially one of the most interesting and important aspects of teaching and learning, is often seen by beginning teachers as a necessary but rather tedious chore; this tends to be even truer in the context of English than in other subjects. Evidence from Ofsted inspections judges this to be the weakest aspect of teachers' work; the Teacher Training Agency's survey of newly qualified teachers identified assessment as the area for which many of them felt least well prepared. Most books on the teaching of English published in the last 15 years either neglect assessment entirely or tend to reiterate some of the standard jargon and received opinions on the subject. Few of the publications engage with some of the more pressing issues pertaining to assessment: that it is potentially damaging, full of tensions and sometimes difficult to reconcile with an arts-based approach to English teaching.

National attempts to improve assessment by making the Standards and requirements increasingly specific and demanding (whether this is through the specification of Standards in Initial Teacher Training or, in the case of experienced teachers, through Ofsted inspections) have had less impact than might be expected. This is because coming to terms with assessment as a teacher has as much to do with attitude and understanding as it has to do with practical competence. English teachers need to realise that in the context of assessment (as much as in planning and teaching) they can employ the sophisticated skills and sensitivity to language which originally attracted them to the subject. Assessment becomes easier if it is viewed not solely or even primarily as the making of disembodied judgements but more as a process of supporting learning through analysis, feedback and response to pupils' work in a spirit of dialogue and discovery.

COMING TO TERMS WITH ASSESSMENT

Before looking in more detail at the requirements of the Standards for Initial Teacher Training it will be helpful to consider why, despite the considerable emphasis given to assessment in national policy and official government documents in the last ten years, assessment presents tensions and difficulties in the teaching of English.

One of the most frequently quoted extracts from the task group's Assessment and Testing Report, on which the original structure for the system of national testing was based, urged that the assessment process 'should not be a simple bolt-on addition at the end' but should be 'an integral part of the education process, continually providing both "feedback" and "feedforward"' (DES, 1988). This is a laudable intention but it is a goal which is not made easy if there is an undue emphasis in the classroom on external testing and formal reporting. The preoccupation with accountability through published league tables of examination results, combined with the imperative to meet local and national targets, does not make it easy to retain a broad conception of what assessment entails. In the current climate, assessment is inevitably in danger of being seen as having the primary purpose of making comparisons between different pupils, classes and schools rather than having the richer aim of improving learning. The challenge for English teachers is to cope with the external requirements without allowing these either to compromise the integrity of English as a subject or to adversely influence their approach to teaching and learning in the classroom.

It is when assessment becomes a 'bolt-on extra' that it tends to be seen largely as a chore. Whereas planning and teaching can more easily be seen as creative and interesting processes, students and teachers often undertake assessment out of a routine sense of duty. Assessment brings to mind images of the overworked teacher faced with endless piles of exercise books or examination scripts to mark and grade. It is little wonder that many newly qualified English teachers find the sheer volume of marking to be overwhelming and debilitating.

The practical solution to this problem is related to the broader theoretical question of how assessment is actually viewed. The image of the teacher constantly collecting in exercise books to be marked derives from a model of assessment that is largely summative (the making of formal judgements at specific times). A more 'formative' approach to assessment that places emphasis on feedback is more likely to involve the teacher intervening in the process of creation rather than simply responding to product. Such an approach also allows the introduction of a wider range of assessment strategies, removing the teacher from the treadmill of having to respond formally to every single piece of work that is completed. Much feedback and advice can take place face to face in the classroom where a wider range of evidence can contribute to forming an opinion about how a pupil is performing in English. Reducing the volume of work that is formally marked and graded will allow more quality attention to specific pieces.

The following list of random suggestions was drawn up by a group of PGCE students who were asked to brainstorm ways in which a teacher might gain evidence about a pupil's performance in English.

- individual discussion with the teacher;
- answers to questions in class ('open and closed comprehension questions – questioning for implicit and explicit understanding of meaning');

- discussion with parents;
- interview about a pupil's reading habits;
- drawings and diagrams;
- group discussions;
- pupil presentations;
- homework;
- drafts of writing;
- notes;
- reading aloud to teacher;
- reading aloud in class;
- finished writing products;
- miscue analysis;
- diagnostic tests;
- brainstorming;
- class discussion;
- video of oral work;
- drama presentation;
- responses to other pupils' writing;
- pupils' own comments on their work.

Activity 1 Can you think of any additions to the list of ways of gaining evidence about a pupil performance in English? Try to categorise the list according to the following criteria:

- the appropriateness of the suggestion as a method of assessment;
- the relevance to specific attainment target (whether the strategy is more appropriate in gaining evidence about reading, writing or speaking and listening);
- the level of formality;
- the likely degree of reliability.

An individual discussion between a teacher and pupil based on a novel that the latter is reading may reveal all sorts of interesting insights about the pupil's strengths and weaknesses in English but does not constitute a reliable form of assessment. The concept of reliability here is being used in a technical sense and has to do with the degree to which the form of assessment is likely to yield the same results if repeated on different occasions and marked by different people. Assessment strategies that are not reliable may however be valid or at least contribute to the validity of a particular judgement based on a variety of evidence. The more valid a form of assessment is, the more likely it is to yield a true picture of what it is intending to measure. A pupil who performs very poorly on a SAT test question, which asks candidates to comment on the way in which the nurse adds humour to a particular scene of *Romeo and Juliet*, may respond differently to the same question in other circumstances. In a subsequent classroom task in which the pupils are asked to work out how a director might dramatise the scene in order to bring out the humour, the pupil might show a much deeper level of understanding and personal response. The formal task has more reliability because the question, timing of the test and mark scheme have all been standardised; the test provides a more reliable means of comparing pupils' performances. The classroom task, however, provides a truer picture of the pupils' understanding of the scene in the play. Reliability and validity are key concepts in understanding one of the tensions at the heart of assessment in English.

Another tension associated with assessment in English has to do with the very nature of the subject. In Chapter 1 the contrast between aesthetic/literary and the more functional aspects of English was explored in the context of Cox's five models for the teaching of English. Assessment seeks to objectify, label and categorise and therefore tends to focus on narrow, more functional and reductive aspects of the subject. Cox (1991, p. 147) recognised this in another frequently quoted comment: 'The best writing is vigorous, committed, honest and interesting. We did not include these qualities in our statements of attainment because they cannot be mapped on to levels.' It is easier to assess what are often described as more 'surface' features of a pupil's performance in English but that does not mean that other qualities need to be ignored. In theory there is no reason at all why the qualities such as those described by Cox should not be included in the criteria for judging pupils' writing.

Assessment then can threaten the nature of English as a subject but it is also potentially damaging to teaching and learning in broader ways. Preparation for tests at Key Stage 3 or examinations at Key Stage 4 and beyond can easily become an end in themselves and a distraction from any sense of intrinsic purpose or worth. This is not a new issue. The following comments from the *Handbook of Suggestions for Teachers* published in 1937 has a very contemporary relevance:

> the importance of the internal examination may, on account of the high place it occupies in an unwisely managed school, become unduly exaggerated in the eyes of the pupils. The fear of an approaching examination has been known to rob school life of a good deal of its spontaneity and freshness.
>
> (Board of Education, 1937, p. 58)

It is important to guard against the assumption that preparing pupils for external examinations and tests must involve endless practice papers and rote learning of prepared answers. Examiners' reports constantly exhort teachers to avoid over-directing pupils to the extent that their personal voice is lost in the delivery of prepackaged answers. Apart from some specific advice on examination techniques, the best way to prepare pupils is by good teaching: engaging them in meaningful and personal responses to texts, challenging their thinking and providing detailed, constructive feedback.

Another danger with assessment that has been widely recognised is that definitive judgements can damage a pupil's sense of self-worth, confidence and motivation. Pupils can easily get the idea that they are simply 'not good' at English with all the potential negative consequences for learning which that entails. In the following quotation Graham (1998) while reflecting on those pupils he met in his teaching career who were judged by external criteria not to be 'good at' English considers what 'being good at English' might mean:

> it all mattered to them, reading, telling stories, talking about them, arguing over ideas, finding ways of exploring their life experiences, and so on. They took themselves seriously as far as 'English' was concerned, it affected their lives and played a vital part in them; in so far, that is, as they could keep sufficient faith alive in themselves, and defend themselves from the belief, so easily and damagingly inflicted by external appraisal, that they were not in fact any good at it.

Activity 2	Reflect on your own personal experience of being assessed and judged either in school or in other contexts. Have any of those experiences been particularly positive or damaging?

MEETING THE STANDARDS

The challenge then in meeting the Standards effectively is only in part to do with acquiring specific knowledge and competences but it is also a matter of finding a way of coming to terms with, if not entirely resolving, the tensions involved. There is a parallel between meeting the Standards as a trainee teacher and developing a coherent approach to implementing assessment policies in the classroom. Both have to be more than mechanical processes designed to fulfil external demands but need to be integrated with personal values and beliefs.

Anyone who has a genuine commitment to teaching cannot fail to be deeply interested in whether their teaching bears any relationship to what the pupils are learning. This seems such an obvious point that it is hardly worth stating but sometimes the emphasis on judging pupils' attainment distracts from the important function that assessment serves in evaluating teaching. Cox's maxim that assessment should be the 'servant not master of the curriculum' and should 'not determine what is taught' is only true to the extent that external examinations and tests should not dictate the content of the curriculum. Defined in its broadest sense, assessment should indeed be 'master' of teaching and learning, informing planning, providing a focus for improving teaching and monitoring pupils' progress.

Activity 3	Examine the generic Standards on assessment and the relevant section in the National Curriculum for Initial Teacher Training for English. To what degree do they acknowledge the importance of assessment as a means of evaluating teaching?

RECOGNISING ACHIEVEMENT

When responding to the work of low achievers in English it is often easier to identify what is wrong with a particular piece rather than to recognise what has been achieved. It is important however to begin by recognising positive achievements whatever the standard of work. When the GCSE was originally introduced an important principle was established that an assessment system should seek to determine an individual's capabilities rather than have as its primary goal the revealing of deficiencies. This important principle also underlies the National Curriculum system of assessment. Assigning pupils to a level is a matter of gathering evidence of achievement and of recognising what they know, understand and can do rather than primarily looking for evidence of what they have not accomplished (although there is inevitably an element of this in making a decision between one level and another).

It is easier of course to identify strengths in the work of higher achievers in English but this sometimes happens in very general ways. Pupils who have been identified as being 'good at English' may go through their school years receiving positive but rather bland praise without any detailed feedback. The value of identifying achievement apart from the obvious influence on motivation is in reinforcing positive traits in pupils' work and making explicit what may have been only partially intentional. For example a pupil may have used short sentences effectively in a written narrative without an explicit intention. By drawing attention to this aspect of the writing and highlighting the way in which the stylistic effect contributes to the creation of tension, pupils are likely to gain more control over their own writing in future and develop their own critical capacity.

IDENTIFYING LIMITATIONS

A useful procedure for responding to the work of all pupils, whatever their level of attainment, is to think in terms of achievements first and then limitations. This prevents low achievers receiving only criticism and high achievers nothing but bland praise. Constructive dialogue and detailed feedback should be informative and thought-provoking. The concept of target-setting has swept educational thinking at national and local levels in the last few years. Setting targets can be helpful because they focus the mind of pupils and teacher on specific narrow goals which makes learning seem less overwhelming. But the emphasis should at all times be on meaningful and purposeful communication and dialogue and not on the mechanical procedures. Targets sometimes appear on pupils' work because teachers are following the expected policy and can be meaningless, repetitive and unproductive.

Writing

The assessment of writing tends to be more straightforward than the other attainment targets in English because it always yields a tangible product which can be analysed and to which a response needs to be made. That does not mean that a teacher has to wait for work to be completed nor that intervention in the writing process necessarily has to come between completed drafts. Engaging in dialogue while work is in progress can be productive. The formative dialogue does not necessarily have to take place with the teacher; peer response also has its place. Pupils do, however, have to be taught to be constructively self-critical of their own and other pupils' work. They need to be taught to apply the same principles that should underpin the teacher's approach of recognising achievements and identifying areas for improvement.

It has been part of the received wisdom of marking pupils' work that teachers should respond to content first and only then comment on other more technical aspects of writing. This advice has much to recommend it and has been incorporated into the marking policies of many schools. It can however, if blindly followed, result in the implicit assumption that content and technical aspects are all that are worthy of comment (neglecting, for example, aspects of style and structure). The policy can also reinforce an artificial divide between content and form.

A typical response following this policy might take the following form:

> I enjoyed your account of your childhood memory very much, Emma. I particularly liked the section where you described the visit to the hospital after your accident. There are one or two mistakes in punctuation that you need to correct and I have indicated these.

An alternative comment might seek to link the punctuation with the content of the writing as follows:

> You convey the fear you felt when arriving at the hospital well in the way you describe the waiting room and the sounds you could hear. This section could have been improved even more by getting the punctuation more accurate and emphasising some of the short sentences which would have increased the tension.

New teachers of English sometimes do not appreciate that their expertise in the subject, derived from several years' study in higher education, can be brought to bear on the process of responding significantly to pupils' work. The use of grammatical terms when providing pupils with feedback can be an effective way of reinforcing their knowledge in contexts that matter to them.

It is often necessary to weigh the different aspects of pupils' writing when coming to a judgement about its overall quality. In making such judgements it is also important to keep in mind the purpose of the writing which should have been made clear to the pupils when the work was being set.

Activity 4	Make a selection of different pieces of written work from high- and low-achieving pupils at Key Stage 3. In each case identify the achievements and limitations of the work. Try to decide to which National Curriculum level the work would contribute evidence. What further evidence would be needed to allow an award of a level?

Reading

As with writing it is quite possible for assessment to remain at a surface level, only addressing, for example, literal comprehension instead of more significant levels of response and understanding. Assessment of understanding at a deep rather than surface level is not easy and more formal assessment activities can sometimes yield misleading results. The teacher needs to be alert to indications from a variety of sources that may contribute to an overall picture of how a pupil is performing and making progress in this particular attainment target. The classroom activities listed below provide opportunities for assessment of reading other than simply setting written questions on a passage. The advantages of some of the informal methods of assessment is that they have more potential for providing diagnostic information that identifies particular strengths and weaknesses. Classroom activities could include:

- Individual conversations with the teacher which may be based on a specific passage (fiction or non-fiction) or complete works.
- Creative responses which are often more informative than a list of simple questions, for example, rewriting a piece from the point of view of another character.
- Parodies (which may provide an indication of the degree to which a pupil has responded to style but also may give an indication of the understanding of content).
- Active approaches to text (choosing favourite lines and providing a title for a piece) which are normally viewed simply as teaching methods can provide insight into pupils' understanding.
- Dramatic presentations may provide valuable alternatives to more analytic writing.
- Representing texts in different forms of media (for example, narrative to drama and poem to newspaper article) may reveal a level of understanding beyond that allowed by more traditional responses.

The importance of building up a picture of a pupil's reading ability through a range of tasks is apparent when one tries to specify what being a 'good reader' entails. Does it mean being able to read quickly and get the gist of a passage, to be able to read aloud with expression, to read in depth and offer critical judgements, or to be able to give a personal response to texts? Clearly it involves all of these and a narrow approach to assessment will not be able to include them all.

Recognising that the assessment of reading involves recognising a wide variety of skills requires the use of a range of assessment strategies that may include the use of specific screening or diagnostic tests. These went out of favour with many liberal minded teachers because they were judged to be so narrow in what they actually assessed. Word recognition tests, for example, simply asked pupils to translate letters into sounds – such phonic knowledge did not offer any insight into understanding. Other slightly more sophisticated reading tests placed more emphasis on context and meaning but rarely engaged pupils in subjects that really mattered to them. Such tests, however, do have their place if used as only one part of the evidence that contributes to an overall judgement on a pupil's performance in reading.

As with other forms of assessment it is helpful to build into the planning stage what the focus of the assessment will be. As suggested earlier, assessment in some form or other is likely to take place in all lessons; the teacher will be constantly alert to how the pupils are understanding and responding to content. By thinking about the focus of assessment the lesson is more likely to have unity. For example if the teacher intends to assess how well the class has understood how the author of a particular narrative text has built up to a climax this is more likely to inform the teaching which precedes the task. Disjointed lessons occur when the assessment task does not relate well enough to the work that has gone before.

Speaking and listening

The assessment of speaking and listening presents particular difficulties for teachers of English. Judgements about a pupil's ability in these areas are even more difficult to standardise than in the context of reading and writing as anyone who has been involved in trial marking moderation meetings will testify. The whole process can seem very subjective and somewhat arbitrary. The fact that a pupil's performance changes with context makes the passing of judgement difficult. Many assessment activities necessarily take place in groups and the social dynamics can influence the outcome. The nature of the content is also likely to have an influence on the way a particular pupil performs; in the novel *Kes* the apparent oral ability of Billy Casper changes considerably when he delivers a speech about his kestrel. The influence of context on performance can make it difficult to discern progression in speaking and listening; even a pupil's mood can make a difference to how he or she performs. Teachers sometimes worry that assessment of oral ability is difficult to distinguish from judgements about personality. Should the shy, retiring pupil, or indeed the pupil who is overbearing and overconfident, be penalised? Passing judgement on pupils' ability to speak can seem like an attack on their self-esteem and identity.

These arguments have some force and suggest some principles on which the assessment of speaking and listening should be based. The fact that performance changes with context points to the need for the teacher to provide a variety of opportunities for assessment: in pairs, groups, individually, formally and informally and on a variety of topics. If each of these opportunities has a clear focus that is shared with pupils then the influence of the contextual factors is minimised. A pupil may not be as enthusiastic about contributing to a discussion about road safety than he or she would be about an increase in the price of season tickets but the awareness of what particular aspect of performance is being assessed means that the activity, although rendered slightly more artificial, is more transparent and equitable. It may be necessary to make particular arrangements for the assessment of an individual.

> **Activity 5**   Create a list of random speaking and listening activities. Try to discriminate between the tasks in terms of level of difficulty, irrespective of content and context. How much agreement do you find in the group?

Recording pupils' work

As with assessment, recording should serve teaching and learning rather than provide a distraction from it. It should therefore avoid duplication of effort. After the first version of the National Curriculum was published it was assumed that detailed check-lists were needed to record pupils' progress through each strand of each attainment target. These bore little relationship to the kind of day-to-day marking and feedback that was necessary within the classroom. A more sensible alternative is to seek to keep the formative feedback as far as possible from the system of record-keeping which will in turn feed the writing of reports. Integrating the system of assessment in this way should ensure that teachers are not too distracted from the central role of assessment in supporting teaching and learning. Portfolios of written work to supplement any more systematic records kept by the teacher, which include all the formative comments and feedback given to pupils, will help serve this purpose. Records of reading need to be more than a list of simple grades but should include a wide range of details accompanied by the pupils' own self-assessment in an appropriate format. Records of speaking and listening will build up a profile of a pupil's achievements and progress over time.

> **Activity 6**   In groups compare the system of reporting and recording from three different schools. Evaluate each one in terms of the demands on teacher time.

PROGRESSION

If the assessment and recording process is working well, this will clearly help pupils to make progress in the subject and will aid teachers in their planning. Progression however is not an entirely straightforward matter particularly in the context of a subject like English. Pupils do not learn in a simple linear way, with one skill, aptitude or level of understanding following neatly after another. Pupils can sometimes seem to regress in their command of technical aspects of writing when they experiment with more sophisticated constructions. Their ability to make inferences and respond to nuances of meaning may change according to the nature of the material presented to them. It is hardly surprising that pupils will often exceed expectations and cope with more challenging material when they are particularly motivated. It is probably fair to say that some English teaching in the 1970s and 1980s was strong on engaging pupils' interest and imagination but less successful in focusing the learning and ensuring progression through an appropriate level of challenge. The most successful teaching does both. The English National Curriculum for ITT provides a list of the ways in which pupils develop and progress in reading, writing, speaking and listening which you will find helpful to assist your own planning. As well as seeking to engage the interest and involvement of your pupils, you need constantly to ask yourself whether the work you are setting is making the right level of challenge. Table 8.1 provides examples of progression statements from the ITT National Curriculum.

Table 8.1   Examples of progression in English

Pupils should progress from	to
reading and responding to straightforward and familiar texts	an appreciation of varied and challenging texts
writing in simple, familiar formats for different purposes	independent composition of texts tailored to their audience and purpose
being able to speak to different audiences with some adaptation	sustained adaptation of speech to the needs and interests of different audiences

When pupils make the transition from Key Stage 2 to Key Stage 3 this can be difficult because for most pupils (other than those in middle schools) this involves a change of school as well. There are clearly social and pastoral issues involved here because making a new beginning can be exciting but may also be stressful. Most secondary schools take steps to smooth the transition such as inviting visits by pupils from feeder schools in the summer term and offering return visits by secondary staff. Curriculum continuity however is also an issue not just in terms of content but also in relation to the culture of teaching and learning in the different phases. It is possible for some pupils to regress in terms of their academic attainment during their first year in secondary school. It is important for secondary teachers to understand progression from the Key Stage 2 programmes of study so that the expectations are appropriate and the teaching builds on prior achievement.

> **Activity 7**   The purpose of this activity is to compare the programmes of study for Key Stage 2 and Key Stage 3 for English. For each of the attainment targets make a list in two columns marked 'from' and 'to' which summarise the intended progression. When you have completed your lists, compare these to the levels of attainment in the National Curriculum.

THE LITERACY STRATEGY

The national Literacy Strategy for primary education was established in 1997 with the aim of raising standards of literacy in all schools. The framework provided specific objectives for each term from reception to Year 6 and detailed guidance on how the designated hour for literacy should be structured. Each term's work was structured around three strands: word level (for example, phonological awareness, spelling and vocabulary extension), sentence level (for example, grammatical awareness, sentence construction and punctuation) and text level (for example, reading comprehension and writing composition). A significant feature of the strategy is that the intended objectives are described very explicitly with, for example, details of which technical terms (like 'suffix') and aspects of grammar (for example, the use of pronouns) are to be taught in specific terms.

Inevitably the introduction of the Literacy Strategy in primary schools raises issues about progression to Key Stage 3. The draft framework for teaching English for Key Stage 3 was published in 2000 and will be the focus for a national pilot in 2000/2001. Its purposes are:

- to set out teaching objectives for pupils in Key Stage 3 which will ensure that they build on their achievements in primary school;
- to ensure that pupils entering Key Stage 3 below level 4 are supported so they catch up;
- to provide guidance on how teachers can use these objectives to plan appropriately challenging work for their pupils;
- to enable headteachers and curriculum managers to set high consistent expectations for achievement;
- to promote continuity and progression between Key Stage 2 and Key Stage 3.

It hardly seems possible to object to this list or indeed to the idea of developing literacy because the concept of 'literacy' seems simple and uncontested but that is far from being the case. Many writers have pointed out that the so-called 'unitary' view of literacy (the idea that literacy is the name for one simple set of skills) should be replaced by a 'pluralist' view (the idea there are different literacies such as that needed for the home, community or workplace). Hannon (2000, p. 37) argues that 'theorists' tastes for unitary or pluralist conceptions of literacy derive from whether their primary focus is on literacy as a skill or on literacy as social practice'. He presents a useful summary of contrasting conceptions of literacy as shown in Table 8.2.

Table 8.2 Contrasting views of literacy

Skills-focused	Practice-focused
Unitary view likely	Plural view likely (literacies)
Acquisition seen as results of individual learning	Acquisition seen as a result of social involvement
Learning seen as transferable	Learning seen as context dependent
Literacy may be measurable	Literacy not quantifiable
Literacy relatively fixed	Literacy continually changing
Literacy intrinsically value-free	Literacy inevitably value-laden

You may notice echoes of earlier debates in this book in relation to ideologies of English teaching (Chapter 1) and attitudes to language (Chapter 3). The important point that has been a theme of this book is that very little can be taken for granted. To succeed as an English teacher you need to think, read and reflect, not just acquire skills or standards in a simplistic manner. The draft framework for Key Stage 3 explicitly acknowledges that literacy is much more than simply the acquisition of 'basic skills' but much will depend on how it is interpreted and implemented. If teachers do not think critically and reflectively about the issues involved, the result could be an implicit acceptance of a very narrow conception of English as a subject.

REFERENCES

Board of Education (1937) *Handbook of Suggestions for Teachers*, London: HMSO
Cox, B. (1991) 'Cox on Cox: An English Curriculum for the 1990s', London: Hodder and Stoughton
DES (1988) 'NC Task Group on Assessment and Testing: A Report', TGAT, London: HMSO
Graham, R. (1998) *Taking Each Other Seriously: Experiences in Learning and Teaching*, Durham: Fieldhouse Press
Hannon, P. (2000) *Reflecting on Literacy in Education*, London: RoutledgeFalmer

9 Conclusion
MICHAEL FLEMING

One of the underlying aims of this book has been to encourage you to think for yourself about the issues related to the teaching of English. This seems to be a fairly obvious intention but it is sometimes difficult to keep faith in the importance of independent thought when so much in education is prescribed and controlled. Professional development should never be simply about putting received ideas into practice. It is the view of the authors of this book that the proper acquisition of the Standards cannot take place fully without some understanding of the underlying tensions, theoretical debates and research.

At the end of your training you will receive a Career Entry Profile which is intended to support the transition from ITT to teaching and continuing professional development. It provides information, in relation to the Standards for the Award of QTS, about each new teacher's strengths and priorities for further professional development. It requires new teachers to set objectives for professional development and develop an action plan for induction.

The specific aims of the Career Entry Profile are to support schools and NQTs, working together, to:

- make the best use of the skills and abilities the NQT brings with them;
- use the Standards for the Award of QTS and the Induction Standards to build on the new teacher's achievements;
- devise a focused and individualised programme of professional development which will improve the NQT's practice in areas identified for development during the induction period;
- recognise the importance of effective professional development from the earliest possible stage in the NQT's career and consider the new teacher's longer-term professional development;
- make sustained and significant improvements in the quality of the new teacher's teaching in relation to the teacher's objectives, the school's development plan and local and national priorities.

This is perhaps the most fitting place to draw this introduction to English teaching to a close; we hope you have benefited from reading this book – and from your experience as a PGCE student more generally – but we also hope that you will be ready, both as a newly qualified teacher and in your longer-term future in education, to continue to develop intellectually and professionally. In doing this, not only will you give more to your pupils but also you will ensure for yourself a rich and fulfilling career.

Appendix A
English NC for ITT

A. PEDAGOGICAL KNOWLEDGE AND UNDERSTANDING REQUIRED BY TRAINEES TO SECURE PUPILS' PROGRESS IN ENGLISH

1. All courses must ensure that trainees are taught that pupils' progress in English depends upon teaching that emphasises:
   a. effective communication in speech and writing, and listening with understanding;
   b. developing pupils as enthusiastic, responsive and knowledgeable readers;
   c. the reading, writing, speaking and listening skills needed to participate confidently in public, cultural and working life;
   d. the use of language for pleasure, thinking, learning and personal development.
2. In order to understand the high expectations that teachers should have of their pupils, to aid planning and to ensure that trainees know how pupils are progressing in English, trainees must be taught the ways in which pupils develop and progress in reading, writing, speaking and listening from the ages of 11 to 16.
   a. As part of all courses, trainees must be taught the importance of ensuring that pupils progress in English:
      i.   from reading and responding to straightforward and familiar texts to an appreciation of varied and challenging texts;
      ii. from inference and deduction of simple meanings to grasping other layers of meaning and an appreciation of writers' techniques in realising them;
      iii. from use of specific evidence from texts to support views to marshalling reasons and evidence for a sustained critical analysis;
      iv. from finding and using accessible information to researching, extracting and synthesising information independently;
      v.   from writing in simple, familiar formats for different purposes to independent composition of texts tailored to their audience and purpose;

vi. from accurate and consistent use of the conventions of grammar, spelling and punctuation in straightforward contexts to accurate use of them in more complex texts;

vii. from being able to speak to different audiences with some adaptation to sustained adaptation of speech to the needs and interests of different audiences, including more formal speech when appropriate;

viii. from identifying the key points of what is heard and how these are presented to a discriminating appreciation of what has been heard, attending to the main messages and their impact, and the detail and techniques used;

ix. from contributing and responding in discussion, taking on a number of roles, to making a substantial contribution to the effectiveness of group discussion, including through taking a leading role;

x. from exploring a range of dramatic forms and conventions to represent ideas and issues to adapting and using these to generate their own dramatic representations of character and action.

b. Trainees on 11–18 and 14–19 courses must be taught how pupils' progression in English post-16 builds upon the progression identified above.

3. As part of all courses, trainees must be taught that, if pupils are to make progress in English, teachers must:

a. develop pupils as critical readers and extend the range of what they read, recognising:

i. the responsibility of the teacher to intervene in pupils' reading, including their independent reading, to ensure that:

pupils' reading competence is developed by building on and extending their current experience and interests;

pupils experience reading which is varied and challenging, and which broadens their reading horizons, including pre-twentieth century prose, poetry and drama and texts from different cultures;

pupils are familiar with a range of information texts, their purposes and forms;

ii. the need for pupils to develop a sense of literary tradition, recognising the influence of social, cultural and historical factors and making links between texts;

iii. that their teaching should stimulate pupils to become active, alert and enquiring readers, able to respond to texts critically and imaginatively;

iv. that it is necessary to teach pupils explicitly the ways in which:

texts are written for a particular readership, purpose or medium;

writers represent authorial and other viewpoints;

texts can be construed and interpreted in different ways;

b. develop pupils' competence in writing, recognising:

i. the importance of diagnosing pupils' specific strengths and weaknesses in writing;

ii. the need to identify the specific knowledge of linguistic structures and genres to be covered and to be taken into account when setting up writing tasks and when diagnosing and remedying pupils' difficulties;

  iii. the importance of planned opportunities for writing which make explicit the conventions of different genres and the usefulness of each for different purposes;

  iv. the importance of writing as a tool for learning, e.g. note making, analysis and evaluation;

 c. develop pupils' abilities in speaking and listening, recognising that:

  i. there must be planned opportunities to develop pupils' abilities to speak and listen and that listening skills need to be taught explicitly;

  ii. task-setting, pupil groupings and the purposes for talk are significant factors in determining the nature and quality of speaking and listening;

  iii. pupils must be taught explicitly about the oral conventions that are appropriate in different situations and for different audiences, including the use of Standard English;

  iv. pupils need to experience a number of roles in speaking and listening, e.g. chair, scribe, spokesperson, advocate, antagonist and supporter, so that they learn to speak in different contexts, and move between roles as the need arises;

  v. purposeful, focused talking and listening assist learning;

  vi. strategies need to be devised to provide the structure and support that some pupils need, e.g. those who are shy, inexperienced or suffer speech and hearing difficulties, to be able to contribute to, and to make progress in, speaking and listening;

 d. develop pupils' understanding of language variety, ensuring pupils know:

  i. how and when to use Standard English, and the differing degrees of formality in Standard English, e.g. how vocabulary choices and grammatical constructions vary between a formal oral presentation and group discussion;

  ii. how to recognise the features of Standard English and common non-standard forms, and how Standard English differs from other dialects;

  iii. that Standard English can be spoken with different accents;

  iv. the main ways in which language changes, e.g. through imports from other languages and because of new technology, and how words change meaning over time;

  v. about attitudes to language use, e.g. attitudes to gender in language;

  vi. the differences between speech and writing;

 e. recognise that pupils are often competent in languages other than English and that teaching should include strategies to build upon pupils' knowledge and skills in other languages in order to improve their skills in English;

 f. provide good models for pupils' reading, writing, speaking and listening;

 g. structure learning for pupils who are below the level of attainment expected for their age, so that they have access to the full English curriculum, as well as making progress in basic skills in English, recognising the factors which may contribute to low levels of literacy, including:

  i. poor phonic knowledge,

  ii. poor use of contextual cues and deficiencies in visual or auditory processing;

  iii. lack of support beyond the classroom;

    iv.   disaffection, poor motivation, low self-esteem or lack of confidence because of previous failure in reading;

    v.   the fact that English is an additional language for the pupil.

B. EFFECTIVE TEACHING AND ASSESSMENT METHODS

4. Trainees must be taught how to place medium- and short-term planning in the context of longer-term planning which indicates how the range of texts and the skills of reading, writing, speaking and listening will be covered and how teaching will be structured to enable pupils to develop and consolidate key skills and understanding.

5. Trainees must be taught how to encourage individuals to read, through:
   a. encouraging pupils' regular, individual, private reading;
   b. providing a range of resources which are likely to appeal to and develop pupils' different interests, e.g. through use of libraries and the School Library Service and through use of book boxes;
   c. choosing texts which will motivate all pupils to read and extend their reading interests, e.g. texts which are likely to appeal to boys;
   d. stimulating individuals to read and supporting pupils' reading, e.g. teachers' recommendations, book weeks, visiting authors and setting aside specific times to discuss pupils' reading and set targets.

6. Trainees must be taught how to teach literary and non-literary texts to whole classes and groups, including how to:
   a. select texts, identifying the chief learning aims and how they will be met through use of a text, e.g. deciding which aspects of a text will be taught and selecting a particular text because it uses specific structures or techniques;
   b. introduce a text, e.g. giving excerpts from the text to whet the appetite;
   c. select those passages or aspects of the text which should receive close attention and how to phase and pace the way the text will be taught, e.g. completing a first reading fairly rapidly so that pupils understand the nature of the text, followed by revisiting different sections in more detail;
   d. decide how and by whom the text will be read, e.g. reading aloud by the teacher to bring out the qualities of the text, followed by group reading of the same text for close study of the language; allowing individual pupils a few moments to read privately, before discussion, to form their own impressions; and sharing reading in a group by taking turns and pausing for discussion;
   e. set up activities which will enhance pupils' engagement with the text and improve their skills in reading, ensuring that the selection of activities is closely matched to the teaching objectives for the section of text being studied;
   f. enable pupils to appreciate and respond in writing and discussion to the text as a whole.

7. Trainees must be taught how to teach poetry, including how to:
   a. involve pupils in appreciating, understanding, responding to and writing poetry, including through teachers and pupils reading poetry aloud;

   b. teach the range of poetic forms and equip pupils with the technical terms they need to discuss poems, their meanings and effects, e.g. metre, metaphor, simile, onomatopoeia, assonance, alliteration, hyperbole, oxymoron, sonnet and ballad;

   c. group poems to enable appreciation of theme, form, period and author's voice.

8. Trainees must be taught how to teach Shakespeare's plays, including how to:

   a. explore Shakespeare's plays as scripts for performance, e.g. by presenting; improvising around the play's theme; directing particular passages attending to action, music and set; and devising and performing modernised versions of the scenes;

   b. ensure that pupils gain access to texts and appreciate the force of the ideas, language and dramatic qualities by using a variety of approaches;

   c. enable pupils to gain an appreciation of Shakespeare's language including its poetic qualities, how character and action are conveyed through language and how it differs from contemporary English;

   d. set Shakespeare's plays in their social and historical context, e.g. performance in the Globe Theatre, the nature of monarchy and the conventions of love and courtship.

9. Trainees must be taught how to teach non-fiction, through:

   a. providing for systematic, structured reading of non-fiction texts using a range of techniques, e.g. skimming and scanning;

   b. teaching pupils how to analyse the organisational and linguistic features of different types of text in non-fiction and use these features in their own writing, e.g. patterns of cohesion in information texts, emotive language in newspaper reports, perorations in speeches and the use of analogy in persuasive writing.

10. Trainees must be taught how to introduce pupils to the analysis and composition of the media within the pupils' National Curriculum for English, including newspapers, television and film through activities which:

   a. demonstrate some of the ways in which meaning is presented by the media and consider how form, layout and presentation contribute to impact and persuasion;

   b. teach about the institutions that produce media and require pupils to evaluate the messages and values communicated by the media;

   c. require pupils to consider the ways in which audiences and readers choose and respond to media.

11. Trainees must be taught how to assess pupils' reading, through:

   a. determining at the planning stage what pupils should know, understand and be able to do better by the end of the sequence of work, e.g. skills of relating one part of the text to another, drawing comparisons and recognising how authors build up to a climax;

   b. identifying the assessment opportunities and the assessment evidence that will be collected, including on what, and on which pupils, to focus for particular purposes;

   c. building up a picture of pupils' reading ability through a range of tasks which enable assessment of different types of skill;

    d. knowing how and when to employ particular assessment tools for particular purposes, including:
        i.   open and closed comprehension questions – questioning for the implicit and explicit understanding of meaning;
        ii. running record or miscue analysis – to assess reading in detail, especially for pupils with low standards of literacy;
        iii. standardised diagnostic tests for detailed information about a particular aspect of reading which is giving cause for concern.

12. Trainees must be taught how to teach writing, including how to:
    a. provide models of writing for pupils to analyse and emulate and use pupils' reading to provide inspiration for their writing;
    b. manage the writing process effectively, including:
        i.   how to help pupils to generate ideas for their written work;
        ii. how to teach pupils to draft, revise and then proof-read their work, e.g. through using a word-processor and by encouraging pupils to read their work to someone else;
        iii. how and when it is appropriate to focus on parts of the writing process only, e.g. knowing when bullet points are sufficient and knowing when more than one stage of drafting is unnecessary;
    c. teach pupils to write in different forms, e.g. the discursive essay, the ballad and the informative article, through:
        i.   providing examples and teaching pupils how to analyse them for their linguistic and other conventions;
        ii. using structured approaches to support pupils' first attempts, e.g. writing frames;
        iii. teaching pupils to consider audience, purpose and context when choosing form and language.

13. Trainees must be taught how to teach spelling, including how to:
    a. teach pupils strategies which help them to learn and retain spellings, e.g. the use of analogy, developing visual memory, phonic segmentation, reference to root words and looking for words within words;
    b. teach spelling families and rules systematically, e.g. by working out spelling conventions from lists of regular words, by grouping words containing the same letter strings together and by repeated practice in spelling misspelt words correctly;
    c. introduce pupils to new words with unusual or irregular spellings;
    d. use marking strategies which draw attention to patterns of error and enable pupils to learn from their mistakes, e.g. by highlighting the incorrect elements and by reminding pupils of spelling rules which have been broken.

14. Trainees must be taught how to teach punctuation, including how to:
    a. use well written texts to demonstrate the function of different punctuation marks and how they should be used, e.g. looking at the use of the semicolon and the colon;
    b. use activities, including reading aloud, through which pupils recognise the role of punctuation in marking grammatical boundaries and in symbolising and replacing the intonation of speech;

    c. review and mark pupils' work constructively, drawing pupils' attention to the omission and misuse of punctuation marks so that pupils can correct them;

    d. teach more complex uses of punctuation marks systematically, e.g. the relationship between commas and clauses and the use of the dash;

    e. teach self-help strategies, e.g. requiring pupils to read back their own work to themselves, looking for sentence breaks.

15. Trainees must be taught how to teach grammar, including how to:

    a. teach the grammatical terms and conventions listed in the pupils' National Curriculum explicitly;

    b. teach pupils the ways in which sentences can be extended, elaborated, abbreviated and manipulated by re-organising their sequence and the way they are worded and by adding or removing phrases and clauses;

    c. give pupils feedback on their written work, including the identification of grammatical errors, e.g. non-agreement of subject and verb and provide guidance for development;

    d. teach pupils to analyse reading materials for their grammatical features and conventions, e.g. the use of long noun phrases and the passive voice in information writing;

    e. set pupils activities which demonstrate the way that grammar works and the factors which influence grammatical choices, e.g. changing a first person account into the third person changes the focus of attention and the level of formality.

16. Trainees must be taught how to assess pupils' writing, including how to:

    a. mark pupils' work to respond to content as well as accuracy, highlighting both the strengths and weaknesses, and intervening to extend pupils' writing competence;

    b. encourage independence and the ability to be self-critical, including self-correction among pupils;

    c. weigh the different facets of pupils' writing when coming to a judgement about its overall quality in relation to its purpose, e.g. weighing narrative coherence against spelling and presentation.

17. Trainees must be taught how to teach speaking and listening, including how to teach pupils:

    a. to fulfil the formal and informal roles taken in groups, through the explicit teaching of the language appropriate to different stages of the discussion, e.g. tentative hypothesis, brief summary, probing questions, summing up and handling disagreement constructively;

    b. to adapt their speech for different purposes, including how to sustain a talk or a monologue, how to use visual aids and organise persuasive points, e.g. by anticipating and preparing for the opposing point of view;

    c. the conventions of different types of speech;

    d. to listen attentively and with discrimination, e.g. by using techniques such as making notes, focused listening and directing attention;

    e. to discern rhetorical devices, irony, persuasive techniques and bias in what is heard.

18. Trainees must be taught how to introduce pupils to drama, in the pupils' National Curriculum for English, through:

a. utilising drama techniques, e.g. small group play-making, teaching in-role and tableaux, to involve pupils in examining themes, issues and meanings;

b. using performance of texts to develop pupils' understanding and appreciation of language, dramatic form, character and performance;

c. using role-play, script-writing, writing in-role and a range of stimuli to develop pupils' reading, writing, speaking and listening;

d. requiring pupils to reflect upon and evaluate features of their own and others' performance in order to develop their understanding of techniques for conveying meaning.

19. Trainees must be taught how to assess speaking and listening, including how to:

a. establish a clear focus for the assessment, e.g. how well a group member uses questions and suggestions to organise and sustain ideas in discussion;

b. make opportunities for the assessment of individual pupils, ensuring that pupils understand the nature and purpose of the assessment;

c. build up over time a profile of pupils' achievements in speaking and listening which recognises progress in the pupils' speaking and listening skills, e.g. moving from talking which is largely scripted and read aloud to speaking from notes of the main points to be made;

d. distinguish between aspects of pupils' personality and the way pupils talk, e.g. not mistaking confidence for a significant contribution.

20. Trainees must be taught how to teach about language variety explicitly through:

a. the planned teaching of different aspects of language variation, linking teaching to both the books pupils read and the texts they write;

b. using contrasting texts to teach points of comparison and contrast in content, language and style;

c. direct comparison between spoken and written forms of language, e.g. a transcript together with a piece of reported speech to illustrate similarities and differences in vocabulary and sentence formation;

d. the study of language variation and change.

21. Trainees must be taught how to develop effective strategies for improving the skills in reading and writing of pupils who achieve below the standard of literacy expected for their age including how:

a. to assess pupils' reading and writing using techniques such as standardised tests, miscue analysis, observation and discussion;

b. to evaluate the quality, readability, content and appeal of texts and to assess their appropriateness to pupils' chronological age, so that those texts and other resources match pupils' needs well;

c. to differentiate classroom tasks and support poor readers with tasks which are being undertaken by all the pupils in a class;

d. with the help of an experienced English teacher and/or SEN teacher if necessary, to provide positive and targeted support for pupils with special educational needs, e.g. teaching pupils who are not yet independent readers the phonic, syntactic and contextual skills they need and helping pupils to apply their knowledge of grammar, spelling and punctuation in independent writing.[1]

---

[1] Providers should refer to the ITT National Curriculum for primary English (Annex C) for more detail on strategies for teaching English to pupils whose attainment in English is below that expected for their age.

22. Trainees must be taught how to use Information and Communications Technology (ICT)[2] to support the teaching of English.

23. In order to understand how to evaluate and assess their teaching and their pupils' learning in English, trainees must be taught:

    a. how to monitor and assess pupils' progress and attainment in English, including how to:

        i. make effective use, in their teaching and in planning future lessons and sequences of lessons, of assessment information on the attainment and progress of pupils;

        ii. set up activities so that specific assessment in English can be undertaken for all pupils, including the very able, those who are not yet fluent in English and those with SEN, through assessment, at an early stage, of pupils' strengths and weaknesses in using language;

        iii. keep records of pupils' progress and attainment across the English curriculum, including recording progress in the development of pupils' skills in English;

        iv. make summative assessments of individual pupils' progress and achievement in English, through the use of National Curriculum tests, teacher assessment and other ways of assessing individual pupils, including the appropriate use of standardised reading tests and spelling tests;

        v. present the outcomes of assessment in reports which make reference to pupils' specific strengths and weaknesses and which identify targets for improvement;

        vi. judge levels of attainment against the expected demands of each relevant level description for KS3 and KS4 in English;

        vii. identify both under-achieving and very able pupils in English and how to set targets and make provision for their development.

24. *Opportunities to practise*

    Trainees must be given opportunities to practise, in taught sessions and in the classroom, those methods and skills described above.

C. TRAINEES' KNOWLEDGE AND UNDERSTANDING OF ENGLISH

25. All trainees enter a course of Initial Teacher Training for secondary English with:

    a. *(for undergraduate courses)* the academic requirements for admission to first degree studies;

    b. *(for postgraduate courses)* a UK degree or equivalent and an educational background which provide the necessary foundation for work as a teacher of English in the secondary phase.

    Although all trainees will have a substantial amount of English in their previous education, and those on postgraduate routes as part of their degree, different trainees will have covered different areas to different extents. For example, some

---

[2] All courses of Initial Teacher Training must cover the ITT National Curriculum for the use of ICT in subject teaching (Annex B). The final year of undergraduate courses will be exempt from this requirement for 1998/99 only. For secondary trainees the ITT National Curriculum applies to their specialist subject.

trainees may have pursued studies that emphasised English literature, while others may have followed courses with an emphasis on linguistics. For some, the narrowness of their background subject knowledge may mean that they do not feel confident about, or competent in, all the English that they are required to teach. All trainees need to be aware of the strengths and weaknesses in their own subject knowledge, to analyse it against the pupils' National Curriculum and examination syllabuses and to be aware of the gaps they will need to fill during their training. Trainees need to be alert to the differences between having a secure knowledge of the subject and knowing how to teach it effectively.

26. *Audit*
    a. *For trainees on KS2/3 courses*, ITT providers should audit trainees' knowledge and understanding of English against the English content specified in the KS2, KS3 and KS4 Programmes of Study.
    b. *For trainees on 11–16 courses, 11–18 courses and 14–19 courses*, ITT providers should audit trainees' knowledge and understanding of English against the English content specified in the KS3 and KS4 programmes of study and the content required to teach English at GCSE specified in paragraph 28 below.
    c. *In addition, for trainees on 14–19 courses*, providers should audit trainees' knowledge and understanding of the English against that required to teach English post-16, specified in paragraph 29 below.

    In each case, where gaps in trainees' subject knowledge are identified, providers of ITT must make arrangements to ensure that trainees gain that knowledge during the course and that, *by the end of the course*, they are competent in using their knowledge of English in their teaching.

    In addition, for 11–18 courses, the subject knowledge set out in paragraph 29 is advisory only. Providers should have regard to it, have provision available in relation to it and audit trainees' knowledge, understanding and skills in English against it. By the end of the course, ITT providers should assess how far each trainee's subject knowledge matches the post-16 content, taking account of the opportunities the trainee has had to practise teaching English post-16. *Capability in relation to the post-16 content should be recorded clearly on each NQT's Career Entry Profile.*

27. In order to teach English effectively all trainees must know and understand:
    a. and use correctly, *technical terms* which, in addition to those in the National Curriculum English Order, are necessary to enable trainees to be precise in their explanations to pupils, to discuss secondary English at a professional level and to read inspection and classroom-focused research evidence with understanding;
    b. *the nature and role of Standard English* as the medium through which all subjects are taught, as well as the general, public English used to communicate within the United Kingdom and throughout the English-speaking world.

28. In order to give trainees a more explicit, critical insight into their own writing; to equip them with tools to help them analyse and evaluate others' writing, including pupils' writing; to give trainees the terminology and concepts to understand processes such as language acquisition and development, and to study research evidence on language; and to teach English effectively to GCSE, trainees on 11–16, 11–18 and 14–19 courses must:

a. *know and understand the principles of spoken and written language as a system,* including:
   i. *Lexis*
      - *morphology and semantics* – word structure, meanings and derivations;
      - *phonology* – the sound system of spoken words;
      - *graphology* – the alphabetic spelling system;
   ii. *Grammatical*
      - the *grammar* of spoken and written English, including:
         word classes and their functions in sentences;
         word order and cohesion within sentences;
         construction of complex sentences to include a variety of clauses and phrases;
         co-ordination and subordination in sentences;
      - *punctuation*
         its relationship to the phrase and clause structure of sentences;
         its use to denote emphasis;
         conventions in writing;
   iii. *Textual*
      - *cohesion* – the way that individual words, sentences and paragraphs work together to convey meaning, including the logic and sequence of ideas;
      - *organisation, structure and presentation* including the structure of written text;
b. a broad understanding of language as a social, cultural and historical phenomenon, including:
   i. historical changes in English and its significance as a world language;
   ii. Standard English and other dialects;
   iii. multilingualism and the learning of English as an additional language;
   iv. the differences between spoken and written English;
c. knowledge about texts and critical approaches to them, including:
   i. analysis of different types of literary and non-literary texts, evaluating their quality and making judgements about them;
   ii. identification of the conventions associated with different types of text including non-fiction and media and how they are used and changed for effect;
   iii. how information and ideas are presented, depending on point of view, context, purpose and audience;
   iv. how to analyse texts for implication, undertone, bias, assertion and ambiguity;
   v. familiarity with:
      - the historical spread of prose, fiction, poetry and plays, including key authors from the English literary heritage;
      - a range of texts written specifically for pupils of secondary school age;
      - a range of texts from different cultures;
      - a range of non-fiction and media texts intended to inform, explain, argue, persuade and entertain;

    vi.   those which emphasise different ways of reading texts depending on whether the focus is on the reader, the writer, the context or the text alone.

29. In addition, in order to teach:

  a. A level English effectively, trainees must demonstrate that they:

    i.   have the breadth and depth of knowledge, understanding and skills required for a post-16 course in literary study;

    ii.   can reflect on their own response to texts and consider other readers' interpretations;

    iii.   can use their detailed knowledge and understanding of individual texts to explore comparisons and connections between them and to appreciate the significance of cultural and historical influences on readers and writers;

  b. A level English language effectively, trainees must demonstrate that they:

    i.   have the breadth and depth of knowledge, understanding and skills needed to apply a range of linguistic frameworks to a wide variety of texts from both the past and present;

    ii.   are able to investigate their own and others' speech and writing and respond critically and perceptively to the different varieties of English they hear and read;

    iii.   are able to select and use the linguistic framework most appropriate for investigation and research into language uses and issues.

Appendix B
Self-audits

The following pages 195 and 197–210 are photocopiable resources for personal use.

As an initial audit task you might like to go through the following list which describes very broad 'areas of English' and number them 1 to 7 in terms of your own level of subject knowledge confidence. We realise that the task is not straightforward (for example you may have specialised in nineteenth century fiction but feel less confident about the modern novel). It might be helpful therefore to use the notes section to record any specific observations about areas of strength or areas for development. You will notice that we separated 'drama' and 'Shakespeare' as well as 'the novel' and 'children's literature' because we think these are areas that are worth considering separately but clearly there is a considerable overlap.

Area	Rank	Notes
Novel		
Children's fiction		
Drama		
Shakespeare		
Poetry		
Media		
Knowledge about language		

Appendix C
Self-audit of Pedagogical Subject Knowledge

You should use the statements in order to identify any gaps in your knowledge and use them as a basis for target-setting as part of your secondary English training. Having completed the audit, you should set yourself targets and discuss with your university tutor and subject mentors how best to address the gaps you have identified (for example, supported self-study, observation, and planning and teaching specific topics/ areas).

TEACHING READING

Do you feel confident about:

	Yes	No
encouraging pupils' regular, individual, private reading?		
choosing texts which will motivate all pupils to read and extend their reading interests?		
stimulating individuals to read and supporting pupils' reading?		
selecting texts and identifying the chief learning aims and how they will be met through use of a text?		
introducing a text to a class?		
selecting passages or aspects of a text which should receive close attention, and phasing and pacing the teaching of the text?		
deciding how and by whom the text will be read?		
setting up activities which will enhance the pupils' engagement with the text and improve their skills in reading and ensuring that the selection of activities is closely matched to the teaching objectives for the section of the text?		
enabling pupils to appreciate and respond in writing and discussion to a text as a whole?		
using Information and Communications Technology to support the teaching of reading?		

TEACHING NON-FICTION TEXTS

Do you feel confident about:

	Yes	No
providing for the systematic, structured reading of non-fiction texts using a range of techniques (e.g. skimming and scanning, and DARTS)?		
teaching pupils how to analyse the organisational and linguistic features of different types of text in non-fiction and use these features in their own writing?		

TEACHING POETRY

Do you feel confident about:

	Yes	No
involving pupils in appreciating, understanding, responding to and writing poetry, including reading aloud to pupils and getting them to read poetry aloud?		
teaching the range of poetic forms and equipping pupils with the technical terms they need to discuss poems, their meaning and effects (e.g. metre, metaphor, simile, onomatopoeia, assonance, alliteration, hyperbole, oxymoron, sonnet and ballad)?		
grouping poems to enable appreciation of theme, period and author's voice?		

TEACHING SHAKESPEARE

Do you feel confident about:

	Yes	No
exploring Shakespeare's plays as scripts for performance?		
ensuring pupils gain access to texts and appreciate the force of the ideas, language and dramatic qualities by using a variety of approaches?		
enabling pupils to gain an appreciation of Shakespeare's language including its poetic nature, how character and action are portrayed through language, and how it differs from contemporary English?		
setting Shakespeare's plays in their social and historical context?		

TEACHING MEDIA STUDIES

Do you feel confident about:

	Yes	No
demonstrating some of the ways in which meaning is presented by the media (including newspapers, television programmes and films) and identifying how form, layout and presentation contribute to impact and persuasion?		
teaching about the institutions that produce media and require pupils to evaluate the messages and values communicated by the media?		
requiring pupils to consider the ways in which audiences and readers choose to respond to the media?		

ASSESSING READING

Do you feel confident about:

	Yes	No
determining at the planning stage what pupils should know, understand and be able to do better by the end of the sequence of work (e.g. skills of relating one part of the text to another, drawing comparisons and recognising how authors build up to a climax)?		
identifying the assessment opportunities and the assessment evidence that will be collected, including on what, and on which pupils, to focus for particular purposes?		
building up a picture of pupils' reading ability through a range of tasks which enable assessment of different types of skill?		
knowing how and when to employ particular assessment tools for particular purposes (e.g. open and closed comprehension questions for the implicit and explicit understanding of meaning, running record or miscue analysis, and standardised reading tests)?		

TEACHING WRITING

Do you feel confident about:

	Yes	No
providing models of writing for pupils to analyse and emulate and use pupils' reading to provide inspiration for their writing?		
managing the writing process effectively including how to help pupils generate ideas for written work, how to teach pupils to draft, revise and proof-read their work and how and when it is appropriate to focus on parts of the writing process only?		
teaching pupils to write in different forms through providing examples and teaching pupils how to analyse them for their linguistic and other conventions, using structured approaches (e.g. writing frames) to support pupils' first attempts?		
teaching pupils to consider audience, purpose and context when choosing form and language?		
using Information and Communications Technology to support the teaching of writing?		

TEACHING GRAMMAR

Do you feel confident about:

	Yes	No
teaching the grammatical terms and conventions listed in the pupils' National Curriculum explicitly?		
teaching pupils the ways in which sentences can be extended, elaborated, abbreviated and manipulated by re-organising their sequence and the way they are worded and by adding or removing phrases and clauses?		
giving pupils feedback on their written work, including the identification of grammatical errors (e.g. non-agreement of subject and verb) and provide guidance for development?		
teaching pupils to analyse reading material for their grammatical features and conventions (e.g. the use of long noun phrases and the passive voice in information writing)?		
setting pupils activities which demonstrate the way that grammar works and the factors which influence grammatical choices (e.g. changing a first person account into the third person so as to change the focus of attention and the level of formality)?		

TEACHING LANGUAGE VARIETY

Do you feel confident about:

	Yes	No
the planned teaching of different aspects of language variation, linking teaching to both the books pupils read and the texts they write?		
using contrasting texts to teach points of comparison and contrast in content language and styles?		
teaching about the direct comparison between spoken and written forms of language?		
teaching about language variation and change?		

TEACHING SPELLING

Do you feel confident about:

	Yes	No
teaching pupils strategies which help them to learn and retain spellings?		
teaching spelling families and rules systematically?		
introducing pupils to new words with unusual or irregular spellings?		
using marking strategies which draw attention to patterns of errors and enable pupils to learn from their mistakes?		

TEACHING PUNCTUATION

Do you feel confident about:

	Yes	No
using well written texts to demonstrate the function of different punctuation marks and how they should be used?		
using activities, including reading aloud, through which pupils recognise the role of punctuation in marking grammatical boundaries and in symbolising and replacing the intonation of speech?		
reviewing and marking pupils' work constructively, drawing pupils' attention to the omission and misuse of punctuation marks so that pupils can correct them?		
teaching more complex uses of punctuation marks systematically (e.g. the relationship between commas and clauses and the use of the dash)?		
teaching self-help strategies (e.g. requiring pupils to read back their own work to themselves, looking for sentence breaks)?		

ASSESSING WRITING

Do you feel confident about:

	Yes	No
marking pupils' work to respond to content as well as accuracy, highlighting both the strengths and weakness, and intervening to extend pupils' writing competence?		
encouraging independence and the ability to be self-critical, including self-correction among pupils?		
weighing the different facets of pupils' writing when coming to a judgement about its overall quality in relation to its purpose (e.g. weighing narrative coherence against spelling and punctuation)?		

TEACHING SPEAKING AND LISTENING

Do you feel confident about:

	Yes	No
fulfilling the formal and informal roles taken in groups through the explicit teaching of the language appropriate to different stages of the discussion (e.g. tentative hypothesis, brief summary, probing questions, summing up and handling disagreement constructively)?		
adapting pupils' speech for different purposes, including how to sustain a talk or a monologue, how to use visual aids and organise persuasive points?		
teaching the conventions of different types of speech?		
teaching pupils to listen attentively and with discrimination (e.g. by using techniques such as making notes, focused listening and directing attention)?		
teaching pupils to discern rhetorical devices, irony, persuasive techniques and bias in what is heard?		

TEACHING DRAMA

Do you feel confident about:

	Yes	No
utilising drama techniques (e.g. small group play-making; teaching in-role and tableaux) to involve pupils in examining themes, issues and meanings?		
using performance of texts to develop pupils' understanding and appreciation of language, dramatic form, character and performance?		
using role-play, script-writing, writing in-role and a range of stimuli to develop pupils' reading, writing, speaking and listening?		
requiring pupils to reflect upon and evaluate features of their own and others' performance in order to develop their understanding of techniques for conveying meaning?		

ASSESSING SPEAKING AND LISTENING

Do you feel confident about:

	Yes	No
establishing a clear focus for the assessment of speaking and listening (e.g. how well a group member uses questions and suggestions to organise and sustain ideas in discussion)?		
making opportunities for the assessment of individual pupils, ensuring that they understand the nature and purpose of the assessment?		
building up over time a profile of pupils' achievements in speaking and listening which recognises progress in the pupils' speaking and listening skills?		
distinguishing between aspects of pupils' personality and the way pupils talk (e.g. not mistaking confidence for a thoughtful input)?		

ASSESSING AND TEACHING SPECIAL EDUCATIONAL NEEDS

Do you feel confident about:

	Yes	No
assessing pupils' reading and writing using techniques such as standardised tests, miscue analysis, observation and discussion?		
evaluating the quality, readability, content and appeal of texts and to assess their appropriateness to pupils' chronological age, so that those texts and other resources match pupils' needs well?		
differentiating classroom tasks and supporting poor readers with tasks which are being undertaken by all the pupils in a class?		
with the help of an experienced English teacher and/or SEN teacher if necessary, providing positive and targeted support for pupils with special educational needs?		

ASSESSMENT, MONITORING AND EVALUATION

Do you feel confident about:

	Yes	No
making effective use, in your teaching and planning future lessons and sequences of lessons, of assessment information on the attainment and progress of pupils?		
setting up activities so that specific assessment in English can be undertaken for all pupils, including the very able, those who are not yet fluent in English and those with SEN, through assessment, at an early stage, of pupils' strengths and weakness in using language?		
keeping records of pupils' progress and attainment across the English curriculum, including recording progress in the development of pupils' listening skills in English?		
making summative assessments of individual pupils' progress and achievement in English, through the use of National Curriculum tests, teaching assessment and other ways of assessing individual pupils, including the appropriate use of standardised reading tests and spelling tests?		
presenting the outcomes of assessment in reports which make reference to pupils' specific strengths and weaknesses and which identify targets for improvement?		
judging levels of attainment against the expected demands of each relevant level description for KS3 and KS4 in English?		
identifying both under-achieving and very able pupils in English and knowing how to set targets and make provision for their development?		

TEACHING A LEVEL ENGLISH LITERATURE

Do you feel confident about:

	Yes	No
the breadth and depth of your knowledge, understanding and skills required for a post-16 course in literary study?		
your ability to reflect on your own response to texts and consider other readers' interpretations?		
using your detailed knowledge and understanding of individual texts to explore comparisons and connections between them and to appreciate the significant cultural and historical influences on readers and writers?		

TEACHING A LEVEL ENGLISH LANGUAGE

Do you feel confident about:

	Yes	No
the breadth and depth of your knowledge, understanding and skills needed to apply a range of linguistic frameworks to a wide variety of texts from both the past and the present?		
investigating your own and others' speech and writing and responding critically and perceptively to the different varieties of English you hear and read?		
selecting and using appropriate linguistic frameworks for investigation and research into language uses and issues?		

Index